Reading *Little Britain*

Reading Contemporary Television

Series Editors: Kim Akass and Janet McCabe
janetandkim@hotmail.com

The **Reading Contemporary Television** series offers a varied, intellectually groundbreaking and often polemical response to what is happening in television today. This series is distinct in that it sets out to immediately comment upon the TV *zeitgeist* while providing an intellectual and creative platform for thinking differently and ingeniously writing about contemporary television culture. The books in the series seek to establish a critical space where new voices are heard and fresh perspectives offered. Innovation is encouraged and intellectual curiosity demanded.

Published and forthcoming:

Makeover Television: Realities Remodelled edited by Dana Heller

Quality TV: American Television and Beyond
edited by Janet McCabe and Kim Akass

The Queer Politics of Television by Samuel A. Chambers

*Reading **CSI**: Television under the Microscope* edited by Michael Allen

*Reading **Deadwood**: A Western to Swear By* edited by David Lavery

*Reading **Desperate Housewives**: Beyond the White Picket Fence*
edited by Janet McCabe and Kim Akass

*Reading **Little Britain**: Comedy Matters on Contemporary Television*
edited by Sharon Lockyer

*Reading **Lost**: Perspectives on a Hit Television Show*
edited by Roberta Pearson

*Reading **Nip/Tuck**** edited by Roz Kaveney and Jennifer Stoy

*Reading **Mad Men**: Dream Come True TV* edited by Gray Edgerton

*Reading **Sex and the City*** edited by Kim Akass and Janet McCabe

*Reading **Six Feet Under**: TV to Die For*
edited by Kim Akass and Janet McCabe

*Reading **The L Word**: Lesbians on TV*
edited by Kim Akass and Janet McCabe, with an Introduction
by Sarah Warne

*Reading **The Sopranos**: Hit TV from HBO* edited by David Lavery

*Reading **Ugly Betty**: TV's Betty Goes Global* edited by Janet McCabe and Kim Akass

*Reading **24**: Television Against the Clock* edited by Steven Peacock

*New Dimensions of **Doctor Who**: Exploring Space, Time and Television*
edited by David Mellor and Benjamin Earl

Third Wave Feminism and Television: Jane Puts It in a Box
edited by Merri Lisa Johnson

Reading *Little Britain*

Comedy Matters on Contemporary Television

Edited by Sharon Lockyer

I.B. TAURIS

LONDON · NEW YORK

Published in 2010 by I.B.Tauris & Co Ltd
6 Salem Road, London W2 4BU
175 Fifth Avenue, New York NY 10010
www.ibtauris.com

Distributed in the United States and Canada Exclusively by Palgrave Macmillan
175 Fifth Avenue, New York NY 10010

ISBN: 978 1 84511 939 3

A full CIP record for this book is available from the British Library
A full CIP record is available from the Library of Congress

Library of Congress Catalog Card Number: available

Printed and bound in India by Thomson Press India Ltd

Contents ································

Acknowledgements   vii

Notes on Contributors   ix

Character List   xiii

Introduction: Britain, Britain, *Little Britain*...   1
Sharon Lockyer

PART 1: Narrative, Genre and Comedic Techniques

1   Analysing *Little Britain* as a Sketch Show   19
    Ian Mowatt
2   *Little Britain Live*   35
    Stephen Lacey
3   'Yeah but No but yeah': A Linguistic Perspective on
    the Humour of *Little Britain*   53
    Julia Snell

PART 2: *Little Britain* and Identity

4   How *Little Britain* Does 'Race'   75
    Sarita Malik
5   Chavs and Chav-nots: Social Class in *Little Britain* 95
    Sharon Lockyer
6   'Mischief and Monstrosity': *Little Britain* and Disability 111
    Margaret Montgomerie
7   'The Only Feminist Critic in the Village?': Figuring
    Gender and Sexuality in *Little Britain*   127
    Deborah Finding

PART 3: *Little Britain* and Inter/national Audiences

8   'I'm Anti-*Little Britain*, and I'm Worried I Might Start
    Laughing': Audience Responses to *Little Britain*   147
    Brett Mills
9   *Little Britain*: An American Perspective   171
    Arthur Asa Berger

10 'In English Please!' Lost in Translation: *Little Britain*
    and Italian Audiences   183
    Delia Chiaro

Postscript: *Little Britain USA*   209
Kim Akass

Film, TV and Radio Guide   215

Bibliography   219

Index   237

Acknowledgements ....

The completion of this book has been in every sense a team effort. The help, energy and enthusiasm of many people has been central to ensuring the completion of this book. Sincere thanks to all of the contributors – Ian Mowatt, Stephen Lacey, Julia Snell, Sarita Malik, Margaret Montgomerie, Deborah Finding, Brett Mills, Arthur Asa Berger, Delia Chiaro and Kim Akass – for their interesting perspectives on *Little Britain* and for adhering to, sometimes strict, deadlines.

Many *many* thanks to Kim Akass and Janet McCabe, series editors of Reading Contemporary Television, for their support, guidance and willingness to respond to my repeated 'favours' and 'quick questions'. Little did I know that as we discussed the idea of a 'Reading *Little Britain*' collection when we first met back in early 2006 that it would actually become a reality – your vision and determination ensured that it came to fruition. I am very grateful to Philippa Brewster at I.B.Tauris for her continual faith in the project and for her guidance and patience.

Colleagues at Brunel University have contributed to the academic context in which the book has been completed, in particular Monica Degen, Lesley Henderson, Leon Hunt, Peter Lunt and Milly Williamson. Thanks also to the students who have taken my 'Comedy, Culture and the Media' module for allowing me to 'test out' ideas in lectures and for indulging my interest in television comedy. Colleagues at other institutions have also supported the completion of the book. Warm thanks to Vincent Campbell, Mike Pickering and Liz Sutton for their intellectual spirit.

Comedy has been and continues to be a staple ingredient of family television viewing in the Lockyer household – thanks to all of you for instilling and maintaining my interest in television comedy and for the love and encouragement you've always given me. Finally, thanks to Alan Devlin for providing the supportive environment in which the book was completed and for ensuring I maintained *some* sense of perspective throughout.

Notes on Contributors ....

Kim Akass is Research Fellow (TV Drama) at Manchester Metropolitan University. She has co-edited and contributed to *Reading Sex and the City* (I.B.Tauris, 2004), *Reading Six Feet Under: TV To Die For* (I.B.Tauris, 2005), *Reading The L Word: Outing Contemporary Television* (I.B.Tauris, 2006), *Reading Desperate Housewives: Beyond the White Picket Fence* (I.B.Tauris, 2006) and *Quality TV: Contemporary American TV and Beyond* (I.B.Tauris, 2007). She is one of the founding editors of the television journal *Critical Studies in Television* (MUP) (www.criticalstudiesintelevision.com) as well as (with McCabe) series editor of '*Reading Contemporary Television*' for I.B.Tauris.

Arthur Asa Berger is Professor Emeritus of Broadcast & Electronic Communication Arts at San Francisco State University. He is the author of more than 100 articles and 60 books on media, popular culture, everyday life, tourism and humour. Among his books on humour are *An Anatomy of Humor* (Transaction, 1993), *Blind Men and Elephants: Perspectives on Humor* (Transaction, 1995) and *The Art of Comedy Writing* (Transaction, 1997). His Ph.D. dissertation was on the comic strip Li'l Abner, published as *Li'l Abner: A Study in American Satire* (Twayne, 1970). He has also published a number of comic academic murder mysteries such as *Postmortem for a Postmodernist* (Rowman and Littlefield, 1997) and *Durkheim Is Dead!: Sherlock Holmes Is Introduced to Sociological Theory* (AltaMira, 2003).

Delia Chiaro holds a chair in English Linguistics and Translation at the University of Bologna's *Scuola Superiore di Lingue Moderne per Interpreti e Traduttori* Forlì, Italy, where she is director of studies of the master's programme in screen translation. She is a renowned humour scholar and combines her interests in screen products through audience-based, data-driven work on the perception of Verbally Expressed Humour when it is translated for television, cinema and the Internet. Her publications include *The Language of Jokes: Analyzing Verbal Play* (Routledge,1992), a special issue of *Humor: International Journal of Humor Research* (De Gruyter, 2005, 18(2)) on humour and translation as well as a chapter on this subject in *The Primer of Humor Research* (Gruyter, 2008) and a number of articles in international journals. She has lectured across Europe, Asia and the USA.

Deborah Finding is currently completing her Ph.D. thesis on sexual violence narratives in popular music at the London School of Economics' Gender Institute. Her research interests focus on the intersections of trauma theory and cultural studies, and her publications include contributions to *Investigating Alias: Secrets and Spies* (I.B.Tauris, 2007), *Encyclopedia of Gender and Society* (Sage, 2008) and interviews with authors including Sarah Waters and Lionel Shriver for the *Feminist and Women's Studies Association (FWSA)*. She holds a B.A. in Philosophy and Theology, and an M.A. in post-Holocaust Jewish-Christian relations, from the University of Cambridge.

Stephen Lacey is Professor of Drama, Film and Television in the Cardiff School of Creative and Cultural Industries at the University of Glamorgan. He has published widely on post-war British theatre and television drama and is the author of *British Realist Theatre: The New Wave in Its Context 1956–65* (Routledge, 1995) and *Tony Garnett* (MUP, 2007). He is also co-editor of *Popular Television Drama: Critical Perspectives* (MUP, 2005) and *British Television Drama: Past, Present and Future* (Palgrave, 2000). He is a founding editor of *Critical Studies in Television*, a peer-reviewed journal of small-screen fiction.

Sharon Lockyer is a Lecturer in Sociology and Communications in the School of Social Sciences at Brunel University. Her research interests are in the sociology of mediated culture and critical humour studies. She is co-editor (with Michael Pickering) of *Beyond a Joke: The Limits of Humour* (Palgrave, 2005) and has published in a variety of academic journals including *Discourse and Society; Journalism Studies; International Journal of Social Research Methodology: Theory and Practice; Ethical Space; Sociology Compass;* and *Popular Communication: The International Journal of Media and Culture.* She was the recipient of the *International Society for Humor Studies* (ISHS) Emerging Scholar Award in 2004.

Sarita Malik is a writer and researcher on issues related to cultural identity and screen representation. She has worked for a range of arts, media and educational organisations and her academic and journalistic writings have been widely published. Her areas of expertise include cultural policy and public service broadcasting and black and Asian British cinema. She is the author of *Representing Black Britain: Black and Asian Images on Television* (Sage, 2002), which offers a critical history and analysis of shifting institutional contexts, images of `race' and ethnic-minority cultural politics in modern Britain.

Brett Mills is Senior Lecturer in Film and Television Studies at the University of East Anglia and an Associate Tutor for the Open University. He is the author of *Television Sitcom* (BFI, 2005), *Television Genres: The Sitcom* (Edinburgh University Press, 2009) and, with David Barlow, *Reading Media Theory* (Pearson, 2009). He recently completed the *AHRC*-funded study 'Funny business: interviews with members of the terrestrial television comedy industry'.

Margaret Montgomerie is Senior Lecturer in Media Studies at De Montfort University, Leicester. Her teaching and research interests include the textual and representational practices of contemporary media, gender, sexuality and identity and the media. She is particularly interested in shifts in the representation of marginalised identities in popular screen fictions.

Ian Mowatt was educated at the Universities of St Andrews and Pennsylvania. In 1973, his first novel *Just Sheaffer or Storms in the Troubled Heir* (Harcourt Brace Jovanovich) was described by the *New York Times* as 'the year's contribution to the light touch in mystery fiction'. He subsequently contributed to two best-selling books: *NOT 1982* (Faber and Faber, 1981) and *NOT 1983* (Faber and Faber, 1982). He has contributed to the Scottish newspapers *The Scotsman* and the *Sunday Standard* and has written sketch material for about 40 radio and television programmes including

Naked Radio (BBC Radio Scotland 1981–1986), *Naked Video* (BBC2 1986–1991), *Spitting Image* (ITV 1984–1986) and *Scotch and Wry* (BBC1 Scotland 1986–1989). He lectures in comedy at Glasgow Caledonian University.

Julia Snell completed her PhD on sociolinguistic variation in the speech of primary school children in 2008 at the University of Leeds. She is now working as a Research Officer at the Institute of Education University of London. Her current research focuses on the use of linguistic ethnographic methodologies to study the social meaning of linguistic variation (especially in "non-standard" English dialects), continuity and change in patterns of classroom interaction, and the role of dialogue in teaching and learning. She holds an MA in English Language and World Englishes from the University of Leeds, and her contribution to this volume is based on her MA dissertation.

Character List* ·····························

Characters Played by David Walliams

Alan
Anne
April
Boris the Babysitter
Carol Beer
Dennis Waterman
Denver Mills
Des Kaye
Desiree DeVere
Dr Lowe – The Psychologist
Edward Grant
Eileen
Emily Howard
Harvey Pincher
Jason
Leanard
Len Boothe
Letty Bell
Linda Flint
Liz
Lou Todd
Maggie Blackamoor
Mathew Waterhouse
Michael Dinner/Man in Restaurant/The Posh Diner
Miss Grace
Mr Dudley
Mr Mann
Mrs B
Mrs Emery
Pat
PC Bryce
Peter Andre
Pianist

Rachel
Ray McCooney
Record Breaker (Ian)
Rod
Sandra Patterson
Sebastian Love
Sid Pegg
Sir Norman Fry
The Minstrels
Whitelaw

Characters Played by Matt Lucas

Andy Pipkin
Ashraf (horse whisperer)
Bubbles DeVere
Clive
Daffyd Thomas
Dame Sally Markham
Don
Doug Ramsie
Dr Lawrence
Florence Rose
Gary
Janet
Jeremy Rent
Joan
Judy Pike
Kenny Craig
Marjorie Dawes
Mr Cleeves
Mr T Lookalike
Neville
Newsagent
Nicola
Orville
PC Lindsay
PC Rawlinson
Record Breaker (Ian)

Reverend Jessie King
Robert
Roy
Sir Bernard Chumley
The Minstrels
Ting Tong Macadangdang
Vicky Pollard
Viv
Warren
Workman

Characters Played by Other Actors

Celia Pincher	Geraldine James
Dr Beagrie	Steven Furst
Jane	Samantha Power
Margaret	Voice of Stirling Gallacher
Michael Stevens	Anthony Head
Myfanwy	Ruth Jones
Narration	Tom Baker
Ralph Patterson	Adam Donkin
Roman DeVere	Rob Brydon
Samantha Grant	Helen Coker

Note: * From the television series 1–3

Introduction: Britain, Britain, *Little Britain*...

Sharon Lockyer

> Every few years there's a television comedy that breaks through to being a phenomenon. That's what Matt and David have become.
>
> —Boyd Hilton (2008) in *New Heroes of Comedy*

Big Laughs in *Little Britain*

Little Britain rapidly filled the comedy void left on British television screens when *The League of Gentlemen* (BBC 1999–2002) and *The Office* (BBC 2001–03) came to an end. Written by and starring Matt Lucas and David Walliams, the character-based sketch show began as a BBC Radio 4 comedy series in 2001 and was transferred to television in 2003, with the first series broadcast on BBC Three, BBC's digital channel, where it garnered 'cult comedy' status. The second series was broadcast on BBC Three in October 2004 and repeated, in edited form, on mainstream BBC 1 later in the same year. Series three was broadcast on BBC 1 in November 2005. *Little Britain Abroad* Christmas specials were broadcast on Boxing Day in 2006, the *Little Britain Comic Relief Sketches – Little, Little Britain* and *Comic Relief: The Big One* (both of which included familiar *Little Britain* sketches with celebrities) were aired in 2005 and 2007, and *Little Britain Live,* a sell-out live stage show, toured the UK and Australia in 2005–07. *Little Britain USA,* the American version, was broadcast on HBO and BBC in late 2008[1]. *Little Britain* moved from 'cult' to 'mainstream mass appeal' comedy faster than Vicky Pollard could say 'no, but, yeah, but, no, but...'.

Described by the BBC Guide to Comedy as 'an off-kilter look at modern life' (2007), *Little Britain* satirises an array of British, Welsh and Scottish fictitious characters from Emily 'I'm a Laydee' Howard (played by David Walliams), to Fat Fighter support group leader Marjorie Dawes (Matt Lucas), through to eccentric Scottish flute-playing hotelier Ray McCooney (David Walliams). Lucas has argued that a celebration of diversity is at the centre of *Little Britain* – 'the concept of the show is that we're everybody tall, short, fat, thin, black, white, straight, gay, man, woman, whatever' (in Barrell 2006). Each sketch combines a range of recurring comedic techniques including caricature, drag, satire and repeatable catchphrases. Delingpole (2004) argues that the *Little Britain* characters 'aren't just a gallery of grotesques with randomly selected quirks. They spring from close observation of real people and, no matter how weird their behaviour, it's always acted out...with a sincerity and conviction that defies the audience not to sympathise with them'. The Lou (Walliams) and Andy (Lucas) sketch popularly referred to as 'Swimming Pool' sketch ('Diving Board', 1: 1) was voted the Greatest Comedy Sketch in a Channel 4 poll, and Vicky Pollard's 'Swimming Pool' sketch (1: 2) was positioned fourth (BBC News 2005b).

The character-based sketches run alongside other bizarre sketches such as unsuccessful attempts to break world records, for example the 'Bath of Beans – World Record Attempt' (1: 1). Individual sketches are linked by a plumy-voiced narration from actor Tom Baker ('the Fourth Doctor' on *Dr Who* [BBC 1963–89, 2005–present]). Baker patriotically announces both senseless and caustic snippets of 'factual' information about Britain. For example, the opening of series 1, episode 6 ran as follows: 'Britain, Britain, Britain. Discovered by Sir Henry Britain in 16010. Sold to Germany a year later for a Pfennig and the promise of a kiss. Destroyed in 183042 and rebuilt a week later by a man. This we know. Hello. But what of the people of Britain. Who they, what do, and why?'

Little Britain has become one of the most talked about programmes on contemporary television. It has received a number of industry awards including British Comedy Awards in 2004 (for Best TV Comedy, People's Choice Award, and Best TV Comedy Actor [David Walliams]), British Comedy Awards in 2005 (for Best Comedy Programme and the Ronnie Barker Writers' Award), a National TV Award 2005 (for Most Popular Comedy Programme), a BAFTA 2005 (for Best Comedy Programme), two Rose d'Or Awards in 2005, and an International Emmy award in 2006. Lucas and Walliams were named the most powerful people in television comedy by a *Radio Times* poll in 2005 (BBC News 2005a; The British Sitcom Guide 2008). In February 2008, Channel 4 included Lucas and Walliams in their *New Heroes of Comedy* documentary series (alongside Ricky Gervais and Sacha Baron Cohen).

In addition to this industry recognition, *Little Britain* captured the public imagination. Series two averaged 1.5 million viewers on BBC Three (which made it the channel's highest-rated show) and when shown on BBC 1 it garnered average ratings of 5.5 million (above average for post-9 pm) (Armstrong 2005). The first episode of the third series had viewing figures of 9.5 million (which accounted for almost 40 per cent of the television audience) (Bennett 2005). Fans of *Little Britain* include Princes William and Harry as well as author/actor Alan Bennett (see Barrow 2004); and *Guardian* journalist Gareth McLean has described Lucas and Walliams as 'national treasures' (2004: 50).

A wide range of merchandising accompanies the show, including CDs, books (scripts of the three series and a memoir/travelogue, *Inside Little Britain*), video games, dolls, key rings, greeting cards, calendars, t-shirts, jigsaws and mugs. *Little Britain* appears in the 2008 Guinness World Records as the highest-selling comedy DVD in the world (Dugan 2007) – the DVD of the first two series sold 645,457 copies between March 2006 and 2007. Such successes have resulted in *Little Britain* becoming one of the most publicly recognised brand images of the twenty-first century.

The Lucas–Walliams Comedy Partnership

It was long road to comedy success for the duo. Lucas and Walliams briefly met at the National Youth Theatre in 1990, and a year later both performed in William Shakespeare's *The Tempest*, when they recognised their shared passion for comedy. They both studied drama at Bristol University and in 1995 started to work together. Their *Sir Bernard Chumley and Friends* shows, which were repeated hits at the Edinburgh Fringe in the mid-1990s, toured across the UK in 1997. These shows were based on Lucas's stand-up comic character Sir Bernard Chumley, an eccentric actor and raconteur who Lucas had performed on the London stand-up circuit in 1992 at the tender age of 18 and had appeared at the Edinburgh Fringe in 1994.

Lucas made his early solo television appearances in *The Smell of Reeves and Mortimer* (BBC 1993–95), performing a number of characters including Mayor Hobson, and in *Shooting Stars* (BBC 1995–2002) as George 'He's a baby' Dawes. He also played Marjorie Dawes, George's mother, who would later appear in *Little Britain* as the fat-fighting slimming-club leader. Walliams' solo television performances include *Games World* (Sky One 1993–98), *Incredible Games* (BBC 1994–95), and the dramedy *Attachments* (BBC 2000–02). Walliams had a cameo role in 1999 in *Spaced* (Channel 4 1999–2001), appeared in *The League of Gentlemen*, and made a brief appearance in 2003 in *Eastenders* (BBC 1985–present).

Their television appearances as a comedy-duo include a number of short episodes as 'Mash and Peas' on *Spoofavision* (Paramount Comedy 1996) and in the Fat Les 'Vindaloo' video for England's 1998 World Cup football anthem. They also co-wrote and appeared in *Barking* (Channel 4 1998), a comedy sketch series; the Sir Bernard Chumley character was introduced to television audiences in the spoof documentary *Sir Bernard's Stately Homes* (BBC 1998), which saw Chumley (Lucas) and his murderer-friend Anthony Rogers (Walliams) investigate country estates whilst searching for a 'golden potato'. This show was negatively received; Lucas has recalled Victor Lewis-Smith's comment that instead of the 10-minute show there should be a 10-minute silence for their careers (*New Heroes of Comedy* 2008). Sir Bernard later appeared in *Little Britain* as a resident of 'Sandy Toksvig House' who looks after his sister, Kitty, who has an accident-related disability.

However, it was *Rock Profiles* (UK Play 1999–2000) that placed the Lucas-Walliams partnership on the comedyscape. *Rock Profiles* lampooned the world of pop and involved Lucas and

Walliams impersonating music celebrities and being interviewed by Jamie Theakston. *Rock Profiles'* influences can be seen in *Little Britain* in the sense that the 'spirit' of Bubbles DeVere (played by Lucas) has roots in the *Rock Profile* interview with Shirley Bassey, played by Lucas (see *New Heroes of Comedy* 2008). The Lou and Andy characters in *Little Britain* also have roots in the *Rock Profile* of Lou Reed (Walliams) and Andy Warhol (Lucas) (see BBC Guide to Comedy 2008). *Rock Profiles* was nominated for a Broadcast and a Cable Guide award in 2001, and its producer Myfanwy Moore (Walliams' university friend who also worked on *Spoofavision* and would later work on *Little Britain*) notes that had the spoof interview show been on the BBC it could have been a mainstream success (*Heroes of Comedy* 2008). However, it was *Little Britain* that, ten years after their first encounter, would result in the Lucas-Walliams partnership being one of the most successful and lucrative comedy-duos. Their combined earnings between 2002 and 2006 were estimated at £20 million (Sherwin 2006; see also Hanna 2005).

Yeah but No but...Big Controversies in *Little Britain*

Despite its popularity, *Little Britain* courted controversy, which has been heavily reported in the mass media. It has been criticised for pushing the boundaries of taste too far, for engaging in the 'humour of humiliation', for being grotesquely un-PC by mocking the disabled, gay, poor, elderly or overweight, and for reinforcing negative racial stereotypes (see Leapman, 2005; Cavendish, 2005). Film director Ken Russell heckled Lucas and Walliams at a *Show Bank Show* award ceremony in 2005 for 'spitting in the face of the public' (Hall, 2006), and Johann Hari in *The Independent Online* argued that *Little Britain*

> has been a vehicle for two rich kids to make themselves into multimillionaires by mocking the weakest people in Britain. Their targets are almost invariably the easiest, cheapest groups to mock: the disabled, poor, elderly, gay or fat. In one fell swoop, they have demolished protections against mocking the weak that took decades to build up. (2005)

Further, *The Daily Mail* reported,

> The creator of the sitcom *Father Ted* [Graham Linehan] has criticised comedies such as *Little Britain*, saying they are crude, cynical and intent on 'trying to humiliate people'...In a thinly veiled attack on *Little Britain*...he added, 'Every second programme seems to be trying to humiliate people and the jokes are becoming very crude'. (2006)

Such criticism was not confined to journalists and media-related professionals. After initial broadcast on BBC Three, the series two sketches including WI (Women's Institute) ladies Maggie and Judy (Walliams and Lucas) were edited before being repeated on BBC 1. The WI complained that its name and logo had been used in the Maggie and Judy sketches. Particular concern was raised following the 'Jam' sketch (2: 1) where Maggie vomits in copious amounts on learning that one set of homemade jam she is judging at a local fete has been made by a woman who 'ran off with the schoolmistress', that another has been made by a woman who 'married a black man', and that the marmalade has been made by 'Sanjana Patel'. The WI chair agued that 'while as an organisation we are happy to laugh at ourselves, we felt we were being portrayed as potentially racist and narrow-minded' (quoted in Robertson 2004: 7). BBC spokespersons retorted that it was not their intention to offend (see Farley 2004; Sherwin 2004) and so the WI logo was removed and replaced with reference to a fictitious 'Women's Association'.

Concerns were also raised in relation to *Little Britain*'s influence on its younger viewers. A primary school head teacher requested that parents ban their children from watching *Little Britain*. This was due to children repeating *Little Britain* sketches in the playground which was interpreted as hindering the maintenance of the school's high behavioural standards (BBC News 2005c; Sapsted 2005). Questions were also raised when DVDs of the show were released with a 15 certificate, when a significant number of potential viewers could be school-age children (BBC News 2005e, Rampton 2005).

Series three garnered a wealth of critical responses, and some audiences began to turn their back on the *Little Britain* duo. Whilst the viewing figure for the first episode of this series was 9.5 million, this figure had fallen to less than 7 million by episode three (see Leapman 2005; Davies 2005). The third series 'sparked a previously unthinkable chorus of criticism' (Sheppard 2005). It was criticised in the press for becoming increasingly offensive, for crossing the boundary of good taste and for its use of toilet humour (see Rudden 2006). Some described it as a 'bile-fest' (Hari 2005) and viewed it as crossing the 'boundary of good taste' (Rudden 2006: 12). Fans of series one and two described series three as 'vicious and cruel' (see Barrell 2006). Some of the new characters were deemed too shocking and offensive. For example, Mrs Emery (David Walliams), the older woman who urinates uncontrollably, received criticism from *Incontact*, an incontinence charity, who regarded the characterisation as 'offensive and in poor taste' (BBC News 2005d). Similar concerns of 'inappropriateness' were raised by *Age Concern* and *The Royal College of Physicians* (Sheppard 2005). Questions were asked whether Lucas and Walliams were 'playing ever more crudely to the gallery and moving away from the sharper, wittier sketches that made them famous in the first place in an attempt to become more mainstream' (Sheppard 2005; see also Leapman 2005). Others pondered whether audiences were becoming tired of repeated catchphrases, and some advised that *Little Britain* should have come to an end at series two, like other 'comedy classics' such as *The Office* and *Fawlty Towers* (BBC 1975–79) (see Brown 2005; Leapman 2005).

This collection grew out of a desire to examine this contemporary sketch show that is simultaneously celebrated and condemned. It brings together for the first time critical, theoretical and socio-cultural perspectives on *Little Britain*. The collection includes chapters exploring the generic features of sketch-shows, *Little Britain*'s narrative techniques and the show's aesthetic forms. It also includes critical readings of *Little Britain* in relation to representations and constructions of race, class, disability, gender and sexuality in its sketches. How national and international audiences have responded to and understand *Little Britain* is also explored. Through their varying and sometimes polemical and contradictory approaches, all of the contributors are united in their attempt to understand how *Little Britain* contributes to contemporary mediated culture and to examine how and where it is located in contemporary society.

Narrative, Genre and Comedic Techniques

Little Britain is firmly placed in the 'golden age' of sketch shows, an age spanning the last 15 years (Hall 2006) and including sketch shows such as *The Fast Show* (BBC 1994–97), *Green Wing* (Channel 4 2004–07) and *The Catherine Tate Show* (BBC 2004–07). *Little Britain*'s ample use of catchphrases has been compared to the 'saturation' of catchphrases in *The Fast Show*, and its caricatures remind many viewers of *The Dick Emery Show* (BBC 1963–81) (Hall 2006: 16), yet other features of *Little Britain* are distinctly original and unique. In the opening chapter of part 1, Ian Mowatt draws on his experience of writing material for around 40 radio and television sketch shows to examine how *Little Britain* is positioned within the history of sketch comedy. Mapping out its generic roots, Mowatt explores the development of sketch show comedy from vaudeville, to early radio comedy, through to contemporary television sketch show comedy and argues that *Little Britain* is a key player in the genealogy of the sketch show. Intertextuality, or 'in-jokes' (e.g., naming a school 'Kelsey Grammar' after the *Frasier* star [NBC 1993–2004]), is a significant and recurring feature of *Little Britain*'s sketches. Mowatt's chapter analyses the similarities and differences in style, content, delivery and comic devices between *Little Britain* and other seminal British sketch shows (e.g., *Monty Python's Flying Circus* [BBC 1969–74]). Sketch shows are inherently fragmented in narrative terms. In the final part of his chapter, Mowatt examines the techniques and codes employed in *Little Britain* to retain audiences and enable them to move discursively from one sketch to the next, and from one episode to another. Mowatt's chapter offers significant insights into the comedic originality and continuities in *Little Britain*.

The radio and television versions of *Little Britain* are only parts of this popular sketch show portfolio. Lucas has explained, 'we always had this dream. The show started on radio and we always wanted it to go to television, then live on stage' (Yeap 2007: 14), which is perhaps unsurprising given his and Walliams' theatrical roots. *Little Britain Live*, the live stage version of the show, was immensely popular. When the live tour was initially announced 100,000 tickets were sold in six hours (Armstrong 2005), and due to popular demand additional locations and dates were added to the original schedule. In his chapter, Stephen Lacey examines the relationship between the mediated and live versions of *Little Britain*. Although on initial inspection the live show may simply be regarded as a linear 'remediation' of the TV show, as it relies on characters, locations, narratives and catchphrases in the TV show, Lacey argues and illustrates that this remediation does not take into account the complexity of the theatrical performance. Lacey examines the fusion of theatrical performance (such as the red curtain and orchestral music) *and* the televisual sketch conventions (repeating the established routines [and pleasures] of the sketches built up across the television series). Lacey unpacks how the live show plays around with the conventions of the TV version (e.g., through its use of filmed projection and special effects), whilst also drawing on specific techniques that remain the preserve of theatrical performance (e.g., direct address, improvisation, references to time and place, and audience participation/humiliation).

The physical comedy of the TV and live versions of *Little Britain* forms only a part of the show's appeal. As it originated as a radio show, much of the comedy and its appeal are based on language use, language play and accent. This is manifest most clearly in *Little Britain*'s comedy catchphrases, such as hypnotist Kenny Craig's (Matt Lucas) 'Look into my eyes, look into my eyes, the eyes, the eyes, not around the eyes, don't look around the eyes, look into my eyes...you're under'. These catchphrases captured the public's imagination, and at the programmes height were repeated across Britain in playgrounds, offices, shops, factories, and on other TV programmes. Three of *Little Britain*'s comedy catchphrases were included in UKTV Gold's 'Top Comedy Catchphrases of All Time' in 2005 – with Daffyd's (Matt Lucas) 'I'm the only gay in the village' gaining the top spot. In the final chapter of part 1, Julia Snell explores the comedy of *Little Britain* from a linguistic perspective. Snell employs schema theory to unpack the construction and interpretation of comedy in *Little Britain*. The process of interpretation, according to this theory, involves textual factors and background knowledge. Through close analysis of the language used in the Emily Howard and the Vicky Pollard sketches, Snell illustrates how comedy is derived from script oppositions and exaggerated prototypes and is related to social schema. Snell also examines how schema theory, in particular cultural schemata and comedy schema, can contribute to determining whether a sketch will be wholly or partly identified and appreciated as comedic.

Little Britain and Identity

Little Britain is a programme of contestation. Supporters and denouncers reflect on the motive, content and impact of *Little Britain* in equal measure. Much of the public debate around the programme centres on its representation of specific social groups and their consequences for inter-group relations and understanding. Thus part 2 interrogates the politics of comedic representations in *Little Britain* in terms of race, class, disability, sexuality and gender. Some of the characters, particularly those introduced in series 3, were regarded by some as too gross and racist (see Peters and Becker 2008). These included Desiree DeVere (a black woman played by David Walliams) and Thai mail-order bride Ting Tong Macadangdang (Matt Lucas). In the first chapter of part 2, Sarita Malik asks 'how is "race" managed in *Little Britain*?' This question is answered by examining key issues such as how time and context contribute to comedic meanings and interpretations, the consequences of this when a local text such as *Little Britain* becomes internationally recognised, and how *Little Britain* contributes to our understanding of the socio-political implications of racialisation in contemporary comedy. Malik agues that *Little Britain* includes routine racialisation through a number of key recurring characters and can be best described as a form of 'ethnic humour' as it is a comedy mainly about whiteness. Through discussion of the white and the few non-white characters that exist in the programme, *Little Britain's* racial ambivalence, complexity, fluidity and ever-changing tone and content is brought to the fore – although there are moments across the series where the representations may be deemed racist, Malik illustrates how others can be equally recognised and interpreted as anti-racist.

In my own chapter, continuing the theme of comedic ambivalence, I examine the ways in which British social class is constructed and represented in *Little Britain* via analysis of characters that can be described as 'chavs' and 'chav nots'. Its representations of social class, in particular the chav teenage delinquent Vicky Pollard, have been widely criticised. To take one example, Barbara Ellen (2004), writing in *The Observer* attacks the show's representations of chavs and advises middle-class Lucas and Walliams that 'if you're going to try your hand at "class tourism" then approach it like any form of travel – accept it's not "your patch" and treat the "locals" with respect'. Ellen goes on to argue that the likes of Les Dawson, Peter Kay and Caroline Aherne 'don't wade in like school bullies, pointing and sniggering at the "freaks"...they give the people they depict a dignity'. Social class differences and tensions have been and remain a staple ingredient of British television comedy. In my chapter, I examine how *Little Britain*'s social class representations compare and contrast to these existing comedic representations, whilst simultaneously exploring to what extent the Vicky Pollard character can be seen as contributing to 'chav hate' evident elsewhere in contemporary popular culture. Representations of 'chav nots', for example, the upper-class Harvey Pincher character, are examined to unpack how they operate comedically. Although there is ample evidence to suggest that Vicky Pollard's appearance, behaviour and language epitomises the chav identity that is mocked across popular culture, the ambivalence underpinning the comic characterisation equally permits alternative readings – where Vicky and the chav identity may be positively regarded, where hegemonic ideologies are resisted and where middle-class identities and lifestyles are mocked.

It is probably accurate to state that wheelchair-user Andy and his carer, Lou, are the most instantly recognisable characters from *Little Britain*. Yet when compared to debates around representational issues of social class, race, gender and sexuality, few have focussed on *Little Britain*'s comedic constructions of disability. In order to redress this imbalance, Margaret Montgomerie's contribution unpacks the ways in which disability and mental illness are used as a source of comedy in *Little Britain* and provides a detailed analysis of the roles and functions fulfilled by characters such as Andy and Anne (David Walliams). Interesting questions raised and addressed by Montgomerie include the following: What is at stake when we laugh at these characters and sketches? Do Andy and Anne's actions offer a critique of disablement by inverting the power relations between the disabled characters and their carers/medical professionals? Do they function as the comedic acting out of the 'disability benefits cheats' and the 'violence done by care in the community of mentally ill people' stories which legitimise the scrutiny and stigmatisation of the disabled as 'other'? Are we laughing because of their disabilities, at their embodiment and enactment of the abject and the monstrous? Montgomerie argues that the programme is characterised by contradictory discourses and contradictory responses. Its characterisation of disability is fluid, moving between and across the medical and social models of disability, simultaneously reflecting and negotiating the ambivalence towards disability in contemporary British society.

Little Britain's representations of gender and sexuality have been criticised by some for pandering to old-fashioned problematic stereotypes. For example, Peter Tatchell (of the Outrage! activist group) argues,

> I feel quite ambivalent about *Little Britain*...While it is irreverent and often very funny, it is also quite dated in its camp, clichéd style of queeny humour. Daffyd is really just a modern, harder-hitting version of Kenneth Williams. The setting and characters are different, but he plays to the same gay stereotypes, where queers are the butt of the jokes. The jokes mostly encourage viewers to laugh at Daffyd, not with him. What they are laughing at is a caricature of a gay man. It inadvertently reinforces old-fashioned, negative clichés about gay people. (quoted in Barrell 2006)

In the last contribution to part 2, Deborah Finding offers a critique of *Little Britain*'s representation of gender and sexuality from a feminist perspective. Examining the programme's relationship with alternative comedy and postfeminism, Finding argues that *Little Britain* is more akin to comedy that characterised the pre-alternative comedy scene – one dominated by sexism (and other isms) – rather than to the progressive and challenging comedy of altcom. Finding illustrates this 'return to hate-for-laughs' through a consideration of the way in which irony can be used as a technique to distance the comedian from the joke content – and to simultaneously pre-empt and shut down any possible critique – and through figurative analysis of key characters. Analysing 'The Mail Order Bride' Ting Tong Macadangdang and 'The Gay Man' figures of Daffyd and Sebastian (the latter played by David Walliams), Finding argues that these figures are dependent on grotesque stereotypes based on disgust at sexuality and gender. The chapter is brought to a close through a consideration of how Lucas and Walliams themselves have been and continue to be figured through their own bodies and their own sexual identities.

Little Britain and Inter/national Audiences

Little Britain has acquired both national and international appeal. It is now broadcast in over 40 countries worldwide. It is shown across Europe, in America, Australia, Canada, India, Israel, Malaysia, New Zealand and Singapore. The final part of the collection examines how these national and international audiences respond to and make sense of *Little Britain* – a welcome relief given the dearth of research and academic debate on television comedy audiences. In the first chapter, drawing on the findings of a small-scale qualitative audience study, Brett Mills offers a useful way into this under-explored territory. Through analysis of three key themes raised by audience participants – *Little Britain*'s social and communal role, the sketch show's pleasures and displeasures, and its link to Britishness – it is clear that *Little Britain* audience responses are complex, contradictory and intricate. Mills highlights how audience participants demonstrate a reflexive, critical and active engagement with *Little Britain*. Pleasure and enjoyment are experienced by the viewers, but they simultaneously acknowledge some of the problematic ways in which certain social groups are represented and the negative consequences of such representations (as discussed in part 2). Comedic pleasures and displeasures relate to ideological, aesthetic and performance-related factors. Audiences question the programme's relationship to national identity and express their apprehension over the consequences of this relationship for how international audiences understand Britain and Britishness. Audiences' discussions of and responses to these questions are again characterised by contradictions. Mills' chapter clearly demonstrates the knotty business of making sense of *Little Britain* audiences in particular and of comedy audiences in general.

Arthur Asa Berger offers an interesting reading of *Little Britain* from an American perspective. In doing so, Berger draws comparisons between the programme and American comic strips such as *Krazy Kat* and *Peanuts.* The 'American comedic sensibility' is discussed and comparisons with other popular American comedies, such as *Seinfeld* (NBC 1989–98) and *Frasier,* are made in order to unpack his personal response to *Little Britain*. The specific humour techniques used in *Little Britain*, such as satire and imitation, are examined. It is argued that *Little Britain*'s references to all things British (grammar schools, rural Welsh life etc.) and different cultural perceptions of sexuality can make it a problematic text for American audiences. Berger notes that when compared to American comic characters, such as Frasier, *Little Britain*'s characters are one-dimensional, and the audience's inability to relate to such hollow characters may lead to interpretative difficulties.

Continuing the focus on *Little Britain*'s cultural-specificity, Delia Chiaro examines how Italian audiences respond to and make sense of *Little Britain*. Few British television comedies are shown on Italian television. Chiaro examines the reasons for this and explores the consequences of the cultural-specificity of British comedy in general and of *Little Britain* in particular for exporting audiovisual comedy to non-English-speaking countries. Through close analysis of Italian translation of *Little Britain,* Chiaro identifies the difficulties that resonate around how culturally specific references are translated (such as places and institutions), how language variation is translated (e.g., accent, regional dialect, verbal ambiguity), and how taboos appear in the translation (e.g., sexual euphemisms). Also considered and illustrated are the consequences of subtitling for the appreciation of comedy (e.g., Vicky Pollard's catchphrases and rants are reduced to a small number of words during subtitling). The second part of the chapter moves on to examine the findings of a qualitative audience study on the opinions of Italian *Little Britain* audiences. Italian perceptions of British humour are explored before considering the mixed responses to *Little Britain*, from 'negative but funny', and 'negative but not funny', through to 'realistic and funny'. Chiaro's chapter offers significant insights into the 'politics of translating *Little Britain*'.

All of the contributors in their own ways, and from their own perspectives, are trying to make sense of the ambivalent text that is *Little Britain*. The collection illustrates that there are lots of 'yeah but no but yeah' moments, frustrations and ambiguities which come with the territory when attempting to understand the pleasures and pitfalls of a contemporary television comedy that has divided audiences and critics alike. For some readers there will be omissions in the book's content, but the aims of the book are to stimulate discussion and to promote further work on British television comedy in general and on *Little Britain* in particular.

So in typical Tom Bakeresque fashion...it is *Little Britain* what we now here look at now today. Who they? What do? And why? Let's do it!

Note

1. As *Little Britain USA* was broadcast after the completion of much of this collection, the programme is discussed in the Postscript.

PART 1

Narrative, Genre and Comedic Techniques

Chapter ONE

Analysing *Little Britain* as a Sketch Show

Ian Mowatt

Comedic Originality of *Little Britain*

Little Britain is an inventive and, at times, highly creative sketch show. Some of the characters are completely original, enormously entertaining figures. Above all, its list of characters includes more gay people and transvestites than most other comedies broadcast in the UK (see Thorpe 2005). Daffyd Thomas (Matt Lucas), the only gay in the village, and Vicky Pollard (Matt Lucas), the 16-year-old Bristolian chav with twelve children, are multidimensional characters that belong distinctively to our age. Other characters that have a distinctive original resonance are Ray McCooney (David Walliams), the peculiar hotel manager who speaks in riddles and plays the flute, Harvey Pincher (David Walliams), the young engaged man who requires breast feeding, and young Jason (David Walliams), who fancies his friend Gary's (Matt Lucas) grandmother so badly that he masturbates over her back and then has a post-coital cigarette. Also splendid are the shop sequences featuring Mr Mann (David Walliams), as well as Roy (Matt Lucas) and Margaret (she of no arms and no legs), who try to deal with Mr Mann's impossibly exact requests for books or pictures. Marjorie Dawes (Matt Lucas), who will jog the memories of everyone who has ever attended a slimming club, as well as the transvestite 'ladies' Emily Howard (David Walliams) and his friend Florence Rose (Matt Lucas) too are brilliant.

Defining the Sketch Show

Steve Neale and Frank Krutnik outline how the modern origins of the sketch are situated within:

> the institutions of nineteenth- and twentieth-century theatrical
> variety: music hall, vaudeville, pantomime, the circus, the
> minstrel show, the medicine show, the fairground attraction and
> American burlesque...[and in] the various types of afterpiece
> prevalent in all forms of nineteenth-century theatre, and again
> in the minstrel show. (1990: 182)

There is no shortage of information to support Neale and Krutnik's argument. Indeed any kind of activity in the nineteenth century that attempted to attract the general public for entertainment or some commercial purpose needed some kind of comic interactivity in order to draw customers. Comic banter was always present at the commencement of a minstrel show and 'it was a central feature of Vaudeville where the verbal content drew upon themes relevant to everyday life – immigration, ethnicity, gender roles, urban life, temperance, women's suffrage, and technology especially the development of the automobile and telephone' (Anon 1996).

This central preoccupation with everyday things would later pass on into radio and television in the form of sketch shows and situation comedies. These Vaudevillian activities, along with burlesque, which also featured comedy acts, were commonplace throughout the English-speaking world.

In the United States, sketch shows are extremely uncommon on network television although the two most prominent, *Rowan and Martin's Laugh In* (NBC 1967–73) and *Saturday Night Live* (NBC 1975–present), were long lasting and memorable, especially the latter which is the most durable televised comedy format of all time. Sketch comedy in British broadcasting is a much more established cultural form. Sketch shows are usually half an hour in length, minus advertisements on commercial channels or station identification and trailers on BBC. Sketches on social, sexual, political or current mores last for up to four minutes; shorter sketches, usually 10–15 seconds, known as quickies, usually connect the sketches to each other. *Little Britain* is an unusual programme since it has very few quickies and tends to have good compact sketches, well under four minutes in length, that move the show along at a good pace.

British sketch shows come from two main areas: The first is the traditional working-class sketch show with profound influence from sea-side comedy – mainly older programmes such as *The Benny Hill Show* (BBC/ITV 1955–89), *The Dick Emery Show* (BBC 1963–81) and *The Kenny Everett Video Show* (ITV/BBC 1978–87) which despite their titles were actually sketch shows, usually featuring the eponymous comedians in each sketch. The second is the more recent and more erudite side of British sketch comedy from the Cambridge Footlights Society, which has provided more graduates to television than any other academic source. Amongst its comedic graduates who have found success in sketch shows are David Baddiel, Sacha Baron Cohen, Stephen Fry, Eric Idle, Hugh Laurie, John Lloyd, Miriam Margolyes, Rory McGrath, Jonathan Miller, Bill Oddie, Griff Rhys Jones and Tony Slattery. Another initiation experience often undergone by actors seeking a contract to make a televised sketch show (including Matt Lucas and David Walliams) is an appearance on the Fringe of the Edinburgh Festival – an annual event that takes place for three weeks every August in the Scottish capital. Performers who have appeared at the Fringe prior to gaining wider success include Peter Cook, Billy Connolly, Dawn French, Eddie Izzard, Graham Norton and Catherine Tate (Anon 2005).

Sketch shows are usually written by some of the people who appear in them. One exception would be the highly unusual satirical sketch show *Spitting Image* (ITV 1984–96) which had a large writing crew but was performed by puppets made by Peter Fluck and Roger Law and voices spoken by impressionists. The subject-matter of sketch shows is very varied but often deals with politics, such as *That Was the Week That Was* (BBC 1962–63) and *Bremner, Bird and Fortune* (C4 1999–present), or with changes in social mores, such as *Smack the Pony* (C4 1999–2003) and *Goodness Gracious Me* (BBC 1996–2001), or with parodies of other types of programme, including *French and Saunders* (BBC 1987–2007) and *The Fast Show* (BBC 1994–97).

Let us now look at *Little Britain* in terms of its contribution to broadcast comedy by looking at its writers, its place in sketch show history and the extent to which it could be said to relate to other broadcasting texts dealing with similar issues. First, it might be useful to look at the position *Little Britain* currently occupies at the chronological end of about 85 years of broadcasting, much of which is completely different in terms of narrative and ideology, but a significant portion of which is remarkably similar but never entirely alike. In that respect, *Little Britain* remains a unique sketch show that has made a distinctive contribution to comedy broadcasting.

Early Radio Comedy in the UK

Whereas the early years of American Broadcasting witnessed the establishment of classic acts involving Jack Benny, George Burns, Gracie Allen and Bob Hope, developments in the UK were much more pedestrian. At that time, the director general of the only broadcaster, the BBC, was John Reith, the son of a Scottish clergyman, who disliked light entertainment in general and comedy in particular. During the Reith years, there was little dedicated comedy as such; when sketches were broadcast, they would usually be part of either a concert party – a group of amateur or professional entertainers, singers, dancers, comics, jugglers, illusionists and the like – or a live relay from a well-known vaudevillian establishment. Thus for the first 17 years of British broadcasting, comedy was never treated as an entity in itself but as a minor part of a collective ensemble. A typical example of this would be *Star Vaudeville* (BBC Radio between 7.30 pm–9.00 pm 29 July 1932). Gillie Potter, the compere of the show, was a comedian. He was immensely popular in the 1930s and his 'plummy voiced' famous opening to his series of radio reports ('Good Evening England. This is Gillie Potter speaking to you in English') mocked the pomposity of the BBC. In that respect, of course, it is very easy to draw a parallel with Potter's voice and that of Tom Baker which is such an essential part of *Little Britain*.

Reith remained with the BBC until 1938 and it is interesting that in the year of his departure there was the first proper comedy series *Bandwaggon* (BBC Radio 1938–39). The narrative of

Bandwaggon was punctuated by orchestral interludes and a talent competition but there was still a significant element of sketch comedy. A distinctive feature of *Bandwaggon*, however, was the surrealistic element – Arthur Askey and Richard Murdoch purporting to live on the roof of Broadcasting House with their pets. This surrealistic element was, therefore, present in British broadcasting comedy almost 70 years ago, an element whose use would eventually peak with *The Goon Show* (BBC Home Service 1951–60), *Not Only...But Also* (BBC 1965–70), *Monty Python's Flying Circus* (BBC 1969–74), *The Young Ones* (BBC 1982–84), *The Fast Show* and *Little Britain* to name just a few. Perhaps the best surrealistic sketch work in *Little Britain* are the wheelchair sketches featuring Lou (David Walliams), the carer, and Andy (Matt Lucas), the seemingly paralysed patient who walks about unaided whenever Lou's attention is diverted.

Scriptwriters worked very hard in those times. There were 54 editions of *Bandwaggon* between 1938 and 1939. Also in 1939, *It's That Man Again (ITMA)* (BBC Radio 1939–49) took to the air where it would remain throughout the Second World War and beyond. It too had extremely strong surrealistic qualities and, after the outbreak of war with Germany, carried anti-Hitler propaganda. It is important, therefore, to recognise that although broadcast comedy took a long time coming, when it did eventually arrive, surrealism played a crucial part in it. *ITMA* ran for ten years and at the time was the longest-running and most loved comedy programme ever heard on British radio. In its heyday, *ITMA* sometimes attracted almost 40 per cent of the British audience, a feat that would be impossible to match in the world of digital television – although Bennett (2005) observes how the first episode of *Little Britain's* third series had viewing figures of 9.5 million, – which accounted for almost 40 per cent of the television audience. Throughout its lifetime it was replete with catchphrases, many of which were adopted by the general public. *Little Britain* is, of course, often singled out by contemporary critics for its ample supply of catchphrases.

The Development of Authentic Sketch Comedy

After the Second World War, it was possible to free up some of the broadcasting frequencies and The Light Programme was developed. It would eventually become home to about 20 new radio comedy series over the next 12 years. Many of these programmes were unmemorable but several played a significant part in modifying the narrative, ideology and discourse of broadcast comedy. Two of the prominent writers were Frank Muir and Denis Norden. Muir died in 1998 but Norden still writes and presents the television show *It'll Be All Right on the Night* (ITV 1977–present). Their series *Take It from Here (TIFH)* (BBC Light Programme 1948–60) ran for nine series from 1948 at a time when a series often meant between 30 and 40 editions. Although there were songs and music in *TIFH*, it eventually had two fairly distinct sketch types – a humorous sketch on a recent news item or topical subject, then a song and a sketch about a contemporary film, book or play. Writing in his autobiography shortly before his death in 1998, Muir commented,

> This last part was something of a small breakthrough in radio comedy because, as far as we knew it was the first time in a prime-time series that the listener was credited with having been to school, taken a newspaper and read a few books... Radio was advancing rapidly on all fronts from the mid-forties on, finding its own voice in drama, pioneering a style of documentary programme which radio only could produce, and *TIFH* (as our programme soon became known) made its small contribution by attempting a humour *different* from end-of-pier, music-hall material...and presenting instead parodies of films and literature. (Muir 1997: 147)

End of Pier Comedy

The last point Frank Muir made is especially significant when evaluating the position of *Little Britain* within British broadcasting culture. Muir refers to end-of-pier and music-hall comedy. That is one clear discourse – one relating to the then still prominent world of the music hall where Max Miller, Little Tich, Sandy Powell and George Formby were all known for their quick-fire delivery and double-entendres.

There is no doubt that a significant element of the ideology and discourse of the music hall – along with other aspects of early to mid twentieth-century culture – has made its way to many comedy programmes over succeeding decades. Commenting on Donald McGill's 'saucy' postcards, the writer George Orwell observes,

> They are on sale everywhere...Your first impression of over-whelming vulgarity. This is quite apart from the ever-present obscenity...the figures in them, every gesture and attitude are deliberately ugly, the faces grinning and vacuous, with bottoms like Hottentots. (Orwell 1941/1994: 193–203)

This form of comedy which is ideologically very close to the comedic side of the music hall – preciously close to some of the more extreme characters in *Little Britain* such as Bubbles DeVere (Matt Lucas) and Emily Howard – survived in alternative forms as well after the Second World War.

Intertextuality and Comedic Devices

Although there have been debates about the precise nature of intertextuality and disagreements about how it might manifest itself in any particular text, its existence is axiomatic. It is totally unthinkable that any text, anywhere, be it a book, movie, television programme or any other cultural artefact, can come into existence without any influence from a previous or relatively current text. As Allen argues,

> The fundamental concept of intertextuality is that no text, much as it might like to appear so, is original and unique-in-itself; rather it is a tissue of inevitable, and to an extent unwitting references to and quotations from other texts. These in turn condition its meaning; the text is an intervention in a cultural system. (2005: 1)

In the case of *Little Britain*, the authors, Matt Lucas and David Walliams, have been very forthright in talking about their favourite comedies; their comments might explain, to a certain extent, what has influenced their writing:

> Matt used to watch comedy programmes on telly with his dad.
> *The Two Ronnies* [BBC 1971–87], *Morecambe and Wise* [ITV
> 1961–68, BBC 1968–78, ITV 1978–83] and *Only Fools and
> Horses* [BBC 1981–2003]. His dad bought *Monty Python* as
> soon as they came out on video and watched them with Matt
> on their VCR. They were one of the first families in the street
> to have a VCR which they rented. (Lucas, Walliams and Hilton
> 2007: 269)

In the early 1990s, David attended the drama department of
Bristol University where he had not shared the taste of many of
his fellow students:

> There was an almost Stalinist atmosphere among David's peers
> in the Drama Department. It felt like you had to subscribe
> to a set of values. David had to keep his liking for *Carry On*
> films a secret, for example, less someone accuse him of gross
> sexism. Anyone admitting to finding something amusing about
> Barbara Windsor losing her bra in *Carry on Camping* would be
> considered to be advocating pornography. (Lucas, Walliams
> and Hilton 2007: 234)

One of the most obvious features about *Little Britain* – certainly not
the only feature but one which is fairly prominent – is transvestitism.
Although this practice dates back to Shakespearian Theatre when
women were forbidden to act, it still maintains a very strong
presence in British television. In recent times, Barry Humphries,
Julian Clary and Paul O'Grady have frequently appeared on prime
time television as women. Matt Lucas comments,

> When I was young there weren't characters who identified
> themselves as gay on TV. You had camp characters like Dick
> Emery but they never identified themselves as having sex
> with other men. So we're quite proud of the Daffyd sketches,
> bringing discussions of the gay sexual acts into primetime
> TV. I imagine there are nine year old boys out there watching
> our show and they might ask their mothers 'What is fisting?',
> and I think that's wonderful. (Lucas, Walliams and Hilton
> 2007: 239)

A contemporary of Dick Emery, the late Benny Hill, was also inclined on occasion to do drag and had done a particularly splendid impersonation of Fanny Craddock, the television chef of his day. Hill is a particularly interesting figure in British comedy since he is one of very few English comedians to have made any real impression on the American marketplace. Much of Hill's slapstick (he worshipped Charlie Chaplin) and non-verbal comedy has permeated British comedy since his day; Anna McCarthy of New York University comments that when comparing *Little Britain* and *The Benny Hill Show*:

> it might be tempting to see the former's satirical take on the didactic moralism of 'a portrait of a nation' genres in British TV as an indication of greater sophistication. But when you watch a complete episode of Benny Hill from ages past it is surprising how much contemporary satire it contained. It may be that the lewd jokes are more enduring, but the programmes that aired in the 1970s were chock full of parodies of news programmes and other British-specific phenomena. (McCarthy 2005)

But Benny Hill's drag acts were only occasional. The first time that we encounter drag being performed extensively on television is *Monty Python's Flying Circus*, which ran for four series. The Pythons in drag were indeed a horrendous sight to behold, but Terry Jones displayed a marvellous talent for playing a middle-aged mother figure. Nevertheless, the general impression of women to emerge from *Python* was not a very attractive one. In most of the drag sketches, femininity is mocked rather than celebrated. A very good example of this would be the 'Spam, Spam, Spam' sketch where the women are all harridans. In the case of *Little Britain,* the most repulsive representations of femininity are probably Letty (David Walliams), vomiting WI ladies Judy and Maggie (Matt Lucas and David Walliams), and the visually nauseating pairing of the grossly obese Bubbles DeVere and Desiree DeVere (David Walliams).

Python was an original definitive comedy sketch series. Nowadays *Python* would be described as iconic. As Mark Lewisohn has commented, 'they decided to virtually do away with the traditional idea of using punchlines to finish a sketch...They also toyed with the established structure of television, some-times running the closing credits of the show half way through' (1998: 249). But although many of the idiosyncratic and drag aspects of Python have been sustained and developed in *Little Britain* – in terms of drag, to a much more sustained level than in any other television programme ever aired in the United Kingdom – there are major areas where intertextuality has *not* occurred.

The Pythons often used unusual episode beginnings as part of their push against conventional comedy, that is, pretending it was the start of a late-night movie. By comparison, *Little Britain* uses a powerful narrative beginning using selective imagery and Tom Baker's booming voice as a means of holding viewers from the previous programme and retaining them. *Python* used sketches of widely different lengths. As Michael Palin recalls, 'the whole show went predictably well, with very few problems and the usual reaction of ecstatic recognition of sketches. The only trouble spot was the "Court Sketch", which was running 15 minutes and failed to work at any stage' (Palin 2006: 340). Although this comment referred to a live show, the sketches had all previously appeared on television. *Little Britain* sketches – with very few exceptions – all tend to be around two to two and a half minutes long with a few shorter exceptions such as the blackface quickies and the Sebastian Love/Prime Minister (David Walliams/Anthony Head) and Daffyd sketches which tend to run to three minutes.

Little Britain is not trying to shock in any overtly political way. Instead its ideology relates to our social and sexual lives. *Python* was taking on the establishment. Nothing in *Little Britain* is as extreme as 'The Undertaker Sketch' where Cleese goes into a funeral parlour with his mother's body and asks for it to be cooked and eaten.

Little Britain's authors and performers have more limited but achievable objectives, continuing the cross-dressing staple of British comedy in a more flagrant and flamboyant way than ever done before. It is also reasonable to assume that the development of the highly eccentric Scottish hotel landlord, Ray McCooney, might have been sparked off by the later John Cleese character

Basil Fawlty in *Fawlty Towers* (BBC 1975–79). It is also quite conceivable that the anarchy of the *Carry on Films* (1958–78, 1992, 2008) and *The Young Ones* – which Lucas and Walliams liked as children – has contributed to the air of anarchy surrounding several sketches in *Little Britain*. An example of this would be all of the sketches involving Sebastian proclaiming his love of the Prime Minister in such an anarchic way as to suggest strongly that it might owe at least a little to Rik Mayall's character in *The Young Ones* almost 30 years ago.

Another very firmly connecting intertextual link between *Python* and *Little Britain* is 'The Cheese Shop' sketch in *Python* – where a man comes in and asks for almost every type of cheese under the sun but the proprietor doesn't have any of them. It is almost identical in comedic terms to the small shop jokes with Mr Mann and Roy in *Little Britain*. Indeed, David Walliams alludes to the Python's comedic influences:

> When I was watching shows like *The Young Ones* growing up and even *Monty Python*. You think of the *Meaning of Life* and the Mr Creosote section in that, you know, like vomiting and the exploding body...I mean it's just incredible, and it was something you know, when I was a kid that we used to talk about endlessly. (Interview with Andrew Denton 2006)

A final word on cross-dressing. Homosexual acts between consenting adults were legalised by Parliament in England and Wales in 1967. Several sketches about gay activities and cross-dressing did appear in *Python* since it was still a topical theme from 1969 onwards. We are now 40 years on from the first series of *Python* and for *some* gay people the world is a much more sympathetic and less hostile place. In recent times in Britain, civil partnership ceremonies have been legitimised, giving gay people the same rights over property as married heterosexual couples. It is within this new context that we must view Daffyd Thomas, 'the only gay in the village', and Myfanwy (Ruth Jones) the lesbian, plus, of course, Sebastian Love the aggressive homosexual (sort of) in love with the Prime Minister. When they were creating this sketch, Lucas and Walliams were thinking of

Peter Mandelson and Tony Blair (see Lucas, Walliams and Hilton 2007). So it is not just textual features but also the passage of time and changing mores that have contributed to the more explicit representations. And, of course, in a less carnal but nevertheless camp way, the sketches are partly a reflection of the attitudes of the scriptwriters and performers themselves, both of whom acknowledge enjoying cross-dressing. In an interview with James Rampton, talking about his new part in *The Wind in the Willows* (BBC 2007), where he had to dress up as a washerwoman, Lucas deadpanned, 'oh that was a challenge...There is clearly no escape from dragging up for me. If I ever play Hamlet it'll be in a dress' (2007). Walliams too has a long history of dressing up in women's clothes since his sister dressed him up in her clothes in his childhood and he clearly enjoys it (Cooke 2007; New Heroes of Comedy 2008).

Narrative Construction

When we talk about the narrative construction of a sitcom, it is much easier than doing the same for a sketch show. That is not to say that it cannot be done at all, but the fragmented nature of the structure imposes certain restrictions. The three television series of *Little Britain* never feature exactly the same characters although there are some characterisations that are clearly more favoured by the authors and producer. Before looking at this, though, it is worth examining where the programme lies in relation to other sketch shows. *Little Britain* is not a topical news sketch show like *Not the Nine O'Clock News* (BBC 1979–82) or *Spitting Image*, the latter having run to more series than any other sketch show partly because of its army of freelance writers and the fact that, because they were puppets, the actors did not fall out with each other. It is also unlike much earlier programmes such as *Sez Les* (ITV 1969–76) or *Victoria Wood as Seen on TV* (BBC 1985–87), which involve sketch material and stand-up, monologue material. Nor is it in any way intended for mass consumption – quite unlike *Morecambe and Wise* or *The Two Ronnies*, which also included substantial musical items. In terms of recent popular sketch shows of a similar anarchic ideology, it reminds one most of *The League of Gentlemen* (BBC

1999–2002) and, most of all, in terms of narrative speed, *The Fast Show*.

Neither Lucas nor Walliams ever appear as themselves in *Little Britain* – only as characters, and, despite the number of guests they have, they act a huge number of parts themselves – small as well as the big ones. An analysis of the three series (20 half hour shows) reveals that Vicky Pollard is the most popular lead-off sketch followed by Lou and Andy as well as Sebastian with the Prime Minister. Other most frequently featured sketches are transvestites Emily Howard and Florence Rose, Kenny Craig (Matt Lucas) the unsuccessful hypnotist and Marjorie Dawes, leader of the dieting class who abuses her members despite being overweight herself. The recurrent characters of the vomiting WI woman and the incontinent Mrs Emery (David Walliams) are both part of slapstick techniques – techniques which can be easily interpreted by audiences, adult and child alike. The *Radio Times* magazine questioned 2,000 6–16-year-olds about their viewing habits (see BBC News 2005e). Concluding on the basis of the result of this survey, the researchers were confident in saying that 86,000 *Little Britain* viewers were aged between four and nine, and 280,000 viewers were aged between 10 and 15 – for a programme that is marketed as a DVD for over-15-year-olds. This survey published in November 2005 was conducted during the previous BBC 1 screening of the programme which was in December 2004. Then four re-edited programmes were shown, all in the post-watershed hours with audiences of 4.57 million, 6.14 million, 5.67 million and 5.45 million respectively. In each of these cases then, over a third of a million children watched a programme that was aimed at older viewers.

Despite the very high standard of most of the sketches, there were the inevitable failures. The two sketches in series one, episode 5 ('Edward and Samantha – Valentine's Day' and 'Edward and Samantha – Evening Out'), about the teacher who marries his pupil, were presumably discontinued because they were old fashioned, and the same can be said of Carol Beer's 'Computer says "no"' sketches in series two and three; computers have been a part of everyday retailing for over 20 years now and these jokes are stale. Also present in all series are the sketches about the mentally ill woman (Anne played by David Walliams) which are completely out of kilter with the light-hearted and camp material in other parts of the series. Good comedy programmes should provoke and attack the establishment and bad taste always makes for more viewers. But the mentally ill are an easy and vulnerable group of people to attack and the shows would be better without these weak sketches which are not funny (see Margaret Montgomerie's chapter for further analysis of the representations of disability in *Little Britain*).

A certain amount of criticism has been levelled at *Little Britain* for some of its subject matter. According to Jonathan McCalmont (2006), the likes of *Catherine Tate Show* (BBC 2004–2007) and *Little Britain* are written and performed 'by comedians with a profoundly reactionary artistic agenda, increasingly supported by the PR infrastructure of the major British broadcasters and retailers'. No detailed explanation is given of this allegation but it may be partly connected with the large amount of money the pair were expected to make from merchandising during their British tour.

One important binding piece of narrative that must be touched upon are Tom Baker's continuity sequences. From the beginning and through the show, he not only tells us, in his booming but ironic voice, that we are about to have a feast of entertainment but also provides useful links to anyone joining the programme midway.

Finally, the narrative codes in the final programme of series three give notice that *Little Britain* is drawing to a conclusion. The Prime Minister resigns, Ting Tong (Matt Lucas) evicts her saviour, having opened Ting Tong's Thai Restaurant in his living room, Daffyd tries to leave the village and fails, Linda (David Walliams), the university lecturer who insults her students, gets her comeuppance, Marjorie's class leaves her in anger, Florence looks as if he will revert to Fred, and the Computer, at long last, says 'yes'.

To conclude, *Little Britain* is a curious mix drawing on many of the genres of comedy entertainment that preceded it – vaudeville, music hall, sea-side postcards, early radio comedy and several seminal television sketch shows which the two writers and performers acknowledge. Lucas and Walliams also have the determination and confidence to present us with more gay and transvestite characters than ever seen before in one programme. In addition, there are two completely original characters: Daffyd, the only gay in the village, and Vicky Pollard, the teenage mum with the many children. Both characters belong uniquely to the world we live in.

Chapter Two

Little Britain Live

Stephen Lacey

At first sight, *Little Britain Live*, the stage incarnation of the *Little Britain* phenomenon, presents few challenges to the theorist of television. It can be seen as a straightforward example of what Jay Bolter and Richard Grusin (2000) have termed 'remediation' – that is, the tendency of emerging cultural forms to refashion existing ones in their own image, providing new technologies, representational strategies and interpretative frameworks. Applying this argument to the troubled relationship between theatre and television, Philip Auslander (1999) contends that the former has been so thoroughly remediated by the latter, which emerged (in a pre-internet age) as *the* paradigmatic technology and cultural form, that the ontological differences between 'live' and 'mediatised' performances are nothing compared to the historical, economic and cultural convergences that happened between them over the last 40 years. 'At the level of cultural economy', he argues, 'theatre (and live performance generally) and the mass media are rivals, not partners. Neither are they equal rivals: it is absolutely clear that our current cultural formation is saturated with, and dominated by, mass media representations in general, and television in particular' (Auslander 1999: 1). In a persuasive argument that embraces early live television on the one hand, and experimental US theatre and rock concerts on the other, Auslander contends that television remediates theatre by both insinuating its technologies into live performance and appropriating 'liveness' itself – and does so in a manner that film could never do. Historically, television can uniquely 'convey sight and sound at a distance in a way no other medium can'

(1999: 13) with the result that 'the ideologically ingrained sense of television as a live medium [has] enabled television to colonise liveness, the one aspect of theatrical presentation that film could not replicate'(1999: 13). *Little Britain Live*[1] could not exist without its televisual antecedent, which so determines its specific content, its technologies and ways of seeing – in short, its distinctiveness as a live event – that it seems to provide a text-book case of what Auslander is describing as a remorseless cultural process.

However, the case of *Little Britain Live* is a complex one, and, on closer scrutiny, it provides an example of a somewhat different kind (though it is not the purpose of this chapter to refute Auslander's general thesis). The stage show – and 'show', with its associations with popular entertainment, seems appropriate – is very much of itself, a live event which cannot be subsumed into a mediated one, no matter how much technology is used and how reliant on the television version it is. Far from demonstrating an inescapable and linear process of remediation, in which the most recent – and dominant – media simply bends an older one to its will, the show illustrates that, on a moment-by-moment basis, it is possible for the favour to be returned. *Little Britain Live* revels in its ability to play with the conventions and expectations of the television version, refashioning them in the act of engaging with an audience in the same shared space, invoking and acting upon common memories and reworking familiar pleasures. Indeed, *Little Britain Live* shows how reliant *Little Britain* the TV show is on the theatre.

Origins and Context

David Walliams and Matt Lucas, the co-creators of *Little Britain*, have said on several occasions that the show was always intended for the radio, television and the stage, with the live version as (in Walliams' words) 'the reward at the end of [the process]' (Lucas and Walliams 2006a). *Little Britain Live* has certainly been a phenomenon, playing to over 800,000 people in 200 performances during the UK tours, and mostly to audiences of between 2,000 and 5,000 in large-scale venues.[2] The UK tour opened on 23 October 2005 and closed at Cardiff in December 2006. This period contained a one-month break (January 2006) and a month-long residency at the Hammersmith Apollo in London in November 2006. *Little Britain Live* also toured Australia from January to March 2007.

Little Britain was by no means the first British television comedy to find itself onstage: indeed, cross-media adaptations have been a consistent thread in television comedy production. From the 1950s onwards, this has often taken the form of cinematic versions of popular sitcoms: for example, *The Army Game* (ITV 1957–61), one of ITV's earliest successes, was filmed as *I Only Asked* (1958), and *Steptoe and Son* (BBC 1962–65, 1970–74) reached the screen in 1972 and 1973. More recent successes such as *Mr Bean* (ITV 1990–95) (*Mr Bean* 1997, and *Mr Bean's Holiday* 2007) and *The League of Gentlemen* (BBC 1999–2002) (*The League of Gentlemen's Apocalypse*, 2005) have followed this path. Stage versions of successful shows have also been common. *Dad's Army* (BBC 1968–77) was mounted as a musical revue in 1975–76, whilst *'Allo 'Allo* (BBC 1982–92), a rather less reverential take on World War II, toured the UK repeatedly from 1986 to 1992, taking in three separate runs on the London stage. Both shows also appeared overseas, notably in Australia and New Zealand, capitalising on the popularity of British television in those countries. The enormous international success of *Monty Python's Flying Circus* (BBC 1969–74) led to a UK tour in 1974, a tour of Canada, a three-week run in New York in 1976 and a high-profile appearance at the Hollywood Bowl in 1980 (a *Python* film spin-off, *Spamelot* opened onstage in Chicago in 2004 and was in London's West End in 2008). Several of *Little Britain*'s immediate predecessors (and influences) were also translated to the stage. A live version of *The Fast Show* (BBC 1994–97), for example, received two national tours in 1998 (with the cast of *Shooting Stars* [BBC 1995–2002]) and a third, 'Farewell Tour', in 2002. Perhaps the programme that bears the most obvious comparison to *Little Britain* is *The League of Gentlemen*, which followed a similar trajectory. Beginning as an award-winning show on the Edinburgh Festival Fringe, *The League of Gentlemen* achieved success on radio, reached a much wider audience on television and was re-worked as a stage production that toured the UK in 2002 and 2005. Live versions of television shows have often been staged at the high point of a show's popularity, relying on the visibility of the television version to guarantee audiences, and have been largely successful in this regard. They also function as a way of perpetuating – and extending – the popularity of their television antecedent and may outlive the immediate life of the programme itself. Indeed, in a multi-channel age the enduring presence of popular comedies from earlier decades on digital channels has given them new life: new stage versions of both *Dad's Army* and *'Allo 'Allo*, both available on television and on video/DVD, toured the UK in mid-2007 to early 2008 and mid-2008 to early 2009 respectively.

Little Britain Live, like other recent stage adaptations, can be placed alongside large-scale musicals and other spectacles. This is not so much an aesthetic judgement as a recognition of the role that *Little Britain Live* plays within the cultural economy of theatre, where large-scale events are marketed and sold (along with the requisite merchandise and an injunction over the tannoy at the start to 'please remain seated throughout the performance') in ways which are similar to those of the rock bands that often play the same venues. The scale of the performance certainly challenges the intimacy that is so often associated with television (Auslander 1999: 15), and it also abandons most of the medium's naturalist habits, with each element of performance – especially acting – reconfigured for the stage.

David Walliams and Matt Lucas are perhaps unlike many other actors who have become known for their work on television before turning, or returning, to the theatre. Indeed, their careers have taken a path across genres and media that is becoming increasingly familiar, if not common. They met as actors in the National Youth Theatre in 1990, appearing in several productions in their teens. They were not conventionally trained, however, both having studied Drama at Bristol University rather than in an acting conservatoire. Their subsequent careers have more in common with the 'alternative' comedians popular in and since the 1980s (e.g., Ben Elton and Rik Mayall), who were similarly university-educated and middle-class, than with the older generation of working-class, vaudeville and music-hall-trained British comics (such as Frankie Howard) who are amongst their main influences. Their relationship as performers was cemented during late-night shows at the Gilded Balloon, a comedy venue at the Edinburgh Festival Fringe, and in subsequent tours in the 1990s. In addition to making appearances in television comedy shows (Lucas in *Shooting Stars*, for example, and *The Smell of Reeves and Mortimer* [BBC 1993–95]), they have performed as actors on stage and the small-screen: Matt Lucas, for example, played Thersites in the Oxford Stage Company's production of *Troilus and Cressida* in 2000, and David Walliams appeared in the dot.com drama series *Attachments* (BBC 2001–02). They can also be seen in music videos for the likes of Blur (Matt Lucas was a support act for Blur's 1995 Great Escape tour) and Fat Les. Further, Matt Lucas and comedian Peter Kay – in the guise of their characters Andy Pipkin (*Little Britain*) and Brian Porter (*Phoenix Nights,* Channel 4 2001–02) – released 'I'm Gonna Be (500 Miles)' as a charity single in the UK to mark Red Nose Day 2007 for Comic Relief, along with its creators, The Proclaimers. They are best described as comedy actors rather than comedians, able to work across genre and between live and mediated modes of performance, and this describes their hybrid identity in the media professions as well as their performance skills.

Television into Theatre: Theatricality and Performance

Little Britain Live references both television and the theatre – indeed, it references different types and traditions of theatre – and this was particularly apparent in the opening sequence, which is worth examining in detail. The audience was greeted by that clearest of traditional theatrical signifiers, a red curtain (in situ in some, though not all, venues). The signal that the performance was about to begin was the recorded sound of an orchestra warming up (a sign for performance in a more general sense), replacing the upbeat rock music that covered the audience taking their seats. The first routine featured Lou (David Walliams) and Andy (Matt Lucas), two of *Little Britain*'s most instantly recognisable characters, appearing not within the frame of a sketch – the dominant pattern of the show – but part of a music-hall-cum-pantomime routine. Lou appeared through the gap in the curtain and addressed the audience directly, introducing himself and asking whether anyone had seen Andy.

What followed evoked two established conventions from British pantomime: Andy was flown in from the wings, much as Peter Pan might have been, with Lou's insistent questioning met by 'He's behind you!' from an audience attuned to what was expected of them. Once Andy had landed, the exchange that followed evoked the established patterns of the TV version, reproducing the pleasures of the original (itself based on the repetition of familiar tropes) with Andy tricking Lou into making a fool of himself. It also evoked popular theatre (which revels in the local and the known) with references to the city/town in which the performance was taking place. The conclusion, which in its different narrative contexts is the conclusion to every television sketch involving these characters, involved Andy deceiving Lou. Here, it was achieved by the specifically theatrical device of Andy running from the stage and hiding amongst the audience. This marked the end of a kind of 'front cloth' prologue, to be succeeded by the show proper, which began with a more direct referencing of both the specific content and the aesthetic conventions of the TV version: the curtains parted to reveal a screen that covered the back wall of the stage area onto which was projected a montage of familiar *Little Britain* images with a music soundtrack and Tom Baker's instantly recognisable voice-over. From this point on, filmed projection onto the screen created the different locations for each sketch, such projection being a device that was both economical and increasingly familiar in the contemporary theatre and a direct evocation of *Little Britain* on screen.

The recurring image of three-dimensional actors moving in front of a two-dimensional screen stands as a synecdoche for the way that *Little Britain Live* worked throughout, inviting a response from its audience that evoked the immediacy and presence of live performance and the filmic realism of locations familiar from the TV version. Indeed, the show was very knowing about this relationship and extracted comedy from the juxtaposition of different modes of performance. At one point early in the show, Emily Howard (David Walliams), the would-be 'lady', lured a plumber into her house and then into her bedroom; the movement between the two spaces was represented by the on-screen projections showing one space move into the other, whilst the actors mimed walking on the spot, to the delight of the audience.

However much one might want to argue that *Little Britain Live* is theatrical, its reliance on the locations, situations and characters of its antecedents is inescapable: characters familiar from radio and television populated the show – Des Kaye (David Walliams), Bubbles DeVere (Matt Lucas), Sebastian Love (David Walliams), Marjorie Dawes (Matt Lucas) and Vicky Pollard (Matt Lucas) – and the cast was mainly that of the television version (including Tom Baker's voice and, for some performances, Anthony Head as the Prime Minister). Individual audience members at *Little Britain Live* will, presumably, have had the pleasures of watching the television version in mind (since it is unlikely that there were many spectators who were coming to it innocently and without preconceptions); the live show continuously invoked and replayed the television show, which (much more than the earlier radio version) is, as it were, a kind of master text.

Many of the visual gags that might seem to be inherently televisual were recreated on stage. They were not, however, simply the *same* gags, characters or situations, since the process of translation from screen to stage reconfigured them. There were, for example, several familiar and repeated sketches that rely on a comedy of excess, which seem to belong to the small screen. A recurrent sketch on *Little Britain,* reworked for *Little Britain Live,* involves middle-aged and middle-class Maggie (David Walliams) adjudicating a home-made produce competition at an English village fête. The central gag of the sketch, which is essentially the same every time, is that the competition is won by someone who is homosexual or from an ethnic minority, with the result that Maggie, a covert homophobe and racist, vomits up what she has eaten in impossibly copious amounts. The gag works as a gross comedy of exaggeration onscreen, which plays against the inherent naturalism of the medium. Onstage, however, the routine was more complex: it was not only excessive but also spectacular, appealing to the audience as a special effect realised under the constraints of live performance. On the screen, large or small, such trickery goes unnoticed – or at least it is accepted, since it is assumed that the camera can deceive. Onstage, however, such effects produced a double response and offered a double pleasure, one related to the comedy of the narrative and the other to the craft involved in making the gag work – 'How did they do that?'. In other sketches, the special effects and visual trickery were drawn attention to in more self-referential – but no less playful – ways. A familiar routine imagined conversations between the British actor Dennis Waterman (played by David Walliams) and his agent (Matt Lucas). Waterman made his name on British television as George Carter, one part of a double act in the hugely popular police series *The Sweeney* (ITV 1975–78), in which he played a young detective whose cynicism, jack-the-lad humour and propensity to use his fists to solve all problems helped to stereotype Waterman as a 'hard man'. In *Little Britain*, David Walliams characterises him as extremely small and having a high-pitched voice, obsessively concerned to write and sing the 'theme tune' of any programme he is offered a part in (a role which Waterman performed on occasion). The visual gags, on which the television sketch relies, concern props – newspapers, pets, furniture – that miraculously grow in size as Waterman/Walliams encounters them. *Little Britain Live* recreated these visual gags as special effects, which had an additional comic dimension because there was no attempt to hide their trickery: Matt Lucas held out an oversized hand to greet David Walliams on his entrance; a wasp became an actor who flew in from above, to terrorise the hapless Waterman/Walliams; similarly, an actor was used to transform a lapdog into a full-size St. Bernard. The actors drew attention to the silliness and impossibility of the gags; 'It'll be interesting to see if this works', Matt Lucas commented of the miraculous wasp. In a remark that further acknowledges the television show, David Walliams observed that 'we never really explain why we make him small, do we?' and 'if Dennis Waterman were here he'd beat the shit out of us'.

One of the pleasures that *Little Britain Live* offered is that it reconnected the performance skills of its principal actors to their theatrical origins. The running order of the show remained more or less the same throughout the UK tour (though there were some changes to the material within individual sketches) and was fixed largely to allow David Walliams and Matt Lucas time to transform between characters. However, playing a succession of different characters, often of different genders, all of whom are realised in full physical and vocal detail, becomes that staple of popular performance, the quick-change routine, when played live. For example, Walliams was required to play the cross-dressing Emily Howard, complete with full dress, wig and parasol, and then, immediately afterwards, Carol Beer, a singularly unhelpful travel agent: Lucas transformed from Ting Tong, a Thai bride, to Kenny Craig the hypnotist in successive sketches, and from Dennis Waterman's agent to Marjorie Dawes, the facilitator of the Fat Fighters Club. Although the paraphernalia of characterisation – wigs, costumes, prosthetics, props – was simplified for *Little Britain Live*, compromises would not have been apparent to audiences, who were presented with the characters familiar from television and radio in a context that drew attention to the actors' skills of mimicry and physical transformation.

Matt Lucas and David Walliams have noted that characters that are defined through a precise and realistic, though exaggerated, physicality find their natural home on the stage. 'The style of performing we do on TV does lend itself to a live show', Lucas has observed, and 'characters like Emily and Sebastian and Daffyd and Marjorie are quite broad and the performances are quite big' (Lucas and Walliams 2005: unpaginated). The characterisation is indeed 'broad', and onstage size and scale were registered in an increased physicality; gestures were larger (comically so), physical tics and mannerisms were exaggerated in a way that drew attention to them and directed out to members of the audience who were invited to both recognise their origins and enjoy the overt display of the actors' skill. However, here too, there was a moment-by-moment balance struck between live and mediated performance, between the theatrical and the televisual – a balance which was represented in the tension between the visual and the aural; as microphones were used, the performances vocally connoted their onscreen antecedents. Apart from being a response to the size of the auditoria in which the show was playing, microphones allowed something of the intimacy and 'scale' of the screen performances to be maintained (the physicality of the acting notwithstanding). These existed, as all stage performances must, within the real space of theatre auditoria and the fictional spaces of the narrative, which in the case of *Little Britain Live*'s fast-moving sketches were largely interior and everyday, with interactions that were required to retain something of the vocal nuances of more naturalistic situations.

Varieties of Improvisation

So far, the focus has been on the theatricality of performance strategies that related to the television show, even as they moved beyond it. However, there were also elements in the acting that belonged more emphatically to the live, notably the use of improvisation. Much of the material for both televised and staged versions was created through improvisation and later scripted (see Lucas and Walliams n.d. [a]) and then frequently ad-libbed on set. However, for all its exuberance and excess, the text of *Little Britain* is invariably fixed before shooting and is finalised in the editing suite. Departures from the original script – and Lucas and Walliams have indicated that there were many – are not acknowledged in the eventual programme, which is presented as a seamless whole, with the fictional world of the sketches intact. *Little Britain Live*, however, was very different; there was considerable disparity between the fictional narrative of the routines – the written text of the script – and the performance text played out in front of, and sometimes amongst, the audience. There is always a disparity in theatre between written text and performance, of course; here it was the result of varying strategies of improvisation and audience engagement, which were woven across the performance text and which continually re-organised the actor/spectator relationship.

The kind of improvisation that characterised *Little Britain Live* is in the tradition of both British popular theatre, such as music-hall, and the alternative comedic performance styles David Walliams and Matt Lucas developed on the Edinburgh Festival Fringe. It is not improvisation that creates character and situation 'in the moment' but rather that which by its spontaneity disrupts them, pleasurably, to draw attention to the performance itself, and may be to a degree pre-planned. Such improvisation stands outside the fictional situations of the narratives and comments on them and is linked to the way that the audience is embraced by the event. Sometimes this was a kind of rehearsed performance in itself, which became a sign of improvisation and not the thing itself. The example given above of the asides thrown out to the audience in the 'Dennis Waterman' sketch is of this type, since it was essentially the same across different shows. Elsewhere, Walliams and Lucas appeared to have given themselves particular moments where improvisation was permissible (that is, it was expected and anticipated by the performers) since it was repeated. In a routine set in a do-it-yourself (DIY) store, David Walliams (the 'Mr Mann' character) was a troublesome customer to Matt Lucas's shop-keeper (Roy). In both the Cardiff Arena and the Blackpool Opera House performances, the actors came 'off script' in the latter half, to improvise an exchange that had nothing to do with the ostensible subject matter of the sketch. In both shows, Walliams engaged directly with the audience; Lucas, called (within the narrative of the routine) to his off-stage wife, Margaret. The laughter that followed was immediately picked up by Walliams – 'Wrong Margaret' – and used as a stimulus to a verbal riff. 'That's just a group of pissed-up Northerners', he said in Blackpool (they became 'pissed-up Taffies' in Cardiff) direct to the audience, before proceeding to explain, with interjections from Lucas, that he, Walliams, could run faster than any Northerner (paraphrasing a familiar music-hall gag – 'the audience was with me all the way – I managed to shake them off at the station'). In Cardiff, the same moment was filled with an extended and competitive exchange about Walliams' supposed bi-sexuality; 'I just help out at week-ends', Walliams observed; 'your penis is gay', Lucas retorted, before noting with reference to Walliams recent swim across the English Channel for charity that he was merely chasing a man that was 'all greased up'. The appeal for the audience had partly to do with the specificity of the local reference (to which we shall return) and the comedy of the material itself. It was also, however, a moment that was created from within the sketch and yet broke from it; the actors remained physically in the situation, retaining fixed positions on stage – this was not a sketch that relies on much physical business – and the physical silhouette of the character, whilst simultaneously displaying their 'in the moment' improvisatory skills. This playful self-referentiality, celebratory of the bond with the audience and subversive of it, was a recurrent element in *Little Britain Live*, as it is in popular performance in general.

Strategies of Audience Engagement

It has been impossible to discuss the performance strategies of *Little Britain Live* without referring to members of the audience, who were central to both television and live versions of the show. Much of the television work Lucas and Walliams have done, independently or together, is performance that directly engages with the audience – that is, in a particular sense 'live' even when it is recorded. Like other television comedians and actor-comedians, Matt Lucas and David Walliams, when given the choice, prefer to play to two audiences, the 'live' studio one as well as the one experiencing it through television sets. *Shooting Stars,* for example, was recorded in front of an audience, and although *Little Britain* was made largely on film, with some sketches recorded in front of a live audience, those same audiences were also shown the filmed footage, their responses providing the broadcast laughter track (see Lucas and Walliams n.d. [b]). The 'live' audience experiences the performance directly as live, being in the presence of the actors in the act of performing; the broadcast audience, however, experiences mediatised performances alongside the live audience responding to those performances, witnessing and sharing in, if only by proxy, a 'live' event (there is an attempt to catch this sense of sharing a performance when a laughter track is added to a programme). Playing to these two audiences – or rather, wishing not to lose the experience of playing 'live' in a mode of performance that is ultimately recorded – is important to Lucas and Walliams (and they are not alone in this regard).

However, it is in the relationship of the audience to the performer, present in the same space and at the same moment in time, that *Little Britain Live* was most clearly itself and most obviously re-configures the narrative conventions and modes of address of the television version. Such 'presence' has acquired the status of an ontological and definitional category, marking live performance out from other forms of representation (see Phelan

1993); in the case of *Little Britain Live*, presence was of more than ontological significance, since the audience was incorporated into the event at almost every stage and in a variety of ways. The means by which the show did this places it in a tradition of popular performance, which, in its British (and, more broadly, European) context, has a long and varied history. As Bourdieu has argued in relation to his notion of the 'popular aesthetic', which, although not specific to theatre, clearly draws on it, audiences for popular performance show 'a desire to enter into the game' with identification with characters and situations relying on 'a form of *investment* [original italics], a sort of deliberate "naivety", ingenuousness, good-natured credulity ("we're here to enjoy ourselves")...popular entertainment secures the spectator's participation in the show and collective participation in a festivity' (1992: 32–3).

'Participation', however, is a broad term and can take many different forms within the context of individual performances. As has already been noted, *Little Britain Live* engaged with its audience consistently through direct address: from the moment David Walliams as Lou walked through the central gap in the red curtains to the encore, where Daffyd (Matt Lucas), 'the only gay in the village', defiantly led the cast in a song (I'm Gay!'), the audience was acknowledged, that is, they not only looked but were also *looked at*, as onstage relationships were opened out – offered up – in a reciprocal act of engagement that was maintained throughout the show. This was a literal engagement, as a performer's look met that of an individual spectator, but it also worked more generally as a sign of engagement, an invitation to participate and an early signal of the dominant acting conventions to be employed and was understood as such even by spectators at the back of the auditorium. It also had no correlation with the television version, since, as Walliams has said, 'in the TV show, apart from Tom Baker, nobody looks to the camera and talks directly to you. The sketches are what you'd call "fourth wall"' (Lucas and Walliams 2005: unpaginated).

Direct address to the audience anchored other modes of engagement, some more complex and specific to the immediate performance context. As the analysis of the opening sequence above indicates, *Little Britain Live* immediately acknowledged the time and place of the performance event, referring directly to the town/city of the specific show in a mock-disparaging manner: 'You always said you hated Blackpool', Lou/Walliams said to Andy/ Lucas' evident embarrassment, 'a pus-ridden carbuncle you called it'. Further local references were inserted throughout the performance, and this continued even when the show toured abroad (in Australia, these were provided by Gina Riley and Jane Turner, creators of *Kath and Kim* [ABC TV 2002–04, 2007]). Clearly, there is pleasure in this for an audience, one of recognition and connection, and this is something that Walliams and Lucas are keenly aware of ('I think there's a frisson for the audience when the place they live in is mentioned' observed Walliams [Lucas and Walliams 2006a]). As Bourdieu has noted, 'everything takes place as if the popular "aesthetic" were based on the affirmation of continuity between art and life' (1992: 32); the acknowledgement of the specificity of place is a good example of this.

In the critical discussion of performance and audiences, terms such as 'active' and 'passive' take on an almost metaphorical resonance, referring to intellectual and/or emotional responses (or, in the case of Brechtian theatre practice, to political engagement): in *Little Britain Live*, participation was often more literal and physical. Some of the most striking departures from the aesthetic of *Little Britain* came in the moments when the barrier between actor and audience was deliberately and provocatively dismantled. There were three notable occasions when this happened. On one, David Walliams as Anne, the talentless Whitney Houston impersonator in a TV talent show, offered an extension to a sketch that seemed to have ended with the drawing of the curtains. As the applause was established, Walliams/Anne appeared through the curtain to reprise the 'song' and extend it into the audience. Like a naughty child, Anne assaulted the front row, baring his/her backside and sitting on one person's lap – an action both outrageous and playful.

There are also two moments where audience members were invited (or, more accurately, were hoisted) onto the stage. The first of these happened during a routine that figured Des Kaye, a children's entertainer with homosexual paedophiliac tendencies, performing at a holiday camp. The theatre audience was cast as the fictional audience for his show-within-a-show and addressed directly. The climax of Des's routine (which were full of double entendres that betrayed, seemingly without intentionality, his sexual proclivities) involved a game of 'hide the sausage', for which two 'boys' from the audience were required. Walliams/ Des chose two men, one of whom was clearly younger and more conventionally attractive than the other, to participate. The humour of the 'game' that ensued (and I leave the reader to imagine what the sausage looked like and exactly how 'hide the sausage' and what followed, 'hunt the sausage', were played) hinged on Des's uncontrollable attraction to one and indifference to the other. The unlucky recipient of Des's attentions was kissed and fondled; he eventually had his trousers pulled down and was bundled off the stage as Des attempted anal intercourse.

The second moment arose out of one of the most familiar of *Little Britain*'s sketches which figures Lucas/Marjorie Dawes and her 'Fat Fighters' Club. In the television version, Marjorie's reluctant members are present on screen as part of the narrative; onstage, the theatre audience became the club members and were addressed as such. A recurrent joke, in which Marjorie feigns incomprehension when she is spoken to by a women of apparent Asian ethnic origin, was re-cast with an audience member (whose ethnic origin was difficult to determine) as the butt of her patronising racism. Another, in which the hapless Fat Fighters are asked to guess the calorific value of various foods (including 'dust'), was directed out to the audience. However, the centre of the routine was when a member of the audience was pulled onto the stage to become the focus of ritual humiliation. Each of the persons chosen in both the performances discussed here was indeed overweight, a woman and the subject of many jibes at her expense ('I see the steps held up' said Marjorie/ Lucas as they moved from the auditorium onto the stage). The culmination of the routine was when Marjorie's victim was presented with a Fat Fighter's T-shirt the size of a double-bed sheet.

The strategy of audience humiliation owed something to British music-hall but even more to the bruising informality of the Edinburgh Festival Fringe shows and the subsequent tours that Lucas and Walliams created in the 1990s, especially in its explicitness and outrageousness. When asked by an interviewer (reported in the *Little Britain Live* programme) whether the show might include improvisation, Walliams replied,

> We've got some audience interaction with Des Kaye and Marjorie Dawes – we say interaction, though it's more humiliation. That's something we've always loved. When we started off doing shows in the Edinburgh Festival in 95, we always liked that element. We started shows at midnight in front of 100 people, when everyone had been drinking all day. It had to be quite in-yer-face and combative so we'd have lots of interaction there. (Lucas and Walliams 2005: unpaginated)

Little Britain Live, however, was not as confrontational as this account of their early shows suggests, since audience participants presumably knew something of what they were letting themselves in for. The television version may not have this kind of direct participation but it signals that (more or less) anything is possible, even the outrageous, and this strategy of audience involvement/humiliation was an extension of this permissive stance. 'Outrageousness' is always a matter of context, and *Little Britain*'s impact is due partly to its existence within the regulated, though not illiberal, environment of British television. *Little Britain Live*, however, was more excessive because it was less policed. It is a matter of frequent comment that after the abolition of pre-production censorship in 1968 British theatre went from being the most regulated of cultural forms to being the most free; *Little Britain Live* took advantage of this openness, as several of the examples above demonstrate. The degree to which the *Little Britain* phenomenon is truly 'carnivalesque', riotously and subversively overturning social and cultural norms and celebrating their alternative, is considered elsewhere in this book. If a case is to be made, then perhaps *Little Britain Live* provides some of the most telling evidence. This is partly because of the explicitness of its content and the sheer rudeness of its attitude towards the audience. It is also because live performance – its physicality, immediacy and presence – is a paradigm of the carnivalesque and the source of its origins is in popular festivals and entertainments.

All of the above does not mean that the audience for the television version of *Little Britain* is uninvolved, of course, but simply that audience engagement takes different forms in different media. Also, although it is convenient and habitual to refer to 'the' audience – as this chapter has done so far – there are/were potentially different audiences, both in the domestic sitting-room and in the theatre auditorium. It is difficult to generalise about the social, cultural, gender and age profile of any of the many audiences for the *Little Britain* phenomenon, but it would be reasonable to surmise that it is fairly broad-based. Indeed, the attendance figures quoted earlier, and an unscientific glance around the Cardiff International Arena on the night of the performance I attended, seemed to confirm this of the live show. Attending a live performance requires a bigger commitment to the show than watching it on television (certainly financially, since tickets for this one were circa £35 each), and it is reasonable to speculate that a high proportion of the audience for *Little Britain Live* would have described themselves as fans. The *Little Britain* phenomenon, in all its incarnations, has its own distinct and committed fan base, in the sense(s) that Matt Hills has usefully explored (2002). (The processes of engagement with a programme are similar even for audiences who are not or would not consider themselves to be, in a strict sense, 'fans'.) Fans are, by definition, involved in the programme to which they commit, enacting their relationship to the series through a variety of means and discourses. As Hills has pointed out, fan identity is not stable or fixed but is rather performative: 'fandom is not simply a "thing" that can be picked over analytically. It is always performative; by which I mean it is an identity which is (dis)claimed, and which performs cultural work' (2002: xi). Although fan/audience identity can be claimed at any stage of the process of engaging with and responding to a programme, it is perhaps most possible in the act of consumption itself – watching the programme and attending the show. In one sense, attending the live performance enhances the ritualistic quality of all audience members' relationship to a programme (and not just of those who might define themselves as 'fans'); one is there not simply to consume a performance but to take part in an event – and ritual is always performative. Watching a regular television programme, often in the company of other fans, has a ritualistic aspect as well, but in live performance, where the audience is in a distinct and public space, in the company of strangers as well as friends and family, the quality of collective participation is much more to the fore. *Little Britain Live* restaged and affirmed, for a collective subject, the audience's engagement with the whole *Little Britain* phenomenon.

Notes

1. For the sake of consistency and to avoid confusion, I will refer to the stage show as *Little Britain Live* and to the television version as *Little Britain*. I will not be discussing the radio version of the show.
2. I shall be referring to the UK tour in this chapter, using the DVD of the show recorded at the Blackpool Opera House on 9 May 2006 and my own experience as an audience member at the Cardiff International Arena on 5 December 2006.

Chapter THREE

'Yeah but No but Yeah': A Linguistic Perspective on the Humour of *Little Britain*

Julia Snell

The appeal of *Little Britain*, originally launched on BBC Radio 4 and then transferred to television, is based not purely on visual comedy; its humour originates in the language used. This chapter[1] will examine the humour of *Little Britain* from a linguistic perspective. In particular, I will show how schema theory, a useful tool for analysing comedy, can shed light on the construction and interpretation of humour in the show.

Schema Theory and Humour

'Schema theory' is 'an umbrella term covering a range of individual cognitive models at the heart of which are situated the core concept *schema* and the attendant concepts *frame*, *scenario* and *script*' (Simpson 2004: 89). These are just some of the terms used by researchers. I will use both *schema* and *script* as unmarked terms for this type of cognitive structure: *schema* (pl. *schemata*) when talking about the concept in general and *script* to refer to specific examples.

Schemata are organised packages of knowledge based on previous experience of objects, events and situations, which are stored in memory; they may be defined as 'mental representations of typical instances' (Guy Cook 1994: 11). Such bundles of knowledge are continually updated according to new experiences, and the basic claim of schema theory is that 'a new experience is understood by comparison with a stereotypical version of a similar experience held in memory. The new experience is then processed in terms of its deviation from the stereotypical version, or conformity to it' (Guy Cook 1994: 9).

According to schema theory, meanings are constructed in the interaction between a text and the interpreter's background knowledge. Schemata are activated by either linguistic items in the text or contextual cues. Once activated, schemata generate expectations, and these expectations fill in what is not explicitly mentioned in the text. Expectations may be subverted, however, resulting in incongruity, and this incongruity may give rise to humour.

Raskin (1985) and Attardo (2001) have formalised the concept of incongruity as opposition between semantic scripts in theories which borrow terminology from schema theory: the 'Semantic Script Theory of Humour' and the 'General Theory of Verbal Humour'. The basic premise of these theories is that a text can be characterised as humorous if it is compatible with two opposing scripts. Examples of script opposition will become apparent in the following analysis.

Social Schemata

Much of the humour in *Little Britain* emanates from 'larger than life' characters often based on recognisable stereotypes. Culpeper (2002: 262) states that first impressions of characters are guided by schemata; people often perceive others as members of social groups rather than as individuals. Such groups, according to Culpeper (2001, 2002), provide the basis for cognitive categories. He suggests that the social categories which people use in their perception of others include three broad groupings:

- *personal categories* (preferences, interests, traits and goals);
- *social-role categories* (kinship roles, occupational roles and relational roles);
- *group-membership categories* (gender, race, class, age, nationality and religion).

(Culpeper 2001: 75–6)

Culpeper argues (2001: 77) that 'generally, when a category is activated, so too is the network of which it is a part'. It is this network, which contains links between the different social categories, that he describes as a 'social schema'. Such links arise as a result of experience: particular social roles tend to be filled by certain kinds of people. Based on their experience of the sorts of people who generally fill the occupational role of an accountant, for example, some people may have a social schema for ACCOUNTANT that includes links to personality traits or to group-membership categories such as gender and class (e.g., 'boring, introverted, middle-class male'). The schema is not necessarily based on direct experience but could be influenced by stereotypical images that appear in the media. Two of the recurring characters from *Little Britain*, Emily Howard (David Walliams) and Vicky Pollard (Matt Lucas), illustrate how this concept can be applied.

Emily Howard

Emily is a failed transvestite: a man who dresses as a woman in a rather unconvincing manner and yet tries to persuade people that he is 'a lady'. Two Emily Howard sketches from the first series of *Little Britain* are reprinted below.

Text 1: Emily Howard ('Pub', 1: 1)

Emily has just wandered into a seaside pub. 'Her' entrance is dramatic and theatrical:

Emily: Ooh, ah! Ooh, ah! Absolutely tipping it down out there. That's the only reason I came in here alone, without a chaperone. I am a lady, you see. Please, pay me no heed. ((Goes to the bar)) I've never been in a pub before. Tell me, what does one do?

Landlord: Well, you can order a drink if you like, mate.

Emily: Yes, I'll have a lady's drink, s'il vous plait.

Landlord: What can I get you?

Vic: I'd like to buy the lady a drink.

Emily: ((Shocked)) What?

Vic: I said I'd like to buy you a drink if that's OK.

Emily: But I'm a lady.

Vic: Yeah, I know. And I'd like to buy you a drink.

Emily: Oh erm- well er er er a drinkypoopoo. Yes, I'll have a slimline tonic water, please.

Landlord: ((Suspicious)) Right you are.

Emily: And um, two packets of crisps. Do you have Barbecued Beef variety? Merci beaucoup.

Landlord: ((Nods and gives Emily two bags of crisps))

Vic: Cheers.

Emily: Chin chin ((takes a tiny sip))

Vic: So tell me a little bit about yourself.

Emily: Well, my name is Emily. Emily Howard. And I am a lady. And because I'm a lady, I like to do ladies' things, like attend the operettas and les ballets imaginaries. Do you like the theatre?

Vic: No, but I like you.

Emily: Well, you must know that I am a lady! I press flowers and stroke kittens and swim in rivers wearing dresses and hats, and shit.

Vic: You're a very lovely looking lady.

Emily: ((Laughs coquettishly for far too long))

Emily: ((Coy)) You embarrass me. I must go and powder my nose....

Text 2: Emily Howard ('X-Ray', 1: 4)

Emily is in the X-Ray room of a hospital waiting for the doctor:

Doctor: Right, sorry to keep you. ((Checking clipboard)) So, Eddie Howard.

Emily: Emily Howard. I'm a lady, Emily Howard, yes.

Doctor: Right, uh, what happened?

Emily: Well, I was disembarking a motor coach when I took a tumble.

Doctor: You fell off the bus?

Emily: Quite.

Doctor: Right, well, I'm going to need to do an X-ray of the whole leg. So if you'd just like to place this over your testicles.

((The doctor hands Emily a small pillow. She is quite alarmed))

Emily: Ooh, doctor, you do amuse!

Doctor: No, it's not a joke. It's got a sheet of lead in it. It uh deflects the radiation.

Emily: But I am a lady. I – I don't have testiclés [pronounced [testıkleı]]. Well, perhaps...little ladies' testicles.

((Emily pulls out a Chinese Fan from her Handbag and moves it around her midriff))

Emily: Might, er, might er this do for me instead?

Doctor: No.

Emily: Or er or this?

((Emily pulls out a Victoria copy of *The Lady* magazine))

Emily: Surely I er hm?

((Emily pulls out a small white fluffy cat))

Doctor: I'm sorry. You need to use this. ((He hands Emily the special pillow))

Emily: Well, would you mind if I brightened it up a little with some appliqué and décollage? Yes I could sew some lace around the edges.

Doctor: We don't really have time for this, Mr Howard.

Emily: But I am a lady.

Doctor: Well I can't give you the X-ray without it.

Emily: Well, do you know, I think I am feeling rather better. Yes, I don't think I need an X-ray at all. Yes.

((Emily climbs off the bed uneasily and in great pain))

Emily: ((Manly)) Aargh! Shit!

When presented with the lexical item 'lady', the audience constructs a cognitive representation by identifying and activating a script, LADY. *Little Britain* plays on an old-fashioned stereotype of 'a lady'. This comes across in the character's language, as well as in her dress (long skirt, high-necked frilly blouse and elaborate period wig) and the props which appear in the sketch. According to Schank and Abelson (1977), 'props' are one of the 'slots' that form part of a script. For the Emily Howard sketches these include a parasol (despite the fact that there is no sun) and a Victorian copy of *The Lady* magazine. These objects belong within a specific track of the script LADY such as VICTORIAN LADY. These scripts generate a network of links and associations that may be said to constitute the social schema. For example, there are links to interests: *attend the operettas and les ballets imaginaries; press flowers and stroke kittens and swim in rivers wearing dresses and hats; appliqué and décollage.* Various traits are also alluded to. Emily's notion of a lady is that she is coquettish, refined and sophisticated. These more abstract attributes cannot be observed but have to be inferred, and such inferences can be made through a character's language. Lexical items such as *chaperone* and *motor coach* and the phrase *pay me no heed* allude to a bygone era where Emily's old-fashioned notions of gentility belong. The lexical items *drinkypoopoo* and *chin chin* are stereotypically feminine and 'upper-class'. Emily uses idiomatic French phrases such as *s'il vous plait* and *merci beaucoup* as well as mock French pronunciation (e.g., *testiclé* [testıkleı]), in order to suggest sophistication.

Emily displays many of the characteristics sometimes thought to be 'typical' of women's speech (Lakoff 1975): super polite forms (e.g., the euphemism *powder my nose*); emphatic stress (e.g., *Absolutely*); and fillers such as *well*. Of course, in terms of linguistic research in this area, conceptions of women's language have moved on significantly. Many linguists have challenged Lakoff's set of 'women's language' features (see Cameron, McAlinden and O'Leary 1989; Coates 1996; Holmes 1995). This is not to say that such features are any less important in forming an impression of a character, however, especially in relation to *Little Britain* where the stereotype that is being created for humorous purposes is not concerned with reality.

Little Britain plays on an old-fashioned stereotype of 'a lady'. Emily Howard's conception of women's speech is similar to that described by Jespersen (1922: 246) where women prefer refined expression and avoid coarse and vulgar language. It is obvious to the audience when Emily switches out of this mode. In order for linguistic forms to carry meanings over and above referential meaning, 'they must be sufficiently salient when they are uttered' (Podesva 2006: 189). In these sketches, the word *shit* has what Podesva (2006: 189) calls 'categorical salience', whereby 'infrequent variants stand out more than frequent variants'. Because expletives are infrequent in the Emily

Howard sketches, they are categorically salient and can thus be used stylistically for humorous purposes. Emily's use of the word *shit* in both sketches is foregrounded against the rest of her language. These examples are evidence of Emily 'slipping out' of character. Her failure to perform the role of 'a lady' is thus heightened.

The social schema that Emily represents is incongruent with the more modern representation of a 'lady' (even more so of a 'woman') that the audience is likely to have constructed to operate in daily life. As a result, Emily is a failure as a 'lady' and the character is also a failure as a transvestite. The script for TRANSVESTITE includes the information that a transvestite is a man who dresses up in women's clothes. This script is unlikely, however, to contain the information that a transvestite should try and actually convince people that he is, in fact, 'a lady' and repeatedly state 'I am a lady'. The incongruity between Emily's perception of herself and what the audience actually sees gives rise to humour. This incongruity is reflected in script oppositions such as OLD-FASHIONED/MODERN, LADY/MAN, REALISTIC/UNREALISTIC, SUCCESS/FAILURE.

Vicky Pollard

In the following sketch, overlapping speech is shown by a square bracket placed at the beginning of the overlap in both utterances.

Text 3: Vicky Pollard ('Magistrates' Court', 1: 4)

Vicky is accused of shop-lifting and is being interrogated by the prosecution lawyer.

Lawyer: Vicky Pollard you have been charged with shoplifting. On the 11th April, it is alleged you went into the Erskine branch of Superdrug. Once there you attempted to steal an eyeliner pencil and can of Red Bull by concealing them in your leggings.... Now in the face of the overwhelming evidence we've heard today against you, do you stand by your plea of 'Not guilty'?

Vicky: No but yeah but no because what happened was right this thing happened what I don't know nothing about shut up I wasn't meant to be anywhere even near there. Then Meredith came over and started stirring it all up started calling me all these things about this thing I didn't even know about or somefink or nuffin'

((The Lawyer is stumped))

Lawyer: Right, but you admit you were in Superdrug at the time?

Vicky: No but yeah but no because there's this whole other thing what I didn't even know about and Meredith said it weren't a thing but it was but don't listen to her because she's a complete slag.

Lawyer: Sorry, Meredith? Who is Meredith?

Vicky: She's the one who done that thing about the thing but if she gives you sweets don't eat 'em because she's dirty.

Lawyer: Thing? What – what thing?

Vicky: Yeah, I know and anyway and there was this whole other thing what I didn't even know about or somefink or nuffin' because nobody told Wayne Duggin that Jermyn fingered Carly round the back of the ice rink.

Lawyer: Right.

Vicky: But I was supposed to be doing Home Ec. But I wasn't right I was on the phone to Jules. But anyway don't listen to her because she had a baby and didn't tell anyone.

Lawyer: Vicky, were you at Superdrug at the time?

Vicky: No but yeah but no but yeah but no but yeah but no because I wasn't even with Amber.

Lawyer: Amber? Who's Amber?

Vicky: Yeah, exactly. I wasn't even with her and anyway I didn't even know who she is so you'd better ask her.

Lawyer: Vicky I don't think you realise the gravity
[of the situation you –
Vicky: [No but there's something right what I don't even –
Lawyer: If you're [found guilty today –
Vicky: [No you definitely can't say that right bec-
Lawyer: You'll have a cri[minal record.
Vicky: [No but I'm allergic to cat hair
so I don't have to go into lessons.
Lawyer: This is a [court of law, you have t – Are you going to
Vicky: [No cos – Towser, right, well he no no no
Lawyer: [keep interrupting me?
Vicky: [no no no no no no I'm not, I'm...going to let you
speak.
Lawyer: Good...Now we've heard from the social [workers.
Vicky: [Oh my
God, right there was this whole other thing I
[completely forgot to tell
Lawyer: [Oh I give up!
Vicky: you about.

You know Craig? Well he felt up Amy on the
corkscrew at Alton Towers and her mum had
an eppy [epileptic fit]. But then Dean went on
the Mary Rose and was sick on Louise Farren's
head.

Vicky represents the stereotype of a working-class teenager or 'chav'. The sort of person whom this word refers to was
(and still is) a current social phenomenon that the writers of *Little Britain* were able to capitalise on. In her book *Larpers and
Shroomers: The Language Report*, Susie Dent (2004) cites 'chav'
as 'a contender for the word of 2004'. The term found its way
into the *Oxford English Dictionary* in June 2006: 'a young person of a type characterised by brash and loutish behaviour and
the wearing of designer-style clothes (esp. sportswear); usually
with connotations of a low social status'. As suggested by this
definition, the script for CHAV makes a number of links between
the group-membership categories of age ('a young person') and

social class ('low social status'), and personal categories ('brash and loutish behaviour'). A brief review of some of the 128 definitions of 'chav' posted on the *Urban Dictionary* demonstrates the public consensus concerning the delineation of this social schema:

> The female chav (chavette) will have peroxide blonde hair scrunched so tight into a pony tail with colourful scrunchies that her forehead stretches. She will wear a dark blue tracksuit with white stripes, an enormous puffa jacket, hoop earrings, and white trainers.

> A young British 'person', bottom bottom class in both status and culture, favouring baseball caps, fake 'sports' 'labels', tracksuit bottoms tucked into their socks, trainers that cost the same amount of money as a flat deposit, and an unspeakably antisocial manner: a juvenile ruffian.

> Most Chav words are mercifully brief, and sentences tend to be punctuated with 'innit' or some sort of expletive.

> Unable to converse in any high form of language and too lazy to communicate the limited vocabulary they have properly.

In terms of appearance and behaviour, Vicky Pollard fits this schema perfectly (see Sharon Lockyer's chapter for more on Vicky Pollard). The last two definitions show that there is also public perception of the sort of language a 'chav' uses. How then does Vicky Pollard's language reflect (or reinforce) the social schema TEENAGE CHAV?

Following the launch of the Bergen Corpus of London Teenage Language (COLT), a number of studies have focused on the speech of teenagers. Using the corpus to research pragmatic markers in teenage conversation, Andersen (1997: 2) notes, 'teenage talk in general is said to be highly expressive and vivid, and teenagers are said to use language as a means of expressing and evoking emotional involvement rather than for the communication of facts and logical ideas'. Vicky's speech certainly conveys very little that is factual or logical. The perception of her language as being incoherent is due in part to her use of pragmatic markers such as *but, right, because, anyway*, which do not add anything to the propositional content of her speech.

Andersen aims to test the perception that teenagers use pragmatic markers in conversation to a greater extent than adults do by comparing conversations from the COLT corpus with a subset of the British National Corpus (BNC), which includes mainly adult speakers. His findings show that the claim that teenagers use more pragmatic markers than adults does not hold: teenagers use certain markers (such as *right, really, actually, anyway*) more frequently, while adults use other markers (such as *well, I mean, I think, I guess*) more frequently. Figure 1 compares Andersen's results with the speech of Vicky Pollard for five salient pragmatic markers. The occurrences of these markers in Vicky's dialogue in the 'Magistrates' Court' sketch were counted and compared to Vicky's total word count in order to derive a figure ('frequency per 1000 words') comparable to Andersen's data. So, for example, Vicky utters 337 words in this sketch and uses the pragmatic marker *anyway* three times. We can say, therefore, that, on average, Vicky uses this marker 8.9 times per 1000 words (3/337 x 1000).

Vicky's speech includes many more pragmatic markers than either the teenage or adult conversations used by Andersen (Figure 1). This is most noticeable with *but*, which is part of Vicky's trademark catchphrase *yeah but no but yeah*. The point is that, although Andersen's data does not support the hypothesis that teenagers use significantly more pragmatic markers than adults,

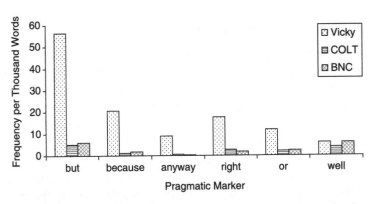

Figure 1 Comparison of Anderson's (1997) results with the speech of Vicky Pollard

the perception that this is the case leads to comedic exaggerations of this particular speech style in characters such as Vicky Pollard; it becomes part of the social schema for TEENAGER or CHAV. The link between pragmatic markers and the social categories of 'teenager' or 'chav' is not direct. Frequent use of pragmatic markers, to use Ochs' (1992) terminology, directly indexes incoherence in discourse and only indirectly indexes teenage or chav language. The link to the social category of teenager or chav is only through a series of ideological conventions which associate incoherence with teenage/chav identity. Such ideologies are not necessarily based in fact, but they still inform our interpretations of language use and other behaviour.

Vicky's speech reinforces other stereotypical assumptions about the language of a 'chav'. She uses taboo language (e.g., *slag*) and non-standard grammatical constructions (e.g., *what I don't know nothing about*). As Culpeper (2001:17) points out, 'knowing what the linguistic stereotypes are is valuable, since these are the currency of the layperson'. The likelihood of stereotypical assumptions not having empirical validity does not diminish their importance in forming character impressions. In fact, this particular social schema may not be based on personal experience at all but be driven by the image of the 'chav' that has been constructed within media and popular discourse. You do not necessarily have to know someone like Vicky Pollard personally in order to be able to access this social schema.

The Importance of Context

Vicky Pollard and Emily Howard illustrate the humour that is created from the exploitation of social stereotypes. But the importance of context for these characters should also be highlighted, for it is often in their inability to act appropriately according to the situation that these stereotypes become more pronounced. Emily Howard and Vicky Pollard have maximum impact in the show not only because they are based on familiar social schemata but also because they surprise the audience through some unusual distortion brought about through interaction with an unexpected context and their inability to act appropriately in that given context. In Culpeper's (2001) terms,

Vicky Pollard and Emily Howard are examples of 'exaggerated prototypes'. Such characters are not simply the prototype of some social category, that is, the average or the norm, but prototypical in some exaggerated way. Characters are perceived as exaggerated prototypes if:

- they fail to exhibit contextually sensitive behaviour;
- they simply appear in situations where they are not expected.

(Culpeper 2001: 88–9)

In the 'X-Ray' sketch, Emily's behaviour (linguistic and other) is inappropriate considering the hospital setting. Faced with strict time constraints, doctors 'typically want to arrive as quickly as possible at a diagnosis' (Wodak 1997: 343), and they require the patient's cooperation in doing this. Patients may be considered 'difficult' if their behaviour disrupts this process (Wodak 1997: 351). With this in mind, the elaborate avoidance strategies that Emily adopts when faced with the prospect of an X-ray appear deviant. The doctor comments on the time constraints that frame this situation: *We don't really have time for this, Mr Howard.* Emily does not adhere to convention, however. Her behaviour in the examination room is contrary to normal expectations. At the start of the scene, even her initial explanation of the accident appears odd: *I was disembarking a motor coach when I took a tumble.* Grice suggests that participants in a conversation are guided by an overarching 'Cooperative Principle': 'Make your conversational contribution such as is required, at the stage at which it occurs, by the accepted purpose or direction of the talk exchange in which you are engaged' (Grice 1975: 45). This principle encompasses four maxims, which are summarised below:

- *quantity*: provide the amount of information that is appropriate given the purposes of the exchange;
- *quality*: do not state that which you know to be false, or for which you lack adequate evidence;
- *manner*: be clear, brief, and unambiguous;
- *relation*: be relevant.

Emily's deliberately obscure explanation violates the maxim of manner and is particularly inappropriate in this context. This point is reinforced by the doctor's simple reformulation: *You fell off the bus*. The use of a periphrasis for 'fell' (*took a tumble*) and the obsolete noun *motor coach* for 'bus' highlight the script oppositions FORMAL/INFORMAL and OLD-FASHIONED/MODERN. At the end of the sketch, Emily actually denies herself medical treatment in order to maintain the role of 'a lady'. As an exaggerated prototype, Emily cannot modify her behaviour, even in a serious medical situation.

We see similar behaviour from Vicky Pollard in the 'Magistrates' Court' sketch. The situation activates the script for COURTROOM, and this script generates expectations about appropriate behaviour. The COURTROOM script is likely to include information such as the following: the lawyer and judge are the only people who are able to ask questions, and these questions should be answered by the witness in an efficient manner. In this sketch, the lawyer addresses direct questions to Vicky, but she consistently fails to provide the preferred response. In fact, Vicky's responses do not make any sense at all in this context. Grice's (1975) Cooperative Principle provides a framework of conversational expectations which when broken may trigger interpretative activity. On this basis, the audience will notice something deviant about Vicky's speech. The lawyer is certainly stumped by Vicky's first turn in the interaction. The lawyer has asked Vicky a direct yes-or-no question: *do you stand by your plea of 'Not guilty'?* Vicky's answer violates Grice's maxims of quantity (by giving far more information than is required), manner (by being deliberately obscure and unnecessarily wordy) and relation (because her answer bears no relevance to the question). The lawyer attempts to get back on track with the pragmatic marker *Right,* but his attempts are thwarted. The lawyer searches for relevance in Vicky's remarks (*Sorry, Meredith? Who is Meredith?*), supporting Grice's (1975) claim that people assume cooperation in conversation (a far greater expectation in this context), but he finds none. Vicky's utterances are deliberately vague: *who done that thing about the thing; this whole other thing; somefink or nuffin*. Her catchphrase *no but yeah but no* is symbolic of the general incoherence of her discourse.

The COURTROOM script also contains information about appropriate discourse routines and activates a turn-taking script whereby the balance of power lies with the lawyer. His discourse role affords him certain rights, such as the right to speak at length without interruption. In this sketch, though, it is Vicky who does most of the talking. Vicky has 337 words distributed over 13 turns (average turn length: 25.9 words), while the lawyer has 150 words distributed over 13 turns (average turn length: 11.5 words). Moreover, Vicky consistently interrupts the lawyer, thereby deny-ing him his speaking rights. The lawyer explicitly refers to the rules that *should* govern this interaction: *This is a court of law... Are you going to keep interrupting me?* This is the only occasion when Vicky responds with a firm 'no' to what appears to be a yes/no question. The irony is that, on this occasion, the lawyer's ut-terance is not functioning as a question but rather as a command with the intended meaning 'Stop interrupting me'. Vicky does not comply with this command, however. The power differential in this interaction has been reversed, and the lawyer, who should occupy high status, actually withdraws from the situation: *Oh I give up*. This constitutes the final punch line. The script for COURT-ROOM gives way to TEENAGE GOSSIP.

Cultural Schemata

The wide appeal of *Little Britain* is evidenced by its being broadcast to a number of countries outside Britain, including the United States, Canada, Australia and Japan. There are many people, both in Britain and outside it, however, who do not appreciate its humour. Can schema theory help to explain why?

I would argue that, to a certain extent, schema theory *can* acc-ount for the different reactions that separate sections of the audi-ence may have. According to the theory, the process of interpre-tation involves a combination of textual factors and background knowledge. Because people have distinct kinds of background knowledge and beliefs, it is possible for different people to con-struct quite different interpretations of the same text. Of course, some people may have very similar schemata and thus extract shared meaning from a text.

Semino (1997: 124) notes that 'the content of schemata will vary from individual to individual, and, more dramatically, from culture to culture'. This is an apt point with regard to humour since many of us may have experienced the embarrassment that results from making a joke which does not successfully transcend cultural boundaries. The changes which Lucas and Walliams will no doubt make to the show's American version will reveal differences in the culture, history and traditions of the US audience compared to viewers in the UK (see Postscript to this collection). Social groups differentiated by age, class, gender and ethnicity as well as by geography may produce different interpretations of texts. Davies (1990: 312), in his book *Ethnic Humor around the World*, makes the point that the (humorous) qualities imputed to a group can be interpreted and evaluated in many ways. He notes that individual members of a ridiculed group could interpret the joke as referring to a subgroup other than the one to which he or she belongs. It is possible, therefore, for members of both the ingroup and the outgroup to appreciate the same joke (albeit through different interpretations). Do the working-class teenage viewers of *Little Britain*, for example, laugh at Vicky Pollard because they see her as a member of a teenage subgroup to which they do not belong?

Comedy Schema

Whatever background the interpreter is coming from, I would argue that most individuals interpret humorous texts under an overarching comedy schema. This concept is similar to Stockwell's (2002: 80–1) notion of a literary schema. He states that a literary schema is 'a higher-level conceptual structure that organises our ways of reading when we are in the literary context':

> Any ordinary schema can appear in a literary context, but once there it is treated in a different way as a result of literary reading. It is this reading angle that 're-registers' the original schema and processes it in terms of literary factors. (Stockwell 2002: 80)

When interpreting a text under the comedy schema, we do not take what we see to be literally true. We would not, for example, update our script for LADY according to the behaviour of Emily Howard.

. After experiencing the *Little Britain* sketches on a number of different occasions, I would hypothesise that viewers create new scripts based upon the characters in the show under an over-arching comedy schema. The mention of the name Emily Howard, for example, would then activate the script for EMILY HOWARD: FAILED TRANSVESTITE. Catchphrases are so closely associated with the characters in *Little Britain* that hearing a catchphrase could easily activate the relevant script. Eventually, when enough people share the same schematic knowledge, it becomes possible to evoke laughter among one's friends and colleagues by the mere repetition of 'I am a lady' or 'yeah but no but' because these phrases are able to activate the relevant script with all its related humorous links and associations. For anyone who does not possess the relevant schemata, there is no evident reason why the catchphrase should be interpreted as funny.

Repetition is a powerful tool in comedy. Although repetition of a joke will diminish its humorous effect, variation on a familiar theme has the double impact of creating humour anew while also evoking memories of previous humour. The laughter is thus experienced on two separate levels. With *Little Britain*, repetition of character sketches creates new schemata based on the characters which can then be used to interpret and reinterpret the humour. With each new sketch, the familiar characters are presented to the audience in a unique context and the audience's existing schemata are reorganised accordingly. After three series, however, the sketches may cease to be 'schema refreshing' (Guy Cook 1994), that is, the sketches would activate existing schemata but lack the novelty required to humorously challenge and then update these schemata. It is at this point that audiences begin to lose interest in the characters and the show. Perhaps this fact influenced the decision not to continue the show into a fourth series.

For many people, the name 'Vicky Pollard' activates not only VICKY POLLARD: WORKING-CLASS TEENAGER but also CHAV; Vicky Pollard has come to symbolise a female chav (or 'chavette'). A definition from *Urban Dictionary* simply states,

> Chavettes (female species if you already didn't know) are summed up perfectly by the one & only Matt Lucas in 'Little Britain' Two words – Vicky Pollard!!

The media certainly exploits this association. British newspapers abound with references to 'Vicky Pollard' which rely on the activation of scripts such as CHAV: 'the Vicky Pollard types who become single mothers' (David Smith, *The Sunday Times*, 7 January 2007); 'a Vicky Pollard community' (Jessica Shepherd, *The Guardian*, 23 October 2007); 'a nation of Vicky Pollards' (Rob Draper, *The Daily Mail*, 20 February 2005); 'a generation of Vicky Pollards' (Sara Wallis, *The Mirror*, 3 May 2007). By activating the script VICKY POLLARD in the minds of their readers, these journalists can tap into a network of associations and images which frame their story.

Interplay between Verbal and Non-verbal Humour

I have so far not mentioned the non-verbal humour in *Little Britain*. Norrick (2004: 401) makes the point that 'many jokes fall outside the province of script theory, because they depend on performance in various ways.' I would argue, however, that some aspects of non-verbal performance can be incorporated into schema-based theories if we consider that both verbal and non-verbal elements are capable of activating schemata. In fact, verbal and visual elements may activate conflicting/incongruous schemata, giving rise to humour. The *Little Britain* sketches involving the characters Lou (David Walliams) and Andy (Matt Lucas), for example, successfully exploit this technique since the humour often lies in the incongruity between Lou's speech and the secret actions of Andy, which the audience (but crucially not Lou) is privy to. In the 'Diving Board' (1:1) sketch, for example, the audience hears Lou make a long request to a lifeguard for help in assisting his disabled friend, Andy, into the swimming pool: *Excuse me, I wonder if you could give me a hand. I'm here with a friend, who you may have seen is in a wheelchair. And I need a little bit of help getting him in and out of the pool... he's not a strong swimmer...So shall we go help him in?* In the background, Andy, unseen by Lou, has climbed the steps to the tallest diving board, jumped into the pool, swum to the steps, got back out and sat down again in his wheel chair. Lou's speech activates scripts such as DISABLED, POOR SWIMMER, CARER, while Andy's behaviour activates the conflicting scripts ABLE-BODIED, COMPETENT

SWIMMER, MISGUIDED FRIEND (see Margaret Montgomerie's chapter for more on Lou and Andy). A useful starting point for an examination of the interplay between verbal and visual humour would be a comparison of the *Little Britain* televisions sketches with the original radio performances. Not surprisingly, the Lou and Andy characters did not feature in the radio sketches.

Conclusion

This chapter has highlighted a number of ways in which schema theory can be applied to research on humour. Apart from giving an insight into the construction of humour in *Little Britain*, schema theory has also been able to demonstrate how *Little Britain*'s audience could construct different interpretations from the same sketches and/or appreciate different aspects of the humour. Through a by-product of this analysis, I hope to have demonstrated how popular texts such as *Little Britain* could be used in the classroom to illustrate the application of a linguistic theory. Indeed, such texts could be used to help people, in particular those learning another language, to understand the humour of other cultures.

Transcription Conventions

Transcripts of the sketches are based on those used in the official compilation of scripts (Lucas and Walliams 2004) with the following modifications:

[completely forgot	Brackets signal the start of overlapping speech
[Oh I give up!	
....	Pause
((Goes to the bar))	Annotation of other verbal/ non-verbal activity
[pronounced [testıkleı]].	Transcriber's comments

Note

1. The chapter is a revised and extended version of an article originally published in *English Today* (Snell 2006).

PART 2

Little Britain and Identity

Chapter FOUR

How *Little Britain* Does 'Race'

Sarita Malik

The relationship between ethnicity and comedy has been widely debated both within popular discourse and in academic study. The question of how 'race' works within the comedy genre raises both sociological (authorship, power and identity politics) and media/communication (textual representation and meaning) concerns. In addition, when comedy that touches on aspects of 'race' is brought into the public arena and becomes dependent on public recognition, for example, through the sphere of public service broadcasting (PSB), further issues are raised around audience reception, intention, impact and the relationship between media policy and cultural production. *Little Britain* – as a popular sketch show which, as I will go on to describe, depends on the routine racialisation of many of its core characters and as a series which is aired on and produced by the UK's leading public service terrestrial broadcaster, the BBC – serves as an important contemporary mainstream media text both for humour research and for studies of race and cultural representation. A number of critical concerns are involved here: how time and context produce meanings around humour; the possible implications this has when a very locally specific text such as *Little Britain* becomes internationally known (most obviously through BBC America); and what we might learn, from our focus on this phenomenally successful comedy series, about the current social and political effects of racialisation within comedy.

Racialisation, an analytical term which emerged in the 1970s, occurs when a racial character or context is imposed on an individual or group. It is a representational process in which this individual or group becomes defined as Other – a political and ideological process that is entirely dependent on context. How this Other is understood, signified and interpreted – although it will produce a *racialized* regime of representation – cannot simply be reduced to being described as a process of racism (Hall in Malik 2002: ix). In this chapter, I will discuss how these representational processes work within *Little Britain*'s three television series and argue that 'racialisation' needs to be maintained as critically distinct from 'racism'. I will situate the analysis within the broader context of 'ethnic comedy' and public service broadcasting in the twenty-first century. I want to argue that *Little Britain* is a comedy primarily about whiteness and is, in this sense, a form of 'ethnic humour'. Its racialized connotations and cultural construction of ethnically inflected comic types are an important dynamic in how its humour works. In addition, this is dependent precisely on the cultural politics of representation centred on ambivalence. *Little Britain* manages, in different ways, to produce a range of readings that might be determined as either inferentially or overtly racist or anti-racist in the same episode, sketch and even representational moment.

Context: Notes on Institutional Context

Ethnic humour has broadly been defined as humour about ethnic groups (Davies 1990). Although it is generally accepted that human 'races' are primarily cultural creations, not biological realities, 'race' and ethnicity are still broadly associated with selected ethnic (minority) groups. As such, television comedies about race, which reached their peak in Britain in the 1970s, more generally refer to those which include ethnic minorities or the topic of racism as the sources of humour. For example, in popular comedies such as *Love Thy Neighbour* (ITV 1972–76) and *Mind Your Language* (ITV 1977–79), racial difference is a key narrative theme.

Since the 1980s, 'ethnic humour' has included 'ethnic sitcoms' such as *No Problem!* (Channel 4 1983–85) and *Tandoori Nights* (Channel 4 1985–87) as well as 'ethnic' sketch-shows such as *The Real McCoy* (BBC 1992–96) and *Goodness Gracious Me* (BBC 1996–2001). The precursor to *Goodness Gracious Me* was

Peter Sellers Is Dead[1], a one-off show with a title that symbolised the end of an era in which white actors 'blacking up' was deemed acceptable.

The socio-political context of the 1980s and the 1990s Britain meant that terrestrial television comedies were approved within a broader PSB policy agenda of supporting Britain's cultural diversity through on-screen representation. Since the mid-1990s, PSB policy has emphasised the importance of a more universalist principle of equal representation for all; ethnic minority representation has become less palpable in British television comedy. Notable exceptions have been the black female-led hidden camera show *3 Non-Blondes* (BBC 2003), the much-criticised *The Crouches* (BBC 2003–04), the one-woman sketch show *Little Miss Jocelyn* (BBC 2006–present) and *Goodness Gracious Me's* successor, *The Kumars at No. 42* (BBC 2001–07). In 2007, it was announced, symbolically perhaps, that *The Kumars at No. 42* (also fronted by *Goodness Gracious Me* stars Sanjeev Bhaskar and Meera Syal) was not to be recommissioned by the BBC. This context is important because *Little Britain*, as a series led by two white Englishmen (David Walliams and Matt Lucas), emerged and became an international brand in the same moment that these minority-led models of 'ethnic humour' on British television, specifically black- and Asian-led television comedy, were on the decline. The industrial context of British television comedy also lays the series open to criticisms that it has helped to sustain an ongoing under-representation of non-White performers in mainstream light entertainment in the post *Goodness Gracious Me* mediascape.

Although the visibility of ethnic minority television comedians has waned in recent years, the limits of 'ethnic humour' continue to be significantly negotiated and contested within British popular culture. In 2007, for example, the UK communications regulator Ofcom (Office of Communications) cleared the public broadcaster ITV of racism following complaints that Sir Trevor McDonald, the presenter of a late night satirical news comedy programme and the UK's first and best-known black television newsreader, had called the controversial comedian Bernard Manning a 'fat, white bastard'. Manning, who had died earlier that week, is well known for having been Britain's most openly racist high-profile comedian. In its ruling, Ofcom stated that McDonald's comments were 'clearly intended to parody' Manning's comic style, that it did 'not believe this specific expression went beyond the likely expectations of an audience' and that 'any offence that may have been caused was justified by the context' (Ofcom 2007: 19–20). Ofcom's verdict that the programme was not in breach of media regulation illustrates the general acceptance, both amongst comedy audiences and now it seems media regulators, that comedy is inextricably linked with issues of intention, impact, subjectivity, performance and context. Thus, it was accepted that McDonald had not *intended* to cause offence; he intended to *parody*; offence *may or may not* have been caused; even if it was, it was politically *justified* because of the broader *context* (of a late night satirical programme? of being topical? of a black newsreader saying it? as an impersonation of the dead comedian's direct comic delivery style?). In these ways, the comedy genre continues to be a key space in which media representations (images, ideas, signs, symbols, discourses and debates) around 'race' are discursively played out. And, therefore, comedy has to be understood as constructed and contested, relational and contextual (Gillespie 2003). It is also clear that despite the surge of new media formats and multi-channel viewing options, traditional PSB remains an important part of our public debate and private domestic rituals and a place where the boundaries of expediency are routinely tested and mediated.

Approaches to Understanding 'Race' in *Little Britain*: Racialising or Racist?

This background leads us to explore some of the possible reasons why *Little Britain* became successful and the ways its representations of race and ethnicity might be connected. Like other BBC television sketch shows which emerged at around the same time such as *The Catherine Tate Show* (BBC 2004–07) and *Tittybangbang* (BBC 2006–present), *Little Britain* features a set of recurring fictional characters that function to satirise British society. *Little Britain*, as its title indicates, parodies an assortment of specifically British character types and, like most satirical humour, depends on its audience recognising which social groups the characters 'belong' to. The making of these social types raises a central question in discussions of humour: why are certain groups chosen to show certain qualities in jokes? (Davies 1990). Satire, with its heavy emphasis on 'the social' and on designated political targets, functions as an important barometer of popular opinion on 'race' at specific moments and over time.

The fact that *Little Britain* is created and performed by two English white men, focuses almost entirely on white characters and is a satire about Little England/Great Britain also inevitably raises questions about how race and the nation are imagined and articulated in the series, and by whom. In any case, this is a broader issue for public service television because it is the primary arena where these matters are played out; the medium defines whether we are positioned as 'in' or 'out', the same or different, British or not. What we don't see is as significant as what we do. *Little Britain*'s focus on England, Britain and 'Britishness' is indeed timely, as the issue has been increasingly prominent in critical debate during the first decade of this century. There are many psycho-social, political and historical factors that are thought to have led to a preoccupation with new kinds of 'anxiety' around national identity. The critical deconstruction of the common interchangeability of 'Englishness' and 'Britishness' has been an important aspect of these debates. That is, it is argued that it is now quite impossible, if there ever was a time, to speak of Britishness solely as 'Englishness' (see Kumar 2003). An approach to understanding 'race' in *Little Britain* has to be informed by a culturalist analysis which positions the programme within these wider contexts of production and reception.

Little Britain is a significantly polarising text because it appears to divide the public according to whether they love it or hate it. Popular responses to its racial politics (to be found in the national press, reviews and internet sites, for example) appear to be similarly discordant. In spite of its largely white portfolio of comic characters, it is rarely considered to be a comedy primarily *about 'race'*. It bears repetition here that within white Western culture, 'race' itself is widely perceived to belong only to certain ethnic groups and considered an 'issue' only when the presence of racial difference is realised through the introduction of different ethnic or cultural types. In spite of the UK's growing multi-ethnic reality, the use of the term 'ethnic' is still routinely applied to those who are ethnically in a minority and most obviously to those categorised as 'non-White', 'people of colour', 'black and Asian' or 'Black Minority Ethnic'. This may help us to understand why most responses to the series have tended to foreground questions of gender, sexuality and class even though *Little Britain* is predominantly a 'white text'. So whilst *Goodness Gracious Me* is unequivocally discussed as an 'ethnic' or 'British-Asian' comedy, *Little Britain* and the discourse that surrounds it produce a neutrality of its own in which there is a refusal to pin it down as a white, English comedy.

One might argue, however, that those British television comedies which rarely profile 'obvious' ethnic characters, such as *Fawlty Towers* (BBC 1975–79) or *The Royle Family* (BBC 1998–2000; 2006; 2008), are, in fact, texts which are themed around and articulated through racial imagery and racial context. In this way, they are *racialized*. It is, I would argue, white English ethnicity, along with other facets of identity such as class, gender and social status, that forms a vital ingredient in how the characters, settings, plots and themes are culturally constructed in these comedies. In turn, characters such as Basil Fawlty and Jim Royle 'make sense' to comedy audiences only because they are both white and English. It is interesting, then, that these comedy texts are rarely discussed in relation to their racialisation techniques or in terms of how they construct 'race'. Although the growth in studies of representation of white people in white Western culture has started to challenge the common assumption that whiteness is itself ethnically, culturally and racially neutral, that it is all and nothing, studies of race and British television comedy have by themselves contributed to this emphasis on the non-white axis of difference focusing primarily on representations of black and Asian communities (Ross 1996; Malik 2002).

In series one and series two, all *Little Britain*'s stock characters are white. In devising a set of recurring characters that are all white *in different ways*, these series acknowledge the multeity not just within 'Little Britain' but also across whiteness. In fact, this allows a thematic focus on the multiplicity of whiteness. In part, the mutations of Englishness are juxtaposed with the strong identities of other nations in the UK. Ray McCooney (David Walliams), the eccentric, riddle-speaking Scottish hotel owner, Vicky Pollard (Matt Lucas), the Bristolian 'chav', Edward 'Emily' Howard (David Walliams), the 'unsuccessful' transvestite trying to pass 'herself' off as a Victorian English lady, Daffyd Thomas (Matt Lucas), the Welsh gay-wannabe who claims he is the 'only gay in the village', all are just some of the white social types that encourage readings which complicate and problematise ideas of white or, for that matter, English universalism and sameness. Through visual and linguistic humour (puns, double entendres, dress, accent play, malapropisms, broad exaggeration, catchphrases) and familiarity and repetition (of both language and characters), the series organises a system of imagery that encourages audience recognition and association. In particular, it produces a *racialized* (not racist) pattern of representation that depends on a familiar stock of cultural, ethnic and national stereotypes.

'Race' plays a constitutive role alongside other vectors of difference. As film theorist Ella Shohat argues, one approach to understanding race in representation is by considering 'ethnicities-in-relation' (Shohat 1991: 220) in conjunction with other facets such as sexuality, gender, religion and class and, therefore, as part of an interconnected relationality. Thus, one possible approach to understanding representation is to not single out 'race' from all other considerations but to analyse the way it works alongside other parts of the whole constructed identity. Relatedly, our readings of these characters are directed by schemata; they are perceived, as Snell outlines in her analysis of *Little Britain*, in relation to the social groups to which they belong (Julia Snell in this collection and 2006). Characterisation is dependent on what Culpeper describes as 'social schema', so that 'when a category is activated, so too is the network of which it is a part' (Culpeper 2001: 77).

The racial basis of *Little Britain*'s characterisation is an important part of this social schema. In this way, the cultural construction of race and ethnicity in *Little Britain* mirrors more typically recognised forms of 'ethnic humour'. Christie Davis, in his study of ethnic humour around the world, identifies racial, nationalist and religious themes, along with other ethnic humour

inflections based around gender, class and region. He also argues
that humour based around stupidity and canniness is a principal
feature of ethnic humour. This is summarised by Bill Russell in his
review of Christie's study:

> The butts usually live in the same country as the jokers and
> nearly always in the same cultural region. 'They are almost
> like us but not quite the same', a sort of modified version of
> the jokers, on whom the jokers can project their own inability
> to cope with the problems of modern society. The butts are
> selected for this purpose because they are on the edge of the
> 'home' culture...They often speak (or are believed to speak) a
> modified version of the 'home' language. (Russell 1996: no
> pagination)

Christie's analysis seems as applicable to *Little Britain* as it
does to 'ethnic' sketch-shows such as *Goodness Gracious Me*.
Hence, any assumption that ethnic humour can refer only to
that which is authored and presented by ethnic minorities is
challenged by *Little Britain*. Although Walliams and Lucas, as
white men, are not necessarily actively racially Othering their
portfolio of white characters, they are nonetheless able to rac-
ialise their cultural constructions – a racialisation which in
other contexts might be considered racist. (How, for example,
would these characterisations be interpreted if they were produced and performed by non-white or non-British performers?).
This illustrates how markers of race are not always markers of
difference. To elaborate, recurrent themes; identifiable settings;
Tom Baker's eccentric 'Queen's English' voice-over and traditional motifs of Englishness (and Scottishness, Welshness) such
as toleration, insularity, eccentricity, provinciality, tea, class, village life, public school and sexual repression occur throughout.
The 'Englishness' of the text is also buttressed by the pompous
(and condescending) voice-over and 'portrait of a nation' claims
in the establishing scenes. Of course, these are also the precise ways in which *Little Britain* produces a satirical take on the
conventional social-issue-led BBC documentaries of the 1950s
and 1960s. These stereotypical signifiers of quintessential 'Englishness' function as a backdrop against which more updated
themes of contemporary Britain – such as multiculturalism,

liberalism, 'urban' culture, anti-racism, political correctness, cultural difference and immigration – are transferred. These target concerns, part of a broader New Labour political agenda of promoting a 'socially inclusive' society, are foregrounded and shown to be filtering down into meaningless, quasi-governmental drives towards social inclusion. This is indicated, for example, in the 'PC' names given to public establishments (such as St. Mohammed's Hospital and St Saddam's Hospital, along with Sandi Toksvig House, Rhona Cameron House[2]). These explicit references in the series signal a broader critique of the so-called PC Britain and its accompanying approaches towards multiculturalism and equal citizenship – a self-reflexive comment on how *Little Britain* itself may be read as working against such ideologies.

The up-to-dateness of these social observations and the misanthropic spin on these themes function in two important ways with regards to race and ethnicity: first, it suggests that the series and its creators are 'socially-engaged' and quite possibly projecting and displacing collective national anxieties about the state of modern Britain; second, for comic effect, these liberal preoccupations and agendas are designed to jar with the traditional versions of Englishness. In relation to the latter, it is specifically cultural (and often racial) diversity that is commonly seen to pose a problem for the white English (always female) character. For example, Linda Flint (David Walliams), in spite of the 'Equality Seminar' posters displayed in her office, is challenged by the physical, racial and cultural difference of her students. Marjorie Dawes (David Walliams) claims that she finds it difficult to comprehend the accent of an Asian sari-wearing member of her Fat Fighters class. Maggie (David Walliams) is driven to projectile vomiting when tasting the raspberry jam made by a black woman, the marmalade made by Sanjana Patel and the fruitcake made by the mother of Judy's future (black) son-in-law, James.

It is through these exhibitive moments that *Little Britain*'s white characters are confronted by racial difference and, in fact, the presence of race is seen to be realised. This works on different levels. In relation to the inner textual dynamic, it functions as a marker of difference and positions racial conflict as entertainment. On a representational level, it cuts through *Little Britain*'s prevailing whiteness and produces a veneer of Britain as a multicultural society. Vicky Pollard's friends and milieu, the students at Kelsey Grammar School, Marjorie Dawes' Fat Fighters class attendees and Linda Flint's college students, all point to Britain as a nation that is both culturally diverse and discordant. There are also regular small appearances by Charu Bala Chokshi as Meera in the Fat Fighters class and Habib Nasib Nader as Gregory Merchant (the PM's new treasury adviser) (these Asian and black actors also appear in other small roles in all three series). However, in broad terms, these representations of non-whiteness are limited – a backdrop to the 'real' comedy fronted by the white stock characters and, therefore, reminiscent of the shallow 'integrated casting' approach commonly found in early cinema and television. However, although their presence is limited, they can also be seen to be included for 'positive', socially progressive reasons because they are set up to expose the predictable traits and foibles, and often bigotry, of the main white characters. The degree to which these representations of ethnic minorities are for better or worse is undecided; such uncertainties are perfectly able to function as part of a cultural politics of representation centred on ambivalence.

Blanket vs. Nuanced Racialisation

Although *Little Britain* depends on this kind of blanket racialisation of its core characters, the programme (until non-white core characters are introduced in the third series) largely transcends readings that acknowledge the intricacies of these racialisation techniques. But the fact that ethnicity can work in relation to other identity positions is recognised. For example, Walliams and Lucas have been accused of producing easy, vulnerable targets which denotes a new form of contempt in British society towards the white poor. The most obvious and commonly cited satirical target here is the dim-witted, working-class, single mother, represented by Vicky Pollard (see Sharon Lockyer's chapter for more on Vicky Pollard). Johann Hari's suggestion in *The Independent* that our current political climate would not allow such public media representations if they were based around non-white characters is revealing:

> Imagine a comedy where a British Asian wearing a sari, or
> naming their child Apu or Karim or Gita, was the joke and
> the punchline. It's (rightly) unthinkable. But abusing the
> white working class is rewarded with viewing figures topping
> 10 million. We look back on Jim Davidson blacking up as
> a head-scratching, imbecile black man with horror. But why
> is a public schoolboy dressing up as a head-scratching,
> imbecile single mother any better? Lucas and Walliams give
> us, the British public, what we want: an excuse to mock the
> vulnerable. (2005)

Hari's argument (published just after the third series began
to air on the BBC) is atypical because it suggests that *Little Britain* produces new racial targets for comic effect – not the Asian
sari-wearing mother, but the white (English) working-class, single mother. And our contemporary society, according to Hari,
tolerates a well-educated, 'well-spoken' man impersonating
a white (English) working-class, unintelligent, single mother
but considers itself to have progressed by no longer accepting a working-class, cockney-speaking man (Jim Davidson[3])
'blacked up' to impersonate an unintelligent black man. The
basic point here is that, as Hari correctly identifies,[4] the 'right
targets' of comedy shift over time and are deemed to 'work' or
be (in)appropriate depending on the historical moment. Humour is also inescapably dependent on who delivers the joke,
how the comedy is enunciated and the context in which jokes
are read. *Little Britain* works against the traditional idea that, in
racial terms, it is only ethnic minorities that can be considered
as a 'vulnerable' social group or be positioned as the 'victims'
of national humour. If an insinuation of *Little Britain*'s (new)
objects of racialisation is apparent here, this has intensified
since more prominent representations of non-whiteness have
occurred.

In series three (first aired in 2005), we are introduced to Desiree
DeVere – a black woman played by Walliams, who is Bubbles'
(Matt Lucas) bitter rival – and Ting Tong Macadangdang (the Thai
mail-order bride, played by Lucas). When these characters were

introduced, one of the principal criticisms aired in the national press and on internet sites was that the series is, amongst other things, 'racist'. Jim Shelley in *The Mirror* refers to the character of Ting Tong, describing 'her' as 'so politically incorrect as to border on racist' (18 November 2005). Hannah Pool, in a piece in *The Guardian* about the resurgence of light entertainment stars 'blacking up' to play white parts, comments on the Desiree character:

> She is fat and has that weird wiry hair and funny skin colour...even if you give Lucas and Walliams the benefit of the doubt and assume they were trying to even up the racial balance of the show, why don't they go the whole hog and employ a black actor instead?...But the underlying message is the same: stop taking yourself so seriously, stop being politically correct, we're only having a laugh. (22 September 2006)

The sight gag of Walliams playing the role of Desiree ('blacked up' in a fat suit, accessorised with a large gold necklace) is arguably what positions 'her' as a creation worthy of recurring status alongside *Little Britain*'s other core characters. The joke is clinched at the moment that we realise that it is Walliams who is behind the black make-up; in order to deliver the joke, Walliams has to 'black up'. Specifically, the issue raised in Pool's commentary about whether a black actor might be both more politically appropriate and institutionally meaningful is important when we consider the 'ethical limits' (see Pickering and Lockyer 2005a) of the series – that is, we need to ask whether white actors 'blacking up' (a passé performance practice that is now commonly accepted as racially insensitive and politically objectionable) should be reintroduced in the name of comedy. A further problem is that this politics of 'blacking up' cannot be disconnected from the context in which it is produced and, arguably, legitimised. Specifically, is the BBC, as a public service broadcaster, formally endorsing what many agree is a racist and inappropriate practice (in a multi-ethnic Britain) and, therefore, colluding in the institutionalisation of racist (not simply *racialized*) regimes of representation? The challenge, of course, is that, in order to be successful, the precise way in which *Little Britain* racialises its characters – white or not – is a key device through which the programme's humour is achieved. So would those who see racism here also suggest that the series is 'racist to everybody'?

It is uncertain whether audiences would be prepared to receive such narratives if they were not dressed, in considerable measure, in the language of ridiculous comedy and impersonation. If Desiree and, for that matter, Ting Tong were played by an African and a Thai respectively, the joke simply wouldn't 'work' or could be deemed (even more?) politically unacceptable. The idea of role-playing in scripted performance (the dramatisation of the excessive Desiree and, we might add, the canny Ting Tong) is a central comic device in how humour is achieved through these characterisations. This suggests, however, that performance and performativity are the only factors involved, leaving little space for the question of 'ethics'? One approach might be to consider the act of 'blacking up' (one of the most ambiguous forms of impersonation) not exclusively in terms of 'ethics' (or racial sensitivity) but also in relation to functionality (or the comedic purpose it actually serves). For example, in the opening episode of *Little Britain*'s first series, 'blacking up' was used by David Walliams and Matt Lucas in a strikingly different way, in order to produce a politically astute sketch about questions of political correctness and forced migration ('Black and White Minstrels – Radio', 1:1). The surreal sketch is outlined here (see Lucas and Walliams 2004: 40–41):

Minstrel Scene

Int. Kitchen
A minstrel couple are eating breakfast. The radio is on.

News Reporter (on radio)
So Home Secretary, what are your priorities for the next twelve months?

Home Secretary (on radio)
I would say the biggest challenge we face now is the increasing influx of minstrels. There are too many minstrels in this country, and I would say there is a case for saying that a good deal of them should be sent back to Minstrel-land.
In my constituency uh uh over the weekend...

> One of the minstrels gets up and changes the station.
> The radio now broadcasts a famous minstrel song.
> The minstrels break into broad smiles, and a minstrel song and
> dance routine

The stereotype is reversed here so that the minstrels, rather than being characterised as racist, are now the vulnerable targets of a broader politics of asylum and immigration. The absurdity of 'Minstrel-land' and the common usage of immigration discourse ('increasing influx', 'sent back' etc.) to refer to minstrels (who are not a social group that could be identified without their minstrel make-up and, therefore, impossible to deport) helps to produce what I would argue is an abstract, satirical take on important contemporary concerns, and does so to witty comic effect. There is a subtext and a different level of alternative meaning is conveyed.

But Is It Racist?

In series three, we see a shift in how *Little Britain* approaches racial difference. There is a new and exploitable kind of ambivalence in which the difference of the raced stereotype is similar to and yet troublingly different from how its other characters are racialised. The starting and the ending of what is designed to make us laugh at Desiree and Ting Tong is more or less the same; they are flat characters with very little detail or function beyond the sight gag (Desiree) and suggestion of duplicity and sexual submission (Ting Tong). Thus it is not surprising that Ting Tong in particular has come under some attack for being nothing more than an insidiously racist character (see *The Guardian*, 'On the Offensive', 20 June 2007). The main problem with Ting Tong is that the character's race is depicted as determining its culture, the character being based around the classic and entrenched stereotypes of a (failed) ladyboy, sexualised Thai woman and 'Thai bride'. The website ThaiFarang.co.uk's comment on Ting Tong and Dudley raises the issue of how television can serve to sanction such otherwise 'unacceptable' portrayals. It also draws attention to how the character of Dudley (as a daft, exploited, sexually inept white man played by David Walliams) serves to double the ethnic stereotype and, therefore, plays a defining role in how nuanced racialisation is produced.

> The yellow makeup, dodgy buck teeth and the comedy value of hearing Ting Tong being unable to pronounce her 'r's are all something akin to racist stereotyping...Lucas and Walliams definitely seem to have been treading a thin line between overt racist stereotyping and poking a jovial sort of fun at a modern phenomenon of UK and Western life – the Thai-Farang relationship...The childish humour practised by the Walliams/Lucas team make them light entertainment for the majority, and their sketches always seem strangely inoffensive when seen on TV rather than spoken about in other contexts. (ThaiFarang, n.d.)

On the one hand, Desiree and Ting Tong represent continuities within trademark *Little Britain* humour. Like many other *Little Britain* characters, they allow grotesque caricature, lurid sexual references, a reliance on drag performance and so on. They also function to expose a big disconnect between who they are and who they think they are/pass themselves off as being. Desiree sees herself as sexually desirable and beautiful; Walliams' depiction of her suggests not. Ting Tong is deceitful, unattractive and a man but passes 'herself' off as an obedient, exotic, Asian woman. Similarly, Vicky Pollard thinks she is more 'street' than she actually is; Emily Howard is far from the Victorian lady she tries to emulate; Linda Flint considers herself to be supportive and politically informed when she unfailingly demeans her students; Daffyd may not actually be gay but dresses and behaves as if he is and so on. Although such incongruities are designed to be a key source of humour, Ting Tong and Desiree appear to be more overwhelmed by their basic and crude characterisations. This lays *Little Britain* open to criticism because they are the only non-white core characters.

Comedy is a particularly tricky genre, 'a double-edged game, in which it is impossible to ensure that the audience is laughing with, not at, the stereotype' (Hall in Givanni 1995: 21). In relation to this, the role of the laughter track (or 'canned laughter') is crucial in how 'race' is managed within *Little Britain*. I use the word 'managed' because the laughter track, which is liberally applied in the series, is a post-production device with a specific aim to supplement natural reactions to a punch-line and, therefore, produce a certain amount of laughter *at the right moment*. It plays a critical role in the relationship between cognition (joke recognition) and appreciation (funniness). Close readings of *Little Britain* indicate that the precise moments when ethnic minority characters enter the visual frame – the moment when the presence of race itself is realised – are quickly succeeded by the use of canned laughter. For example, in the Maggie and Judy 'James' sketch (3: 3), Maggie drops in at Judy's house and is thrilled at the prospect of meeting Judy's daughter's fiancée, a Cambridge-educated barrister. The audience gets to see James (a black man) before Maggie and, knowing from previous sketches how she is repulsed by her racial Other, we are directed by the canned laughter to anticipate her reaction and, therefore, find humour in that moment. But the fact of James' blackness, yet to be revealed to Maggie, is also set up to be additionally comical because it subverts the audience's expectation of the traditional black male stereotype (James is well-dressed and well-spoken, polite, highly educated, professional and so on). A similar use of canned laughter occurs when Desiree DeVere first appears in series three ('Roman' sketch, 3: 1). We (the audience) see Desiree before her arch-rival, Bubbles. Although we have no previous knowledge of Bubble's racism and, therefore, there is no expectation about her reaction to finding out that Roman (her ex-husband played by Rob Brydon) has married a black woman, the canned laughter is used in the moment just before Desiree is revealed to Bubbles. The double punch-line comes from Desiree's blackness (the most extreme visual mismatch to the way Walliams really looks), and because she is an exaggerated version of Bubbles (also naked but bigger and, therefore, more desirable to Roman). Desiree, as a fusion of the 'black momma' and African queen caricatures – big hair, rolling eyes, layers of fat, former Miss Botswana and so on – is, quite simply, *more* funny because she is black. The display of rivalry between Bubbles and Desiree is also given a particular visual edge (white vs. black) because of their extremely different colouring.

The changes within *Little Britain* as an evolving text need to be registered. In spite of its monotonous, repetitive structure and style (same format, same characters, same voice-over etc.), its approaches to representations of race and ethnicity are not constant or fixed. Rather, it is a moving production that can best be understood as having been, being and becoming. This is important with regard to race because the nuances within and across each episode and series suggest variations in how race and ethnicity are represented. The first series, for example, is far more abstract and overtly politically astute than the subsequent series. The third series (when Ting Tong and Desiree are introduced) sees a marked turn towards characterisation that is cruder, 'flatter' and arguably less 'politically correct'. How it was and what it has since become need to be carefully mapped in relation to context and the conditions of production and reception. What difference does it make to how the comedy is constructed and interpreted once audience identification and loyalty have been secured? How does this relate to perceived risks that can or cannot be taken? Such ambiguities will inevitably take on new dimensions as *Little Britain*'s influence spreads internationally. Would Ting Tong be deemed an appropriate characterisation in Thailand? Does it matter if it's not shown there? How does the Thai diaspora respond to it within its own local contexts? What kind of global readings do national jokes produce? And who, if anyone, should carry the burden of how race and ethnicity are represented, not just for local but also for global audiences? These questions are especially pertinent since *Little Britain* is a comedy highly dependent on the cultural competence of the British viewers who are expected to 'get' the cultural references and be sufficiently literate in the codes and conventions of British television comedy.

Was the introduction of Desiree and Ting Tong at a moment of intense popularity and fame a conscious attempt by the creators of the series to appeal to the sensibilities of the viewing public in a moment when they were less likely to be constrained by an over-arching 'politically correct' politics and 'get away with it'? Do Walliams and Lucas draw upon their accumulation of symbolic capital – their professional kudos, their network of connections and their track record of success – to overcome the ideological limitations of what this particular moment might otherwise consider objectionable? It certainly seems that the impact of *Little Britain*'s growing popularity, its 'promotion' to a BBC1 prime-time position in series three and a changing politics which might be described as 'post-multiculturalism' are all likely to have had an impact on how the series was developed and received in different ways to when it was first launched on television in 2003. The institutional politics of PSB – or the role the public media plays in platforming certain kinds of comedy – is significant here. These boundaries of political and cultural expediency are always shifting, and broadcasters play a key role in how the cultural production and visibility of particular kinds of race-related humour are framed. Within a media history context, it is generally agreed that television can be defined by certain historical moments in which the types of representations produced were framed within the cultural limits and expectations of that particular moment. The ethnic sitcoms and black- and Asian-led sketch shows of the 1980s and the 1990s were products of their time, emerging at a time when *Little Britain*, which plays recklessly with the boundaries of political acceptability, arguably would not have won such critical and popular favour.

In research conducted in 2007 by the Open University and the BBC involving a nationwide joke survey, the most popular subjects of jokes were national, ethnic or racial identities and sex. The axis of a large proportion of British comedy has rested on notions of racial difference (Malik 2002). There is much to suggest in interviews with *Little Britain*'s creators that they not only are (increasingly) in tune with this historical and political context of British humour but also have a strong understanding of how humour can become popular in contemporary British society. This has led to it being positioned as 'anti-PC' comedy or as a contemporary critique of political correctness. Steve Bennett, editor of Chortle, Britain's largest comedy website, argues that in live *Little Britain* shows, he does

> feel a little uncomfortable when the crowd roar at Ting Tong
> sketches...But I do think it is different from the 70s where you

had white comics saying, 'We don't like black people and we want them to go home'. *Little Britain* is playing with what is acceptable in our PC world. (quoted in Armstrong 2007)

Any judgement about whether *Little Britain* can be determined as a racist text will depend precisely on how racism is defined – on whether it is considered as an ideology or a set of beliefs dependent on intention or something that is more institutionalised, unforeseen and hidden. The emphasis on the supposed intention of Walliams and Lucas not to offend or 'be racist' but instead to test the boundaries of the nation's tolerance is important. It raises the question of why certain representations are licensed to offend today, whilst others are not (e.g., *The Black and White Minstrel Show* (BBC 1958–78), or the humour of Bernard Manning, Jim Davidson, and Benny Hill). What is the difference – real or imagined – in their comedy? In particular, the characterisation of Ting Tong and Desiree, in spite of the satirical lens through which they are claimed to be produced, casts significant doubt that the degrees of difference in *Little Britain* go far enough to be endorsed uncritically. The sketch-show, possibly more than any other format, accommodates such contradictions, because it can 'give with one hand, then take away with another' (so, for example, we are encouraged to laugh at Maggie's racist intolerance and Ting Tong's inability to produce her 'r's in the same episode). This particular reading of *Little Britain* suggests the need to build on the analysis, foregrounding the 'ambiguities of interpretation' (Pickering and Lockyer 2005b). What are the meanings of *racialized* identity in *Little Britain* and how does this connect with how it is both encoded and decoded in everyday life? Research on how *Little Britain*'s humour is not just constructed but also interpreted, particularly in relation to social background (ethnicity, gender, class etc.) would be valuable in trying to work through some of these concerns (see section three of this collection for analyses of audience responses to *Little Britain*).

Notes

1. *Peter Sellers Is Dead* was a one-off stage show at Riverside Studios in Hammersmith, London, in 1995. Following its success, Jon Plowman,

BBC head of Comedy and Light Entertainment, commissioned a series for Radio 4 which began in July 1996.

2. Sandi Toksvig and Rhona Cameron are famous lesbian entertainers in Britain.

3. Jim Davidson's comedy career reached its peak on British television in the 1970s with *The Jim Davidson Show* (ITV 1979–82). In September 2007, he was expelled from the celebrity reality TV show *Hell's Kitchen* (ITV 2004–present) after making what the broadcaster called 'unacceptable remarks' about homosexuality. He subsequently referred to himself as an 'un-PC fossil'.

4. Hari does not include a discussion of how Walliams and Lucas 'black up' to play The Minstrel duo seen in Series one. Desiree and Ting Tong would probably have been introduced into the programme shortly after Hari had written this piece.

Chapter FIVE

Chavs and Chav-nots: Social Class in
Little Britain

Sharon Lockyer

Ridiculing class struggles, differences and tensions has been a prominent trend in British television comedy since the 1950s (Medhurst, 2007). As television comedy audiences, we have laughed at the 'Class' sketch in *The Frost Report* (BBC 1966–67), at the benefit-dependent couple Wayne and Waynetta slob in *Harry Enfield and Chums* (BBC 1990–92, 1994–97), and more recently at the middle-class Harpers in *My Family* (BBC 2000–present). *Little Britain* continues this focus on class comedy through a number of class-based characters including 'chav' teenage delinquent Vicky Pollard, and 'chav not' Harvey Pincher, an upper-class 30-something man who is still breast-fed. This chapter examines *Little Britain*'s comic treatment of social class identities in order to explore how these representations reproduce or challenge stereotypical portrayals of social classes, and to examine to what extent *Little Britain* reproduces conventional comedic class discourses.

Contemporary British Class Identities

Despite British comedy's 'obsession' (Medhurst 2007: 145) with social class, when compared with other spheres of identity, such as gender, race and ethnicity as well as sexuality, a relatively small number of detailed critical analyses of British class comedy exists (Crowther and Pinfold 1987; Medhurst 2007; Wagg 1998a). And this is despite the fact that conceptualisations of and tensions between social classes continue to dominate British socio-political agendas. Whilst there are political and theoretical claims of the 'death of class' or that we are living in a 'classless society' (Clark and Lipset 1991; Holton and Turner 1989; Pakulski and Waters 1996), evidence points to deepening class divides due to increases in British working-class inequality and poverty and decreases in social mobility (Dorling et al. 2007; Blanden et al. 2005). For many, class continues to be an important and significant means of analysing inequality which encompasses not just economic categories or occupation but also symbolic and cultural class signifiers, such as knowledge and taste, or, in Bourdieu's (1984) terms, 'cultural capital' (see also Crompton 1998; Mount 2004; Lawler 2005; Skeggs 2005; Hayward and Yar 2006). Thus working-class people:

> are not primarily marked as lacking and disgusting through their poverty, but through their assumed lack of *knowledge* and *taste*. To be sure, they may be implicitly vilified through a suggestion that they are not spending their money properly – as in critiques that they are now the prey of a vacuous consumer culture – but this implied lack of thrift is in itself assumed to come from a lack of knowledge and taste which would, presumably, enable them to 'see through' consumerism. (Lawler 2005: 800 emphasis in original)

This increasing importance of symbolic and cultural class markers (which supplement economic markers) has led to a new British social class vocabulary (Tyler 2008). The term 'chav' has become prevalent in popular discourses to describe socially marginalised groups.[1] 'Chav' is frequently used as a term of disgust towards white (often unemployed) British working-class people (Lawler 2005; Tyler 2008).

One of the perceived 'problems' with chavs is that in the sphere of consumption they are regarded as consuming in 'ways deemed "vulgar" and hence lacking in "distinction" by superordinate classes' (Hayward and Yar 2006: 14). They wear the 'wrong' types of clothing (e.g., Burberry caps), wear too much jewellery (e.g., large hoop earrings), wear too much gaudy cheap make-up (or wear too much tango-orange fake tan), binge-drink on cheap larger, and listen to the 'wrong' kinds of music (e.g., rap music). Acronyms such as 'Council Housed and Violent', slang vocabulary including 'chavellers cheques' (i.e., benefit payments), books such as *The Little Book of Chav Jokes* (Bok 2006) and YouTube chav-hate videos including '5 Ways to Kills a Chav'[2], all illustrate the class-based disgust and contempt held towards chavs (see Tyler 2008; Hayward and Yar 2006). Such class hatred, which columnist Julie Burchill (2005) refers to as 'social racism', has been criticised by the Fabian Society which in the summer of 2008 called for a ban on the word 'chav' as it believed that the term denounces a 'voiceless group'. It noted that although middle classes 'have always used language to distinguish themselves from those a few rungs below them on the ladder...this is something new. This is middle class hatred of the white working class, pure and simple' (2008). The Fabian Society attacked televisual representations of chavs, including 'comedy chavs', for contributing to this class hatred.

Comedy Chavs

'Comedy chavs' include teenage schoolgirl Lauren Cooper in the sketch show *The Catherine Tate Show* (BBC 2004–07), the Gallagher family in the dramedy *Shameless* (Channel 4 2004–present), and *Little Britain*'s Vicky Pollard character. Comedy chavs have socio-cultural resonance, for example, in the Channel 4 'Britain's Favourite Celebrity Chav' poll, Vicky Pollard was positioned in 11th place out of 20 (Channel 4, n.d.). Vicky Pollard (played by Matt Lucas) appears in both the radio and the television series: she was included in the pilot television episode and cast in the opening sketches of both series one and two of the television series; she is included in the Comic Relief sketches in *Little Britain Abroad* and *Little Britain Live*. Vicky Pollard is a teenage delinquent single mother from the West Country. She is an ASBO enthusiast and represents the most inarticulate person in Britain (see Lucas 2005). Her catchphrases include 'no but yeah but no but yeah but no', 'shut up!', and 'don't go giving me evils'. She speaks in a thick Bristolian accent and at such fast pace that much of her talk is incomprehensible, all of which serves to symbolically convey a lower social status (Medhurst, 2007) (see

Julia Snell's chapter in this collection for more on Vicky Pollard's language use). Vicky Pollard's humorous responses to legitimate and serious questions asked by upper- and middle-class authority figures, such as barristers, police officers and teachers, creates much of the comedy. In the 'Social Worker' sketch (1: 7) when her social worker asks Vicky where her baby is, Vicky replies, 'Swapped it for a Westlife CD'. The social worker questions Vicky, 'How could you do such a thing?' to which Vicky replies, 'I know, they're rubbish'.

Vicky's carnivalesque appearance epitomises the chav identity that is criticised and mocked on chav-hate websites, on popular television, and in newspapers. This includes her signature bright pink Kappa shell-suit which zips tightly over her portly stomach, her large gold hoop earrings and numerous gold chains, and her long strawberry-blonde hair which is tightly scrapped up in a scrunchie (colloquially known as a 'Croydon facelift'). Vicky is sexually active, excessively so. She has twelve children fathered by numerous men, constantly talks about her and her friends having real or imagined sex (going to 'third base', making 'fanny farts', people seeing her or her friends 'wookey hole'), and refers to herself and her peers as 'slags', 'slagbags' and 'bitches'. In the 'Call Centre' sketch (3: 2), Vicky is working for a telephone sex line and explains to the caller (her uncle Pete), 'So the whole thing is right, we're all covered in Chambourcey Hippopotamouse and we're all like well licking it off each other and I'm like totally lezzing everyone up...'. Vicky's interest in sex could also be interpreted as part of Vicky's chav-loutishness. This thus serves to strengthen the stereotype that due to their limited cultural capital and inability to enjoy other activities or interests, chavs are preoccupied with sex and sexual activities. Such chav characterisations mirror other representations of working-class bodies and sexuality. Skeggs (1997) argues that working-class sexualities and bodies are typified as excessive and vulgar, and Weeks (1981) observes how working-class sexualities are often constructed as animalistic. In their analysis of working-class portrayals, Dodd and Dodd (1992) identify how working-class distinctiveness is situated in an undisciplined physicality, for example, through prostitution. In this sense Vicky Pollard epitomises representations of working-class sexualities evident elsewhere in popular culture.

Additional evidence to suggest that Vicky Pollard's character reinforces this class-based contempt of chavs can be seen in the sketches which serve to ridicule chav stupidity and their perceived lack of knowledge. Taking the 'Supermarket' sketch (2: 1) as one example, we see Vicky attempting to steal pic-n-mix sweets by putting them down her tracksuit trousers (although most of the sweets are simply falling through the tracksuit legs onto the floor). Noticing a security guard watching her, Vicky asks, 'What are you looking at, pervert?' to which the security guard replies, 'I told you before, you've got to put the pic-n-mix in a bag'. Vicky replies, 'God you're so racist', as she puts sweets into a pic-n-mix bag. She then continues, 'Alright now?!' as she puts the entire bag down her tracksuit bottoms. Later in the sketch as Vicky pushes her pram through the security barriers to exit the supermarket, the security guard pulls back the baby blanket to reveal a cash register full of money, to which Vicky explains, 'I bought that earlier'. This sketch may be read as a modern twisted manifestation of 'the tipster, the travelling salesman, the wheeler-and-dealer' theme evident in comedic class discourses (Wagg 1998a). However, due to her delinquent status Vicky does not use legitimate means to generate money; instead she opts for criminal or deceitful behaviour, which helps to construct the view that chavs offer a threat to the moral ordering of British society.

In his analysis of American television comedy social class constructions, Butsch observes how the portrayal of working classes as 'dumb, immature, irresponsible, or lacking in common sense' (2003: 576) persists across the limited number of working-class representations portrayed. Vicky's demeanour and interaction with authority figures reflect such portrayals. Conveying chavs in this manner legitimises their social and cultural position – such representations may imply that chavs simply do not posses the skills and knowledge to be anywhere other than in their low cultural place. Although this comedic class representation can be seen in other television comedies, such as *Steptoe and Son* (BBC 1962–65, 1970–74) and *Only Fools and Horses* (BBC 1981–2003), the representation of Vicky

Pollard has particular social and cultural resonance as it taps into the contemporary stream of abuse of white working-class groups and individuals. Such comedic chav representations reinforce Harding's (2006) observation that all groups and individuals who are 'othered' are constructed as threatening social and moral order. Given the perfomative dynamics of a male middle-class actor playing a female delinquent unemployed single mother, the Vicky Pollard sketches may be interpreted as 'a symptom of a middle-class desire to re-demarcate class boundaries' (Tyler 2008: 22) – through comedy chavs and audience laughter at them, a distinction is made between them ('chavs') and us ('chav-nots').

The Vicky Pollard character has created a wealth of controversy and critical attention. For Tyler, she has 'become entrenched and condemned as a negative figure' (2008: 28). Vicky Pollard's negative comedic connotations have been used to deny individuals and groups opportunities. The term 'Vicky Pollard' is often used instead of 'chav' as a term of abuse. On the reality television show *The X-Factor* (ITV 2004–present), judge Simon Cowell prevented a contestant going through the next round of the contest because she looked like 'Vicky Pollard'; in political debates, measures designed to prevent creating 'a generation of Vicky Pollards' have been proposed (see Tyler 2008). Johann Hari maintains:

> A few years ago, the 1990s backlash against single parents living on crumbling estates – like my sister – was slowly receding. Then Vicky was born. Matt Lucas and David Walliams used the clothes worn by poor people (Kappa, Burberry) and even the names they give their children (Destiny, Shannon, Bethany) as cheap punchlines. They unwittingly incited their armies of child fans to hunt down the Vickys in their playground. (2005)

Yeah But Is It All That Straightforward?

So far we've seen how the characterisation of Vicky Pollard can be situated in the widespread vilification of chavs seen elsewhere in contemporary British culture; to some extent, her characterisation can be mapped onto existing comedic representations of class. Yet, these readings do not acknowledge or take into account the complexity of comedic texts. Comedy depends on ambiguity, contradictions and interpretive diversity. Unlike the singularity of interpretation in serious discourse, comedy 'depends on the discursive display of opposing interpretive possibilities' (Mulkay 1988: 25; see also Fine 1983; Koestler 1964). 'Comedy controversies' are often caused by such ambiguity surrounding meaning, motive and intent of comedic texts. Opposing interpretations were made of Alf Garnett, the central character in the 1960s television situation comedy *Till Death Us Do Part* (BBC 1965–75). Although comedy writer Johnny Speight argued that Alf Garnett ridiculed the stupidity and ignorance of bigots, some viewers interpreted the programme and the character Alf Garnett as celebrating racism (Husband 1988). Pickering and Lockyer refer to this as the 'Alf Garnett Syndrome', where 'what is being satirised becomes a source of celebration among at least a section of the audience' (2005a: 16–17). Interpretive diversity also accounted for the conflicting ways in which Ali G's comic persona has been interpreted (Pickering and Lockyer 2005b; Malik 2002). Ali G, played by Jewish Cambridge graduate Sacha Baron Cohen, is a wanna-be gansta wrapper from the South East of England, first seen on *The 11 O'clock Show* (Channel 4 1998–2000) and then on *Da Ali G Show* (Channel 4 2000). Due to the ambivalence in Ali G's persona and performance, questions were raised about who exactly Ali G was meant to represent: a white man pretending to be a white man pretending to be black, a white man pretending to be an Asian pretending to be black, or a Jewish man pretending to be an Asian pretending to be a white man pretending to be black (Pickering and Lockyer 2005b). Concerns were also raised regarding whether Ali G served to reinforce or undermine racist stereotypes.

Vicky Pollard is an equally ambivalent character. Her performance is based on opposing and often contradictory readings. There is an alternative manner in which her diegesis can be read, offering a more positive interpretation of Vicky Pollard and the 'comedy chav'. Additionally, there are moments in the *Little Britain* series when Vicky Pollard is used to mock the idiosyncrasies of middle-class identities and lifestyles. Vicky Pollard can be viewed as a character of rebellion and resistance to social control and hegemonic ideologies that are repeated and reinforced elsewhere in British contemporary popular culture. As Matt Lucas argues, 'people talk about Vicky Pollard and sometimes we get criticised as if we're sending up somebody from a poor background but I think Vicky Pollard is a real winner and she's celebrated. She's never a victim' (Lucas and Walliams 2005: unpaginated).

Vicky Pollard may be interpreted as offering a contemporary manifestation of Kathleen Rowe's (1995) 'unruly woman', whose body resists and challenges middle-class control and decorum. Vicky's physicality is reminiscent of other large female comic characters, such as Dawn French's character Geraldine Grainger in *The Vicar of Dibley* (BBC 1994–2007) (see Hole 2003; Chambers 2005).[3] Examining the progressive qualities of Roseanne Barr in *Roseanne* (ABC 1988–97), Rowe explains that it is her body size and shape and the '*looseness* or lack of personal restraint her fatness implies, that most powerfully define her and convey her opposition to middle-class and feminine standards of decorum and beauty' (1995, 60: emphasis in original). This hegemonic opposition manifests itself in similar ways through the Vicky Pollard character. Vicky's corpulent figure, garish make-up, spotty face, bright pink tracksuit and long scrapped back hair transgresses many of the boundaries regarding female appearance that contemporary Western makeover programmes, such as *What Not to Wear* (BBC 2001–07), *10 Years Younger* (Channel 4 2004–present), and *Ladette to Lady* (ITV 2005–08), attempt to fix. Through mockery and ridicule these makeover-type programmes humiliate working-class bodies for lacking taste, style and refinement. Through the course of the makeover programme, such working-class bodies are replaced and re-sculptured so they look more middle class – reflecting bodies that are controlled, policed and disciplined (see Wood and Skeggs 2004) – and become distanced from their working-class bodies of excess. Vicky Pollard does not ascribe, neither does she attempt to ascribe, to the desire or need to re-sculpture her body so it reflects middle-class decorum and discipline. Further, neither does her small, untidy and cluttered bedsit subscribe to the clean and tidy living spaces endorsed on lifestyle programmes such as *How Clean Is Your House?* (Channel 4 2003–present) or

The Life Laundry (BBC 2002–04). As an 'unruly woman', Vicky may be interpreted as actively rejecting and resisting middle-class modesty and disciplined behaviours. Yet, such unruliness may be read by some viewers as a consequence of Vicky's chav stupidity and lack of self-awareness, thus limiting the political potential of the Vicky Pollard character – she simply lacks the knowledge that if she dressed, spoke and behaved in a more middle-class refined manner then she may be able to climb the steep social ladder.

Comedy Chav-nots

Sitting alongside *Little Britain*'s comedy chav Vicky Pollard is an assortment of characters that are positioned somewhat differently on the social class hierarchy and are clearly 'chav-nots'. Middle- and upper-class characters are peppered throughout the series, from Conservative MP Sir Norman Fry (played by David Walliams) who is frequently issuing press statements explaining his latest 'compromising position' in an attempt to regain his respectable appearance (e.g., 'However, shortly after my arrival my clothes accidentally fell off. At that moment I slipped on a glacé cherry and landed inside one of the men' ['Gaydar' sketch, 3: 5]), to wealthy romantic novelist Dame Sally Markham (played by Matt Lucas) who has difficulty dictating more than about 70 pages, through to Mr Cleeves (Matt Lucas), a teacher at Kelsey Grammar School, who has difficulty reading and confuses his pupils by writing his name on the chalkboard as 'Mr Wells' and his subject biology as 'French' (1: 7).

Another class-related character is Harvey Pincher (played by David Walliams), a 30-something upper-class mummy's boy. Unlike Vicky Pollard who appears in the radio series and every television series, Harvey Pincher appears in only four episodes of television series two. Across the four episodes, we follow the blossoming of Harvey's new relationship. We first encounter Harvey as he introduces his new girlfriend, Jane (played by Samantha Power), to his parents, Gerald (Matt Lucas) and Celia (Geraldine James) ('Meet the Parents', 2: 1), and we follow the development of his romance through to his wedding day ('The Wedding', 2: 6). Despite being a grown adult, Harvey is still breast-fed and when he wishes to be breast-fed says 'I want bitty' or demands 'bitty' (a combination of 'breast' and 'titty'). His mother (and sometimes his grandmother) obliges by breast-feeding him wherever they are, or whoever they are talking to, which is the climax of each sketch and where much of the comedy lies. In 'The Wedding' sketch, for example, instead of saying 'I do', Harvey says 'Bitty' and summons his mother from the church pew to breast-feed him at the alter – all in front of the stunned wedding guests. Following the vicar's announcement 'I declare you man and wife. You may kiss the bride', Jane reluctantly kisses Harvey, who, as a result of his recent feed, possess a milk moustache.

When we first meet Harvey and Jane ('Meet the Parents', 2: 1), they are driving up a long gravelled drive to a large grand country house, which we later learn is the Pincher family home that Gerald explains has 'been in the family for years'. We're informed by Tom Baker's voice-over that 'posh people are much better and cleverer than common people, and so they live in nicer houses, like this' – a very different living space to Vicky Pollard's bedsit. Harvey Pincher's class identity, like Vicky Pollard's, is marked through his appearance, parole and demeanour. University-educated Harvey dons formal suit and tie attire (whether he is visiting his parents, dining out or meeting the wedding caterer), speaks in formal polite language, and drives an expensive vintage sports car – again a characterisation that is far removed from Vicky Pollard's classed identity. His parents are equally formal. Celia wears buttoned-up shirts, flowing skirts, pearls and broaches, and his father – a wine-drinking member of the local golf club and a supporter of cricket – wears argyle cardigans, or tweed jackets, with a shirt and tie.

As with the Vicky Pollard sketches, there are a number of different interpretive possibilities surrounding the intent and meaning of the Harvey Pincher sketches. In his analysis of class comedy, Medhurst (2007) identifies a trend of ridiculing the experiences, lifestyles and behaviours of specific social classes. This trend proffers a useful way of understanding the Harvey Pincher sketches. In a similar vein as television comedies such as *Absolutely Fabulous* (BBC 1992–96, 2001–05), *Fawlty Towers* (BBC 1975–79) and *The Good Life* (BBC 1975–78), which unpicked and satirised middle-class values, behaviours and lifestyles, the Harvey Pincher sketches ridicule upper-class idiosyncrasies, values and manners. When Jane is asked by Celia whether or not she has her own place in London, the following exchange takes place ('Meet the Parents', 2: 1):

> **Jane:** No, no, my brother and I still live at home with our parents.
> **Celia:** Really?
> **Jane:** Yes, we have tried to move out but...Mum and Dad don't want us to leave.
> **Celia:** Oh I think it's terribly important to let go.

This exchange takes place whilst Harvey is being breast-fed by Celia. At the end of the exchange Celia slaps Harvey on his back in order to burp him, to which Harvey dutifully replies, 'Thank you, Mummy'. The incongruity between Celia's response to Jane ('Oh I think it's terribly important to let go') and her actions (breast-feeding Harvey) serves to ridicule Celia's pomposity and hypocritical behaviour and to highlight her lack of self-awareness. The Harvey Pincher sketches may also serve to highlight the family-specificity of much behaviour. As Terri Apter observes, 'each family has its own set of norms that usually fade into the background of their lives but tend to come to the foreground when two families merge' (quoted in Farouky 2008). To outsiders, the Pincher family norms are extraordinary and bizarre and onlookers are always shocked at seeing a grown man being breast-fed by his mother. Jane is 'initiated' into the Pincher family norms in the first Harvey Pincher sketch – at the end of the 'Meet the Parents' sketch, after Harvey has been breast-fed and 'burped' by Celia, Gerald says to an astounded Jane, 'Welcome to the family'.

Other examples of sending up upper-class values and behaviours in the Harvey Pincher sketches include the desire to portray a wide social circle of acquaintances and to exert or attempt to exert social influence (as with Hyacinth Bucket in *Keeping Up Appearances*, BBC 1990–95). In the 'Restaurant' sketch (2: 2), for example, Celia explains to Jane's parents, 'When our eldest daughter got married, she decided she wanted to have it in a very small village church...the problem was that the church only held a hundred...'. Further, when arranging Harvey and Jane's wedding, Gerald asks, 'do you want me to see if the golf club's free for the reception?' to which Jane's father replies, 'Thank You. That would be great'. The Pincher's intolerance of anything or anyone deemed 'different' to their own values in summed up in Gerald's response to the wedding caterer's statement that a vegetarian option will be available – 'Oh bloody vegetarians, string up the lot of 'em I say' ('Wedding Caterer' sketch, 2: 4).

Harvey's man/boy persona may be read as an attempt to highlight and critique the dependency of young upper-class adults on their parents. Despite Harvey's adult status and his new found love, he is physically and emotionally dependent on his parents, which is symbolised through his need and desire for 'bitty'. If this need is not immediately gratified, he exerts tantrum-like behaviour. Butsch has observed that this immature childlike persona is often characteristic of working-class comedy characters (e.g., Homer Simpson in *The Simpsons* [FOX 1989–present], and Alf Garnet in *Till Death Us Do Part*), whereas middle-class and upper class characters are conveyed as mature and responsible, thus reinforcing ideological hegemony – 'blue-collar workers are portrayed as requiring supervision, and managers and professionals as intelligent and mature enough to provide it' (2003: 576). *Little Britain* turns this immature childlike persona on its head so that it is the upper-class man who is infantilised.

The childlike characterisation of Harvey may shift audience attention away from the social class dynamics of the characters and sketches towards the impending relationship between his mother and her soon-to-be daughter-in-law. It is widely recognised that relationships between female in-laws are often more challenging and tense than relationships between a man and his mother-in-law due to struggles over their position and status in the family (Farouky 2008; Wardrop 2008; Levy 2008). Posed with the threat of 'losing' her son Harvey to his new love Jane and of being excluded from their relationship, breast-feeding Harvey could be read as a way of Celia asserting her maternal love towards her son, undermining the perceived threat posed by Jane to their existing mother–son relationship. In this sense, the classed identities are complexly intertwined with gender, status and familial role identities.

More than 'Somefink or Nuffin'

Class inequalities and class identities are fluid and dynamic, continually being socially negotiated, renegotiated and reconfigured through both macro (capital) and micro (symbols and representations) processes (Skeggs 2004; see also Lawler 2005). British television comedy has played and continues to play a significant role in articulating and negotiating class identities. Class politics continue to be symbolically exercised in television comedy in complex and sometimes contradictory ways. *Little Britain* has maintained British television comedy's 'obsession' (Medhurst 2007: 145) with class through its 'comedy chav' Vicky Pollard and an array of other middle- and upper-class characters, including upper-class mummy's boy Harvey Pincher.

Little Britain's conceptualisations of British class identities reflect and maintain some of the comedic trends identified by Wagg (1998a) and Medhurst (2007), yet they invert others. Vicky Pollard's chaviness and the Pincher's upper-class pomposity serve to ridicule the experiences, behaviours, norms and lifestyles of particular social classes, which Medhurst recognises as a key discursive mode of comedic class representations. However, *Little Britain* inverts another trend in comedy class representations identified by Wagg (1998a), who observes that class comedy privileges middle- and upper-class representations Unlike the Harvey Pincher character, Vicky Pollard has become one of the most popular and talked-about comedy characters in recent television comedy who has wider cultural resonance. Although middle- and upper-class characters are peppered across the *Little Britain* series, it is comedy chav Vicky Pollard who appears in every *Little Britain* television series and has gained much popular attention and whose catchphrase is positioned at number 5 in *UKTV Gold's* top 20 'comedy catchphrases of all' time poll (The Guardian Online, 2005).

Vicky Pollard's popularity may be due to the 'cultural temperature' existing in the early years of the new millennium.

Medhurst (2007) has described comedy as a 'cultural thermometer', as comic characters often draw on wider socio-cultural beliefs about individuals, groups and societies. For example, the characters in *The Frost Report* 'Class' sketch, mentioned in the introduction to this chapter, were/are funny not only because of the way in which the three characters from different social classes interact, but also because they each individually relate to wider dominant social assumptions and understandings of the upper classes (Bowler-hatted John Cleese), the middle classes (trilby-wearing Ronnie Barker), and the working classes (flat-capped Ronnie Corbett) of post-war 1960s Britain. The popularity of comedy chav Vicky Pollard reflects wider British interests in the ways in which class identities have been recently reconfigured and echoes concerns surrounding new and emerging class identities which are deemed to threaten the social and moral fabric of contemporary middle England (e.g., state-dependent teenage mothers, young working-class 'hoodies', binge drinkers and ASBO cultures).

For some *Little Britain* audiences, Vicky Pollard will be a problematic character as she represents an extension of the pervasive chav vilification observed elsewhere in popular culture. However, other audience members may read Vicky as more politically progressive and resistant to the 'middle-class-ification' of appearance, demeanour and behaviour. Equally, for some audiences, the Harvey Pincher sketches may be read as an attack on upper-class behaviours, norms and lifestyles, yet for others they may articulate the tensions between female family roles and status. However the audiences may choose to make sense of these classed characters, it is clear that there are few 'nos' or 'buts' when considering television comedy's significant socio-political role – television comedy has been and continues to be a significant discourse through which concerns, anxieties and questions about British class identities are discursively constructed, mobilised and challenged.

Notes

1. The etymology of the term is largely contested (Skeggs 2005). Some believe that the word is based on an old Romany/Gypsy word for child (Devereux 2007), a community that has experienced marginalization

and social inclusion (Hayward and Yar 2006), whereas other believe the word derives from a combination of the characteristically lower-class names Sharon and Trevor (Shar/vor) (see Nayak 2006).
2. http://www.youtube.com/watch?v=FqLyVEAGoBo
3. Interestingly Dawn French appears in the *Comic Relief Does* Little Britain Live (2007) charity sketches as Vicky Pollard's mother, Shelly Pollard.

Chapter SIX

'Mischief and Monstrosity': *Little Britain* and Disability

Margaret Montgomerie

Watching *Little Britain* is the ethical and ideological equivalent of riding *Submission* at *Alton Towers* theme park. 'Are you up or down? You'll lose all sense of balance on this double inverter. Don't fight it this ride won't be satisfied until it has you screaming at the ground below' (Altontowers.com 2007). Viewing the series is rarely a comfortable experience; it turns our sense of ourselves as decent fun-loving people inside out and upside down, often simultaneously provoking uncontrollable laughter, recognition, guilt, shock and distaste. At times this involves a troubling recognition of our desire for entertainment and exhilaration at any expense including the temporary suspension of our better judgement.

Amongst the material that elicits this confusion of responses is a set of recurring representations of disabled characters. Through catchphrases such as Andy Pipkin's (Matt Lucas) 'Yeah I know' and Anne's (David Walliams) 'Eh eh eeeeh' and iconic images such as that of Andy's tracksuit trousers slipping off his wobbling backside as he leaps out of his wheelchair to perform some athletic act behind Lou's (David Walliams) back, the series has entered popular culture. These characters are often involved in sketches which resonate with risky pleasures. What is at stake when we laugh at these sketches? Are we laughing at what Andy and Anne do? Is it the mischief they perform that amuses us? Is it their pranks? Andy leaping out of his wheelchair, dancing and laying in the wet cement patio that Lou has laboriously smoothed whilst Lou turns away to stretch his aching back

('Patio', 3: 5). Anne hanging fish fingers on a Christmas tree as Dr Lawrence (Matt Lucas) discusses her progress in response to his psychiatric regime with Dr Beagrie (played by Steven Furst) ('Christmas Decorations', 3: 6). Or is it the mischief that they represent? Do such actions invert the power relations between the disabled characters and their carers and medical profession-als through farce and thus provide a critique of disablement? Or do they function as the comedic acting out of the 'disability benefits cheats' and 'violence done by care in the community of mentally ill people' stories which regularly find a place in the British local and national press and which legitimise the scru-tiny, classification and stigmatisation of the disabled as 'other'? Are we laughing at Andy and Anne because of their disabilities, at their embodiment and enactment of the abject and the mon-strous? Disabled actor Paul Henshaw is clearly worried that this is the case:

> Those programmes make me feel slightly uncomfortable. To be honest – my partner finds it offensive because she only uses a wheelchair for part of the time. Ever since *Little Britain*, people stare at her when she stands up, wondering if she's faking it. I guess you can use comedy to point out people's prejudices, but it can be an excuse sometimes just to take the piss out of us. (in Calvi 2005)

Is This All Too Familiar?

Paul Henshaw's ambivalence about the sketches becomes signifi-cant when we recognise that Andy and Anne are part of a long tradition. Tracing evidence of traditions as far back as Elizabethan joke books, Laurence Clark argues that 'society has been deriving humour from disabled people for centuries' (2003: 1). Whilst Tom Shakespeare states that:

> much of the repertoire of traditional comedy focuses on flawed performance or deformed physique, from Quasimodo jokes onwards. Such gags perhaps even become more prominent in the 1980s, as political correctness eroded the acceptability of sexist and racist humour. (1999: 48)

Television comedy provides us with a wide range of memorable characters defined by their impairment: Arkwright in *Open All Hours* (BBC 1973, 1976, 1981–85), Rigsby in *Rising Damp* (ITV 1974–78) and Jim Trott in *The Vicar of Dibley* (BBC 1994–2007) are all distinguished by speech impairments. The central joke in *Clarence* (BBC 1988) was that the main character (played by Ronnie Barker) was a visually impaired removal man, whilst Albert Riddle in *Robin's Nest* (ITV 1977–81) was a one-armed dishwasher. Much of the humour of Peter Cook and Dudley Moore's 'One Leg Too Few' sketch (*Not Only...But Also*, BBC 1965–70), Martin, Frasier's father in *Frasier* (NBC 1993–2004) and the *Monty Python* 'Ministry of Silly Walks' sketches (*Monty Python's Flying Circus*, BBC 1969–74) derives from walking difficulties. Stevie Kenarbum, Malcolm's best friend at school in *Malcolm in the Middle* (FOX 2000–06), exemplifies the notion of the multiply impaired super-geek: he uses a wheelchair, wears thick-lensed glasses, and has chronic asthma and damaged lungs. Alice Tinker in *The Vicar of Dibley,* Mickey in *The League of Gentlemen* (BBC 1999–2002), Frank Spencer in *Some Mothers Do 'Ave 'Em* (BBC 1973–78), Trigger in *Only Fools and Horses* (BBC 1981–2003), Baldrick in *Blackadder* (BBC 1983–89), Earl's brother Randy in *My Name is Earl* (NBC 2005–present) and Caleb Applewhite in *Desperate Housewives* (ABC 2004–present) represent adults with learning difficulties. Victor Meldrew from *One Foot in the Grave* (BBC 1990–2000) and Grandpa in *The Simpsons* (FOX 1989–present) provide humour by displaying the symptoms of dementia, whilst mental distress is central to the comedy of Basil Fawlty in *Fawlty Towers* (BBC 1975–79), Reggie Perrin in *The Fall and Rise of Reggie Perrin* (BBC 1976–79) and Letitia Copley in *The Vicar of Dibley.*

In a poll of TV's most popular disabled character carried out by the online magazine *Ouch* (2005a), Andy Pipkin of *Little Britain* was voted third by disabled participants (Timmy from *South Park* [Comedy Central 1997–present] came first and Dr Kerry Weaver from *ER* [NBC 1994–present] was second) and fourth by non-disabled participants (Brian Potter of *Phoenix Nights* [Channel 4 2001–02] was first, Timmy of *South Park* second and Penny Pocket of *Balamory* [BBC 2002–05] third). However, it is difficult to gauge what popularity means in this context, especially when you find out that some of the other characters voted for were Davros from *Dr Who* (BBC 1963–89, 2005–present) (who, severely scarred and wounded in battle and living through a cyber body, was a megalomaniac scientist responsible for the creation of the Daleks. At the time of the poll, he had not been seen on our television screens in a broadcast episode since 1988) and the Emperor Claudius from the 1976 BBC production of *I Claudius!* The poll could be read to indicate that there is a lack of representation of people with disabilities on our screens. However, this impression is countered by the recognition of the pivotal role of impairment in comedy and by Darke's claim that 'images of the disabled as the abnormal are everywhere in film and television' and that they are used to 'define the parameters of normality' and to 'create the simulacrum through which most apparently "normal people" live their lives' (in Shakespeare 2003: 183). Darke (2003) and Longmore (1987, 2003) offer extensive evidence of the disabled as support characters who motivate the heroic acts of the able and also as malevolent and monstrous villains, of prosthetic limbs as a short-circuit sign for evil and of the maladjusted disabled character who comes to terms with his/her disability through the guidance of an 'able' mentor. Clark (2003: 3) argues that in television comedy the disabled are represented through 'standard comic devices', ridicule, physical comedy, the monster, the fool and the clown, exposition of impairment, disablist language, relationships with non-disabled characters and the satirising of disabling barriers. From this perspective, what the *Ouch* poll indicates in telling detail is not a lack of representation on our screens but rather the paucity of engaging and developed representations of people with disabilities.

Surely Things Must Be Getting Better?

The 2005 *Ofcom Report: The Representation and Portrayal of People with Disabilities on Analogue Television* revealed that despite a raft of European and British Government initiatives and media institutional policies and pledges designed to improve the place and experience of disabled people in our society, the 'proportion of people/characters with disabilities fulfilling major roles in sampled programmes had decreased since 2002'

(2005: 1.4). However, the proportion of people in incidental and minor roles had increased, the 'most commonly represented disabilities were those that are most easily recognised (mobility, sensory impairment and disfigurement/physical impairment)' (2005: 1.5). The implication here is that it is easy to meet a quota requirement or obligation by putting some easily recognisable disabled people in the background of the action, whether it is for entertainment, drama or current affairs. *Little Britain* seems to play on this at times by filling the screen with incidental characters with improbable injuries. An obvious example of this is the man in the street with a plaster cast on his penis which a woman signs at the beginning of a Daffyd (Matt Lucas) 'The Only Gay in the Village' sketch ('The Test', 1: 5). A variation on this theme of the disabled as providing the opportunity for the playing out of the dramas and desires of the unimpaired is evident in the 'St God's Hospital' sketches, featuring the unscrupulous couple Joan (Matt Lucas) and Rod (David Walliams), who use the bedside of a seriously ill child as a pretext to meet celebrities. The Executive Summary of the *Ofcom Report* goes on to note that 'roles filled by people/actors with disabilities were more commonly those of children and retired people both of which can be associated with vulnerability' (2005: 1.6) and 'disability was "central" or "relevant" to the majority of the representations of people/characters with disabilities' (2005: 1.8).

Pathology or Prejudice?

In this context, we can see that Andy and Anne are important and innovative characters. Although they and the sketches they are in do reproduce some of the typical traits and conventions of the representation of people with disability, discussed in depth in Longmore (1987, 2003), Koblas (1988), Barnes (1992), Norden (1994) and Darke (2003), they broaden the paradigm significantly. *Little Britain's* depictions of disability raise a number of questions which underpin broader debates about disability and disablement. Central to these discourses is the question of how disability is defined and by whom. Disabled activists (primarily) have made a distinction between the medical and the social models of disability. The medical model, pathology, is the terrain of the experts who see disability as an anomaly, which should be examined, classified, cured and eradicated, and who have the 'good fortune to receive a salary for their efforts', as Brisenden noted (in Shakespeare 2003: 22). The social model was developed by disabled activists and is informed by their experiences. The central argument is that disability is a social, cultural and political problem which should be addressed by breaking down prejudice and material obstacles to inclusion (Davis 1997: 9; Shakespeare 2006: 2). Just as the rhetoric of state intervention and support fluctuates between the two models and often seems to result in 'mix and match' tactics, so does the discourse of *Little Britain*.

Cheats or 'Tricksters'?

Fundamental to the humour and resonance of the Lou and Andy as well as Anne and Dr Lawrence sketches is the common-sense idea of the binary opposition between true and faked disability. Within this lurks the notion that 'true' disability is pathological and should be all pervasive and fixed, constant or subject to permanent 'repair' and normalisation. The discourse of fakery, of the fraud who masquerades as a disabled person for personal gain, is a recurring story line in the national and local press. A story which is further elaborated by a voter in the BBC website *Ouch*'s *Greatest Disabled TV Character* poll through the following anecdote which reads this representation of 'fake' disability as a welcome portrayal of despicable behaviour:

> I would have to vote for Andy, as he reminds me of a neighbour who has a blue sticker for his car but also has a window cleaning job. He is also a part-time pall-bearer for a local funeral director. It always gives me a laugh when I'm out in my wheelchair and he comes running up the road, because when he sees me he starts limping! (*Ouch*: 2005b)

An alternative reading of Andy's 'faking' can be found in discussions of the role of disabled 'trickster' characters in literature. Tricksters are described as marginal but highly visible characters who live by their wits, often through deception, and who entertain by disrupting hegemonic expectations (Smith 1997). Albrecht notes that disabled characters in this role manage to 'span the mainstream and disability worlds providing insight into both and illustrate the difficulty in moving back and forth between these two frames of reference' (1999: 70). Hynes and Doty develop the discussion through the identification of six recurring traits of the 'trickster', several of which can be recognised in *Little Britain* sketches. They suggest that the trickster is fundamentally ambiguous and anomalous, a deceiver and a trick player, a shape shifter, a situation inverter, a messenger and an imitator of the gods and is a sacred and lewd bricoleur (1993: 34–42).

Shape Shifting

The humour in the sketches in part stems from the shared joke between the audience and Andy and Anne as deceivers and trick players, and from the situation that the supposed experts, Lou (Andy's helper) and Dr Lawrence (Anne's psychiatrist), are seemingly taken in by the temporary performance of disability. This involves 'shape shifting' from wheelchair user to able bodied, from 'mad woman' to sane-sounding man (Anne). Andy regularly abandons his wheelchair to perform outrageous and often joyous physical acts, for example, running naked across a pebbled beach to swim whilst Lou fetches him an ice-cream ('Seaside', 2: 6), or swimming with the fish in the aquarium whilst Lou buttonholes a passing aquarium employee ('Aquarium', 3: 1). This discourse of fakery or trickery is brought to a head at the end of series three ('Mrs Mead 4', 3: 6) when Lou has to abandon Andy to go to his mother's funeral. Lou's replacement, Mrs Mead (played by Imelda Staunton), tests Andy's need to use the wheelchair by whacking his legs repeatedly with a brass candlestick to see if he has any feeling in his legs. In the final sketch of the series, Mrs Mead voices the scepticism and judgement so often expressed in the press about those on incapacity benefit:

> If you ask me I see no reason now why you can't do your own cooking and cleaning. And that TV is going off and

staying off. And no more chocolate or potato crisps. And why don't you get yourself a job? There's plenty of things you can do. First thing tomorrow I'm going to take you down the job centre and find you something. (Lucas and Walliams 2006b: 255)

Andy, however, manages to 'invert the situation' by 'taking care of' Mrs Mead by pushing her over the edge of a cliff.

We never know whether Andy and Anne are personifications of 'real' or 'fake' disabled characters. The terrain of verisimilitude constantly shifts, the characters remain 'fundamentally ambiguous and anomalous'. Andy does not seem to need his wheelchair but some disabled viewers seemed to recognise his situation. They seem to interpret the sketches from a position similar to Tom Shakespeare's in his analysis of the role of disability cabaret, where he argues that:

> comedy is used to identify the barriers which create difficulty for disabled people, and to challenge the cultural values and taboos which dominate everyday interaction. By revealing the underlying relations of power and oppression, jokes like this give disabled people permission to be angry and redirect frustration from impaired bodies, to the contexts which construct impairment as a problem. (1999: 51)

Participants commenting in support of their votes for Andy in the *Greatest Disabled TV Character* poll (*Ouch* 2005a) read his 'faking' or 'trickery' in turn as a response to a limited life and as an expression of autonomy:

> Andy causes all sorts of 'kafuffles' [sic] with his seemingly deliberate indecisiveness when choosing a book from a library or a holiday to go on. As viewers, we assume that this is Andy's way of relieving pent-up boredom and is the only small way in which he is capable of rebelling – though beautifully petty. (*Ouch* 2005b)

'Faking' and 'trickery' may also be interpreted as a way of testing and challenging people's low expectations of those with disabilities: 'because Andy knows he is taking advantage of his mate Lou. Which so many people with disabilities do all the time...not for attention but to see how much others think we cannot do' (*Ouch* 2005b).

Inverting Situations

The wheelchair has become synonymous with public discourses about disability, operating as the visual sign for spaces and services accessible for the disabled. However, in the Lou and Andy sketches the wheelchair can be read more sinisterly as a metaphor for the ways in which Andy's carers try to push him about. He is patronised and constrained by his carer's actions and expectations. This happens literally in the 'Bathroom' sketch (1: 2) when Lou wants Andy to see the changes he has made to Andy's bathroom. Andy is sitting in his wheelchair eating a bag of crisps and watching *Monster Trucks*, he doesn't want to move so Lou pushes the wheelchair into the bathroom; keeping his eyes on the screen, Andy exclaims, 'I'm watching that.'

Although Lou seems to be well meaning, he does, like Mrs Mead, try to tell Andy what he likes, what he wants and what he should do. Lou assumes he knows better than Andy and stands in judgement over him. Longmore (2003: 137) identifies the recurring trope of the 'maladjusted disabled person' in film and television. He argues that, 'typically, disabled characters lack insight about themselves and other people and require emotional education, usually by a non disabled person'. The Lou and Andy relationship seems to elaborate and play on this theme. The typical structure of a sketch is that Lou tries to persuade Andy that he likes something or wants to do something which Andy then rejects and replaces with his own, entertaining but ridiculous choice. The 'Holiday' sketch (1: 6), where Lou and Andy discuss holiday plans, is typical of this. Lou tries to persuade Andy by attributing unlikely phrases to him. Andy has pointed at Helsinki as his choice of place to visit, Lou responds, 'But you always said Finland had a maudlin quality about it rendering it unsuitable as a holiday destination'. The sketch often ends with Lou being right but the joke is on him because he is left being responsible for rectifying the situation; in this instance, we hear the aeroplane take off for Finland as Andy says, 'Don't like it. I want to go to Florida'. A similar scenario is evident in the 'video' sketch (1: 3) when Lou takes Andy to choose a video. Andy points aimlessly without looking (his strategy when Lou tries to get him to expand his cultural horizons), the video he points at is *Pride and Prejudice*, Lou comments, 'I'm not sure you'd like that one' and 'You like your Chuck Norrises and your Steven Segals'. Lou is right; as soon as the film starts, Andy says, 'Don't like it.' Lou takes a tough line and leaves Andy supposedly stuck in his wheelchair watching the film. However, as soon as Lou leaves Andy gets out of the wheelchair and changes the video for *Monster Trucks*.

Learning Disabilities and Mental Illness: Still Fair Game for Ridicule?

Although Andy does not seem to need a wheelchair, he does seem to have learning difficulties. Learning difficulties are never directly referred to but inferred through his speech, demeanour and behaviour and Lou's interactions with him. Andy's catchphrase 'Yeah I know', his slack-jawed smile and his scruffy, outdated and ill-fitting clothes, his sly delight in corporeal pleasures, his lack of judgement – in insisting on having breasts like the ones in the British soft-porn magazine *Razzle* so that he's 'got something to play with', but then having to have them removed because he looks 'a pillock' ('Breasts', 3: 3) – all of these can be read as stereotypical caricature of the adult with learning difficulties who is being cared for in the community.

In the BBC Radio 4 discussion programme *'Should We Be laughing?'* (2004), the presenter, Francesca Martinez, commented that 'it seems many people are still very happy to laugh at the disabilities involving mental distress and at the survivors of the mental health system. These disabilities, including learning difficulties, are still fair game for comedy and ridicule'. The examples cited to illustrate this claim included Alice Tinker in the *Vicar of Dibley*, Father Dougal in *Father Ted* (Channel 4 1995–98), Bubble from *Absolutely Fabulous* (BBC 1992–96, 2001–05), Mickey Love in *A League of Gentlemen*, Frank Spencer in *Some Mothers Do 'Ave 'Em*; Pike in *Dad's Army* (BBC 1968–77), Trigger in *Only Fools and Horses*, and Baldrick in *Blackadder*. The only differences between these representations and that of Andy Pipkin are that his disability is the overt substance of the comedy and that he often gets the last laugh. Despite Lou's supposed superior knowledge and understanding of Andy's needs and desires, it is Andy who knows how to enjoy himself behind Lou's back, whether it is water skiing behind a tourist cruiser ('Boat trip', 3: 2), skydiving at an air show ('Airshow', 3: 1), or watching *Monster Trucks*.

In the same broadcast (17 February 2004), Colin Barnes argued that there are historical precedents for the use of people with learning difficulties and mental health problems as a suitable subject for entertainment and noted that, 'when asylums came into existence across Europe it was not uncommon for asylums to open their doors to the general public so that people could actually come in and laugh at people with mental health problems.' This tradition is blatantly carried on in the Anne and Dr Lawrence sketches which are set in the Steven Spielberg Hospital in Little Bentcock, where she is, as the *Little Britain Character Guide: Anne* website tell us, 'under the care of the progressive Dr Lawrence, despite her incoherent speech and random acts of destruction Dr Lawrence forges ahead with his programme to assimilate Anne into the community' (BBC 2007).

Anne's disability is never defined but implied. Her disorder registers through violence, incoherent screeching and a lack of sartorial and gender conformity. She appears to be a man in drag; no attempt is made to disguise David Walliams' body shape, features, hair, demeanour or voice. She wears a cotton nightie, a pink cardigan and carpet slippers. In the company of Dr Lawrence, her behaviour is often at odds with his assessment. As he explains to the visiting expert, Dr Beagrie, that she is responding well to his regime, she counteracts his comments with violent and antisocial behaviour. An example of this is the sketch when he introduces Dr Beagrie to Anne when she is working in the library (1: 4). They meet as Anne pushes a trolley of books towards them. She rips pages out of a book and places them on Dr Beagries' shoulder and rubs a book on her breasts to which Dr Lawrence responds, 'As you can see, she blends in very well'. Anne's actions are often violent and destructive but are intercut with oddly jarring moments of rational response. An early example of this is the 'Garden' sketch

(1: 2) when she is destroying plants from a flower bed, her mobile rings and she answers it with 'I'm in the middle of something, I'll ring you back'. Just as the library sketch can be read as an ironic critique of the behaviour of librarians, the garden sketch opens up a whole range of interpretations. Anne may be read to be faking mental illness, as she clearly has people she interacts with in a way that accords with social expectations, but equally it could be argued that her behaviour is not fixed but is the product of her interactions with others, particularly with Dr Lawrence. This links into several popular myths about mental health. The first of which is that the lunatics are in charge of the asylum. An interpretation which can be justified through the analysis of recurring examples of Dr Lawrence's seemingly inappropriate assessment of Anne's condition, her suitable treatment and his responses to her often threatening behaviour. When Anne appears on *Stars in Their Eyes* (3: 1) with Cat Deeley, she performs her version of Celine Dion's *My Heart Will Go On* from the film *Titanic* (1997) which consists of a tuneless rendition of her catchphrase 'Eh eh eeeh'. Dr Lawrence listens and comments, 'She sounds quite a lot like her, doesn't she'. This could be a statement of his musical taste, his tone deafness or his total lack of discernment. The latter reading is endorsed as Anne loses interest in performing and proceeds to demolish the stage set. Dr Lawrence does not seem to notice this. Such scenes underline the irony of Dr Lawrence's statement in the 'Dining Room' sketch (1: 2) when he explains to Dr Beagrie that 'We are not trying to implement any sort of hierarchical structure here', as Anne reaches over and removes his bread roll from his plate, and that 'I think it is no small tribute to us here that when people come to visit us here they do say who are the doctors and who are the patients', as Anne proceeds to pour tea and coffee all over him and Dr Beagrie. As Anne drags him away on his chair mid sentence, his only response is to Dr Beagrie, 'We can talk about this later'.

It is interesting to note that there are rarely sympathetic depictions of psychiatrists in screen fictions, the stigma attached to mental health problems seems to pervade all aspects of the representation of people in the mental health system, whether doctors, nurses, orderlies, social workers, administrators or patients. Dr Lawrence is the latest in a long line of representations of incompetent and/or malevolent physicians (*The Cabinet of Dr Caligari* [1920], *One Flew over the Cuckoo's Nest* [1975], *Frasier, An Angel at My Table* [1990], *Copy Cat* [1995], *Cracker* [ITV 1993–96, 2006], *Hannibal Lecter* [see *Manhunter* 1986; *The Silence of the Lambs* 1991; *Hannibal* 2001; *Red Dragon* 2002; *Hannibal Rising* 2007]. His bumbling panglossian response to Anne's violence may seem sweet and ineffectual until it is placed in the context of the negative association which is constantly reiterated in the press of the relationship between mental illness and violence. This association is refuted by mental health pressure groups (e.g., the UK-based schizophrenics support and campaigning group *Voices Forum*) and professionals (*The Institute of Psychiatry*) whose research indicates that the mentally ill are more likely to be subject to violence and ill treatment than to perpetrate it. Although the Anne and Dr Lawrence sketches may open up questions about the power relationships within mental health institutions and regimes, they simultaneously perpetuate the discourse of 'normalcy' which Darke (2003: 187) argues works to integrate audiences into the medical model of disability as abject and abhorrent.

Abject Freaks?

The humour of *Little Britain* is embodied and relies upon the exaggerated and grotesque characterisation of a whole range of abject physical and social anxieties through typage, which is in turn reliant on the currency of the stereotypes mobilised. This resonates with Garland Thomas' argument (1996: 2) that the medical model of disability shares a common and often intertwined history with the freak show, through the development of teratology – the study, classification and manipulation of exceptional bodies as monstrous. In both instances, the exceptional body was exploited, whether for science or commerce. She argues that the essence of the freak show's discourse was in the way in which it 'ranged over the seemingly singular bodies framing them and heightening their differences from viewers, who were rendered comfortably common and safely standard by the exchange' (1996: 5).

Singular bodies populate *Little Britain*. Our current obsession with obesity and the overvalorisation of the slender body is played out through the various characters performed by Matt Lucas. Examples range from the obese Marjorie Dawes and her Fat Fighters to Daffyd, 'The Only Gay in the Village' in his excessively tight and skimpy hot pant suits stretched over his rotund body displaying large amounts of flesh. From Vicky Pollard, the archetypal 'Chav', teenage Mum and delinquent, with her spotty face and perpetually pregnant body encased in her signature pink track suit top, to Andy Pipkin who is described on the *Little Britain Character Guide: Lou and Andy* website as 'a fat, balding, semi-naked spring lamb' (BBC 2007).

Mrs Emery (David Walliams), who was introduced in series three, offers perhaps the ultimate image of the abject. She is depicted as an elderly woman who has no bladder control or awareness. The joke in all the sketches she appears in is that she conducts remarkably civil and mundane conversations with people seemingly unaware that a gushing torrent of yellow liquid is pouring from between her legs. Further, the politeness of her interactions and her obliviousness to the problem renders her various acquaintances unable to discuss the matter. In the 'Doctor' sketch (3: 6), Mrs Emery goes to the doctor with a bad knee, but even he, kneeling in a puddle of urine, is unable to broach the subject. This representation of the abject body, like so many others within *Little Britain,* can be interpreted in a number of different ways. It can be read as a critique of British manners and taboos, particularly of our inability to discuss bodily functions and dysfunctions, especially in 'polite company'. Alternatively, it can be seen simply as an offensive representation of the ageing female body, the stigma of the lack of bodily control made overt. The Mrs Emery sketches act out the obverse of the Tena Lady adverts which suggest a way to keep the secret of incontinence and enable fulfilling lives. It's difficult to know which is most offensive!

Mrs Emery's lack of physical self-control and self-awareness is echoed in several of the other characters. The joke in the Bubbles DeVere (Matt Lucas) sketches appears to be that she does not realise that she is the epitome of the unattractive in contemporary discourse. She is middle-aged, obese, flabby and saggy, but she is not ageing gracefully, nor is she fading into invisibility. Rather Bubbles perceives herself as vital and attractive, offering her body to the manager of the health spa in return for weeks of unpaid bills. In these instances, the excessive body is made 'monstrous' and 'freakish' through its association with marginal identities (the disabled, teenage mothers, the elderly, the obese), lack of control and the characters' failure to conform to acceptable codes of behaviour. Garland Thomas argues that 'freak' discourse is exaggerated and sensationalised:

> because such bodies are rare, unique, material, and confounding of cultural categories, they function as magnets to which culture secures its anxieties, questions, and needs at any given time. Like the bodies of female slaves, the monstrous body exists in societies to be exploited for someone else's purposes. Thus, singular bodies become politised when culture maps its concerns upon them as meditations on individual as well as national values, identity and direction. (1996: 2)

Little Britain provides us with a contemporary freak show parading before us; for our entertainment and reassurance (and the profit of the exhibitors), a range of contemporary singular bodies. The sketches act out and play with contemporary ambivalence towards the disabled, disability and impairment. The emphasis on abject impersonation, on the humorous embodiment of recognisable stigmatised and marginalised stereotypes, functions to secure and endorse the medical model of difference as abnormality. The 'Lou and Andy' and 'Anne and Dr Lawrence' sketches present us with a potential critique of this. They offer popular and engaging but ultimately ambiguous representations of entertaining tricksters, people who *may* choose to be seen as disabled or who are disabled by their carers. The traditionally subordinate and 'othered' disabled characters *may* have the last laugh. Such scenarios and interpretations would call the social model of disability into play. But is this possibility enough? When we get off the *Little Britain* roller-coaster and struggle to regain our sense of equilibrium, to what extent are we invited to think through our contradictory responses and reactions? However we may interpret the characters and their actions, our sense of ethical disorientation must surely force us to acknowledge that there is much more to *Little Britain* than just having a laugh.

Chapter SEVEN

'The Only Feminist Critic in the Village?': Figuring Gender and Sexuality in *Little Britain*

Deborah Finding

Introduction

I started writing a feminist critique of *Little Britain* with a certain amount of trepidation. *Little Britain* is a comedy show, and – in the mainstream at least – feminism and humour are rarely mentioned in the same sentence, unless 'humour' is followed with 'less'. At a time when post-feminism is more popular than feminism and a criticism of any media output for its sexism, racism, classism, ageism or homophobia is met with a chorus of 'But it's ironic!', the temptation to ignore the discomfort and laugh along with the majority is compelling. However, the figure of the humourless feminist (or 'Millie Tant' as *Viz* magazine would have it) who 'cannot take a joke' in itself is one reason to explore comedy not just for its appeal but also for the identity constructions and potential silencing practices inherent in that appeal.

In this chapter, I will place *Little Britain* within a wider context, in order to see its relationship with alternative comedy and post-feminism. I will argue that *Little Britain* has far more in common with the pre-alternative comedy, now known for its racism and sexism, than it does with the provocative and challenging nature of alternative comedy. Drawing on the work of Whelehan (2000), Skeggs (2005), McRobbie (2004) and Gill (2007 and 2008), I argue that this back-step mirrors the cultural transition from feminist sensibilities to post-feminist ones in the media more generally and show how irony, or the assertion of it, is used to pre-empt any potential critique. I consider the characters of *Little Britain* through an engagement with Imogen Tyler's (2008) figurative analysis of asylum seekers and 'chav mums' and argue that the majority of the characters are stereotypes produced through disgust at class, sexuality, race or gender. As many of these figures are heavily reliant on the body (to create the disgust), I also briefly explore the ways in which female comics have approached the body, especially the fat body. Kathleen Rowe (1990) argues that Roseanne [*Roseanne*, ABC 1988–1997) represents an unruly and disruptive challenge to the prescribed codes of female appearance and, by association, behaviour. The kind of dysfunction presented in Roseanne's body, sexuality and family is actually a very functional one, which is recognisable and comforting. I will return to this idea when looking at those characters in *Little Britain* who might be considered disruptive or unruly. I also look with interest at the ways in which David Walliams and Matt Lucas themselves are figured through their bodies in the media. Finally, I question the potential for true alternative comedy through the sporadic moments in which *Little Britain* does subvert or challenge these figures, and I ask whether or not these can overcome the 'pleasures of hatred' (Billig 2001: 267) as the show's primary legacy.

Alternative Comedy

British 'Alternative Comedy' developed from the 1980s in response to the racist and sexist comic material seen on the live comedy circuit and on mainstream television (see Finding 2008 for a detailed discussion of alternative comedy; see also Wilmut and Rosengard 1989; William Cook 1994, 2001; Wagg 1996; Double 1997; Littlewood and Pickering 1998). Alternative comedy replaced sexist and racist jokes (made by comedians such as Bernard Manning) with observational humour and personal narratives, and audiences were required to be intellectually and emotionally involved in the comedian's train of thought in order to laugh. Both 'old' comedy and alternative comedy relied on an audience's identification or agreement with the comedian – however, the targets of the jokes became more complex with alternative comedy. Punchlines were somewhat passé, and audiences started responding to the intellectual shift taking place. Alternative comedians were sending themselves and people like them up, rather than holding up a particular stereotyped 'other' as an object of ridicule (e.g., Jo Brand and Jenny Éclair). Where the target was outside the comedian's immediate experience, it tended to be a person (or an institution) of power, rather than one belonging to a marginalised group (e.g., Ben Elton's political jokes), and a more surreal approach was often adopted (exemplified by comedians such as Paul Merton, Alexei Sayle and, later, Eddie Izzard). Towards the late 1980s/early 1990s, alternative comedy moved from the preserve of 'cult' comedy to 'mainstream' comedy via programmes such as *Newman and Baddiel in Pieces* (BBC 1993).

If the cultural changes instigated by feminism, civil rights movements and a new era of political freedoms were meant to render the sexism and racism of the past nothing more than a pitiful 'joke', then the cultural danger lies – at least for comedians – in failing to 'get it'. Yet identifying oneself as 'feminist' necessarily acknowledges sexism not as a joke, but as a problem. It's not surprising, therefore, that any female stand-up who comments on sexism must preface her joke with 'I'm not a feminist but...'. Many of them prefer to either take on the persona of the ladette or identify more as a *Sex and the City* Carrie type. There seems to be little room for any other position in the mainstream. This is hardly surprising given the consequences of critiquing the 'new sexism' or 'new cruelty'. After all, a comedian cannot be thought of as humourless, or as not clever enough to get the joke, or she will not be accepted as a comedian. Worse, she may be thought to be critiquing sexism through her comedy because she is not pretty enough to reap the benefits of the critical male gaze and is, therefore, bitter. Some comedians, such as Jo Brand, have addressed this directly in their stand-up shows – her best-known heckle-putdown being, 'the reason I keep my weight up is so that tossers like you won't fancy me' (quoted in Wagg 1998b: 112). Others, however, seem to have internalised this myth and suffer under it. In Dawn French's ITV programme *On Big Women* (1994), she stated, 'If I was alive [in Reuben's time], I wouldn't have to be a comedian to earn a living. I'd be celebrated as a fabulous model' (quoted in Hole 2003: 319–20). As Hole points out, the logical conclusion to draw from this statement is that it is more desirable or worthwhile to be a model than a comedian, and that being a comedian is some sort of a fallback position for women unlucky enough to live in a time where their particular body shape is not celebrated. One might note here that the self-deprecation of the female comic here is linked with being bitter, resentful and envious, whereas the self-deprecation associated with the New Lad/New Man male alternative comedians was simply accepted as funny.

It seems that when alternative comedy became mainstream, a return to the old traditional comedy became the knowing, naughty, ironic alternative. If, as seemed to be assumed, the battles over racism and sexism had been won, then there could be nothing new or interesting in talking about them or challenging them. The discourse of 'political correctness' and the tabloids' insistence that 'you can't say anything nowadays' meant that making racist or sexist comments became the new (old) alternative. I believe that we can position *Little Britain* right here. Rather than sending themselves and people like them up, the *Little Britain* creators rely primarily on the stereotypical Other and his/her grotesqueness for the humour of the show. Before examining the show's characters, it is important to understand how this backslide to a hatred-based humour came about and look at the justification for this return – irony – and then to set both within a context of feminist critique.

Humour and Hatred

Billig's (2001) work on the racist jokes of the Ku Klux Klan provides some interesting insights into the links between humour and hatred. In examining some websites providing lists of racist jokes, he often found disclaimers that these were 'just jokes' and that it was not possible to genuinely take offence at them because of this. The creators of the site are not 'real life racists' – the implication being that these are just words and that 'real life racists' would be more action-oriented. Catherine MacKinnon's (1994) work provides a clear critique of the 'only words' defence with regard to pornography, and Billig makes a similar point with regard to its racism application. Writing about the disclaimer, 'This site contains racial jokes, slurs, and an overall negative view to the black race', found on a site entitled 'Nigger Jokes', he argues:

> The overall negative view is not claimed to be a joke. The jokes themselves are presented as 'just jokes'. But they are labelled as 'nigger jokes'. The category labels the jokes and is not part of the jokes. It belongs, as such, to the meta-discourse of the joke. The appellation itself cannot be justified as 'just a joke': it is a serious label whose semantics are not neutral. The extra word, as the ultimate word of racist hate, comes with ideological, historical and emotional baggage. (Billig 2001: 275)

I include this not because *Little Britain* can be labelled in a similarly obvious fashion but because words and phrases which have been used to oppress, shame and mock people from marginalised groups cannot be justified or explained away by the 'just a joke' defence because they produce meaning in themselves. And although the BBC (and possibly the *Little Britain* creators themselves) would shy away from using a word such as 'nigger', there is no such problem with 'chav' or 'slag', for example (see Sharon Lockyer's chapter for more on chavs). However, although words or phrases alone can and do constitute a certain figure, such as the 'chav', the format of the comedy sketch show allows these figures to be constituted in a variety of (stereotyped) ways, including clothes, hairstyle, style of walking and voice, as we will see when examining the *Little Britain* characters.

This return to hate-for-laughs is not confined to comedy. Angela McRobbie's (2004) work on post-feminist symbolic violence in makeover programmes such as the BBCs *What Not to Wear* (2001–07) examined in detail the expression 'Pramface' – a phrase coined by the gossip email site *Popbitch*, originally to describe Kerry Katona (previously of the girl-band Atomic Kitten, and also ITV's *I'm a Celebrity, Get Me Out of Here* [2002–present], more famous for her tabloid-friendly sex/drug exploits) but applicable to any girl who looks cheaply dressed and is pushing a child in a pushchair. It follows other expressions too, for example, 'Croydon facelift', referring to a council-estate girl whose hair is scraped back so tightly that her face appears lifted. As McRobbie points out, this sort of bitchy comment regarding style, body shape and taste is far more closely associated with pre-feminist times. She argues that up to around 2005, teachers would have condemned this sort of talk in the playground as a type of bullying, and (liberal) adults would not have thought it appropriate to snigger at someone because she lives in a council estate or sneer that her mother does not look well off (McRobbie 2004).

Gill has described this pattern of nastiness and extreme criticism (with specific reference to women's appearance) as 'the new cruelty' (Gill 2008). It is exemplified by TV makeover shows, in which the subject is routinely humiliated and criticised at the beginning of the show for her bad haircut/poor taste in clothes/lack of style and other such 'deficiencies'. We might feel a sense of relief when the cruelty stops, when the woman emerges at the end and is praised for having followed a set of rules and changing herself. No such relief exists in the comedy sphere of the sketch show. Comedy characters are not 'real people', and as such the level of cruelty that is appropriate to exhibit is not tempered by any sort of redemptive moment. However, as we will see through the figurative analysis of the *Little Britain* characters, this 'not real people' justification does not work, given the ways in which these character types are represented (figured) to be both recognisable and hated.

Imelda Whelehan (2000) suggests that this back-step, or cultural undoing, of the reforms that took place from the late 1960s until the mid-1990s, although something to be extremely concerned about, was inevitable. She argues that the short-lived 'honeymoon period' of acceptance with regard to what is now condemned as 'political correctness' would always be replaced once it was realised that attitudes and practices needed to be changed after they were challenged:

> Feminists assert that language and intention as well as behaviour matter: since this implies that men in particular have to modify their attitudes, it is hardly likely to be popular. (Whelehan 2000: 70)

However, an unthinking return to the old ways was not possible. Critiques were already in place that meant that one could simply not get away with the type of racist, sexist, homophobic and classist attitudes and slurs that had been acceptable in the past. Something would have to be added in order to make these representations palatable again. That something was irony.

Irony and Post-feminism

As both Whelehan (2000) and Gill (2007) have pointed out, irony has become the 'get out of jail free' card that acts to close down the possibility of critique. Irony establishes a safe distance between the speaker and what is being said. Once this distance has been created, the speaker can say absolutely anything, no matter how superficially offensive, because we should all know that they 'didn't really mean it'. With much of this output, the critique is pre-empted and addressed in the text. This is done either by positioning the speaker as a nostalgic guardian for the good old days when you could be 'a bit naughty', or by making the potential critic a party-pooper, telling us what we can and can't say in this sensitive age of 'political correctness gone mad'. Feminists become the 'thought police' or rail against Page 3 girls because they are not attractive enough to pose for the *Sun* themselves. Or they are simply taking everything too seriously and don't get the joke.

Irony and the assumption of it have been *the* cornerstone of New Laddism. The tagline of *Loaded*, James Brown's first 'lad's mag', was 'for men who should know better'. *Loaded* spawned a host of similar monthly magazines and, recently, two weeklies, *Nuts* and *Zoo*. The ad campaign to launch *Nuts* set out its (ironically) sexist position from the start. In one of the adverts, the man (Matthew Morrison) is sitting in a broken down car, engrossed in *Nuts* magazine, while his girlfriend fumbles ineffectually under the bonnet of the car, in the pouring rain (in a miniskirt, naturally). The tagline reads, 'Women, don't expect any help on a Thursday'. The *Nuts* website offers a 'service' called 'Assess My Breasts', whereby women can upload a picture of their breasts to the site, and the male readers are invited to compare photos as better or worse by using their 'expert knowledge of lady breasts to rate every pair!'. Of course, there are plenty of topless models and reality TV stars on the website, as in the magazine, to boost this 'knowledge'.

There are still those who are willing to critique magazines like *Nuts* and *Zoo*, such as the feminist activist group Object who produce reports on lad mags and encourage campaign letters to protest against the content. However, these groups receive little, if any, media attention, and, as Gill rightly notes, second-wave slogans such as 'This ad objectifies women!' are literally extinct (Gill 2007) due to the assumption that these women are sexually and financially empowered by appearing naked in these magazines. 'Upload your breasts!', *Nuts* online encourages us, and either feminist computer hackers are being thwarted in their attempts to change the text to, 'Actively participate in your own exploitation!', or potential complainants are silenced before the complaint is even voiced.

Not getting the joke or, even worse, being considered humourless is one of the most effective ways to silence criticism. When the critic's target is a television show as popular as *Little Britain*, it is important to look at all the ways in which the criticism is already pre-deflected. Favourable reviews of the show, playground and office repetitions of catchphrases, and identifications of the characters as figures, all act to make *Little Britain* an integral part of our shared popular culture. To criticise it is to stand outside something that is both mainstream and popular, and also to invite suggestion that the critic takes everything too seriously. However, if we agree that representing certain groups in certain ways might not be 'only words' or 'just a joke', then it is worth examining those figures more closely to see how they map onto 'the real world'.

Figurative Analysis

I follow Tyler's use of 'figure' to 'describe the ways in which at different historical and cultural moments, specific bodies become over determined and are publicly imagined and represented (are figured) in excessive, distorted and/or caricatured ways that are expressive of an underlying crisis or anxiety' (Tyler 2008: 18). Her work draws on the fetishisation of the stranger as theorised by Sara Ahmed (2000) and Claudia Castaneda's (2002) work, which inextricably links the semiotic and the material. The corporeal nature of figurative analysis is well suited to a character/stereotype-driven sketch show, as it allows exploration not just of nasty ideas *as* ideas, but also of the ways in which they are projected onto actual bodies.

Tyler uses figurative analysis to explore the figures of the asylum seeker (2006) and the 'chav mum' (2008), the latter of which I reference with regard to the character of Vicky Pollard (Matt Lucas). The framework has recently been applied to the figures of the 'vengeful woman', the 'hot lesbian' and 'the midriff' in Rosalind Gill's (2008) work on advertising. In the next section, I examine the characters of *Little Britain* so far as they pertain to two figures in particular: 'the mail order bride' (Ting Tong Macadangdang played by Matt Lucas) and 'the gay man' (Daffyd played by Matt Lucas, and Sebastian, played David Walliams). I then look briefly at some other characters of interest who might warrant figurative analysis of their own – Emily Howard ('the transvestite' [Walliams]), Bubbles DeVere ('the fat woman' [Lucas]) and Mrs Emery ('the old woman' [Walliams]) – and suggest where such an analysis might lead in terms of *Little Britain*'s presentation of gender and sexuality.

In exploring issues of gender and sexuality through figurative analysis, there is no escaping its intersections with class and race. As there are chapters in this book dealing with class (see Sharon Lockyer's chapter) and race (see Sarita Malik's chapter) separately, I have tried to only highlight these intersections, rather than fully explore them. See Finding (2008) for an in-depth analysis of how class and gender stereotypes amplify and intersect with one another, especially with reference to the character of Vicky Pollard.

Figures

Figure 1: 'The Mail Order Bride'

The first episode of Season 3 of *Little Britain* introduced us to a Thai mail-order bride named Ting Tong Macadangdang. A mocking name, bad yellow makeup, buck teeth and an inability to pronounce 'r' certainly do nothing to set this character aside from every bad South-East Asian stereotype we have been subjected to in the past. However, there is a disturbing political element to this figure that goes much further than a racist physical representation.

Ting Tong is seen as the more powerful one in the relationship she has been bought for, as she convinces Dudley (David Walliams) to marry her despite her not being as attractive as he thought she was going to be. This manages to accomplish two things. First, it muddies the water with regard to the power dynamics inherent in buying a woman for sex. Second, it removes the potential for critique on the grounds of exploitation of Ting Tong, as she is given a potential exit but actively chooses to stay with Dudley. The idea that actually *she* is the one exploiting *him* is not new; in fact, it seems to be suggested in every *Bravo/Channel 5* TV show (posing as documentary) about lapdancing, stripping or prostitution. Its popularity surely owes a great deal to its appeal – after all, if the opposite were true, then those activities would no longer be accessible as sexual titillation or naughty fun where no harm is done.

Brother:	You must be Ping Pong
Ting Tong:	It's Ting Tong
Brother:	From the Philippines?
Ting Tong:	Thailand
Brother:	Thailand. That's right. They're cheaper over there, aren't they? Well, welcome, King Kong.
Brother:	Did you ask for a fat one?
Dudley:	No, it's just how she came

(*Little Britain Abroad* Part 2)

The dialogue once again shows a horror of the imperfect female form, in keeping with the way the other female characters in *Little Britain* are presented. However, it also acts to do more than this. It desexualises Ting Tong by pointing out her undesirability, so that we do not have to think about the reality of a woman being bought for sex. It is impossible that Ting Tong is being exploited, because she is simply not attractive or thin enough for anyone to *want* to exploit her.

We might consider a small reprieve for Lucas and Walliams here – however distasteful and problematic this representation is, at least they have not relied on the 'exotic other' stereotype utilised by those same *Bravo/Channel 5* documentaries, and films such as *Birthday Girl* (2001). However, this reprieve would be short-lived, as they immediately go on to reap the benefits of this recognisable figure by introducing another character. After this scene, we find that Dudley's brother Les (played by Peter Kay) also has a mail order bride, the blonde Russian Ivanka (Julia Davis) who was 'only £200' and is later discovered to have worked in pornography. The men discover this through the machinations of Ting Tong, who is presented as being jealous of the more attractive woman, suggesting once again that she actively wants and chooses to be Dudley's mail order bride and is even willing to fight for the privilege.

Needless to say, there is absolutely nothing challenging or new about these characters. The figure of the mail order bride is sexual, exotic and neither damaged nor capable of being damaged. Given that this makes her not quite human, we do not have to worry about her. Links between mail order brides and women trafficked for prostitution are well established, and the available narratives of the lives of those women (e.g., see Dickson 2004), including rape, beating and imprisonment, are anything but a joke. *Little Britain* uses the characters of Ting Tong and Ivanka to imply that, far from doing any wrong or harm, it is Dudley and his brother who are hard done by, because they have overpaid (£200) for women who are not worth the money because they are either not attractive enough (Ting Tong) or 'shop-soiled' through previous sex-work (Ivanka). The laugh comes from the audience's agreement that they would not pay £200 for 'that' either, and that Dudley and his brother have been hoodwinked. The 'we' here is clearly defined as heterosexual men, and the 'other' as women who are not attractive enough or have had too many sexual experiences (whether these are consensual or not does not seem to matter) to be worth paying for. Again, the idea that men desire beautiful virgins is neither new nor challenging.

The website Thai-UK.org, which exists to 'promote positive relations between Thailand and the UK', ran a survey (entitled 'Stereotype or Fun?') in December 2005 about the character of Ting Tong Macadangdang to see how its Thai readers responded to this sketch. Out of 70 respondents, 25 thought it was 'stereotyping' and 45 thought it was 'fun'. It is interesting to note the binary presented in this choice – *either* it is a stereotype *or* it is fun. One option describes the type of representation made, and the other describes the effect or intention of the representation. 'Stereotype' and 'not fun' are not synonymous, nor are 'fun' and 'accurate description'. If the choices had been 'stereotype' or 'accurate description', this result may have been very different. After all, not ticking the 'fun' box could mean that the respondent does not get the joke, does not have a sense of humour or is simply not fun, rather than being someone who might be all three but finds this particular representation offensive. Again, this is a clear example of the threat of being found humourless being used to prevent any potential critique.

Figure 2: 'The Gay Man'

Surely, one might think, Daffyd, the 'only gay in the village', is *Little Britain*'s trump card, when it comes to deflecting feminist critique. This sketch could not possibly be homophobic, because it is played by Matt Lucas and Matt Lucas is gay. The premise of the sketch is that Daffyd runs around trying – and failing – to find homophobia in his village, when, in fact, a number of locals are either gay themselves or seem to be reasonably fine with it. However, this sketch works only if one believes that we are, in fact, living in a pro-gay, homophobia-free utopia. If this were the case, then indeed it would be ridiculous to see prejudice where it no longer exists. Daffyd would then represent the sort of gay man who actively wants to be a victim, who feels that there is something lacking when there is nothing to complain about any more. One need look no further than the tabloid demonisation of left-wing gay activist Peter Tatchell to see that this is a recognisable figure.

However, the figure of the gay man in *Little Britain* goes further than this. Being gay in *Little Britain* is also associated with being ridiculous. Daffyd's outfits and demeanour ensure that this holds true for him and mean that, after Lou (Walliams) and Andy (Lucas), and Vicky Pollard, he is probably the most recognisable of all the *Little Britain* characters. Discourse around Matt Lucas's portrayal of Daffyd is interesting not only because of the focus on Matt Lucas as a gay man but also because of the focus on the body of Matt Lucas, that it was very brave of him to embody Daffyd in this way because of his own physical shortcomings – too fat, too bald and, one might add, too gay. I will return to this briefly when discussing the differences in the figures of Matt Lucas and David Walliams themselves. The other gay character in *Little Britain*, Sebastian, the Prime Minister's aide, is also positioned as ridiculous. He is the bitchy, jealous queen, so obsessed with the Prime Minister that he concocts petty schemes in order to be closer to him. Both Sebastian and Daffyd are incredibly camp, which in *Little Britain* is equated with ridiculousness.

In his analysis of Channel 4's *Terry and Julian* (1992), Mark Simpson (1998) argues that the excessive campness of Julian Clary is necessary to make the show funny, because homosexuality is less intrinsically funny now that it is more public and, therefore, less frightening. Although I agree with Simpson that the mere connotation of homosexuality is no longer naughty or taboo enough to provoke (nervous) laughter, I am not sure I agree with his conclusion that the idea of overly-camp-for-laughs is entirely ironic. If irony works from a safe distance, this would mean that no one could *really* think gay men were like that – as camp as Clary's character. Not only does this deny the possibility of varied gay subjectivities but also assumes the same position as the Daffyd sketch, that is, that everything is all right now. Although the homotopia that *Little Britain* paints is seductive, we must be dragged, however unwillingly, back into the world we actually live in – the one in which people in many countries are not only still denied access to legal partnerships and parenthood (and other such rights) but also beaten and killed just for being gay. The lack of a gap in content between pre-alternative, alternative and post-alternative comedy with regard to homosexuality (and, as we will see more briefly with regard to Emily Howard, transvestism) means that ironic representations are simply not applicable yet. Both Daffyd and Sebastian clearly rely on and feed into the existing stereotypes and figure of 'the gay man', rather than providing the sort of challenges that characterised alternative comedy.

Other Notable Figures

Space does not allow for an in-depth analysis of some of the other interesting figures in *Little Britain*, however, it is at least interesting to note three more: Mrs Emery ('The Old Woman'),

Bubbles DeVere ('The Fat Woman'), and Emily Howard ('The Transvestite').

Mrs Emery is presented as an OAP, which we are told stands for Old and Putrid. Mrs Emery can't control her bladder and ends up experiencing much humiliation urinating in supermarkets and other public places. A generous interpretation of this sketch might position it as crossing a social taboo – our fear of aging and having our bodies fail us. A less generous reading might see this as a cheap shot: an abuse of an easy target that is unable to fight back against its dominant creators (see Margaret Mongomerie's chapter for more on Mrs Emery).

Bubbles DeVere is played by Matt Lucas in a fat suit (and in the case of Bubbles' sister, Desiree, we have Walliams blacked up and in a fat suit). The comedy value of Bubbles DeVere is contained within her unruly body and its implicit out-of-control sexuality. When she cannot pay for her stay at the spa, she offers her body to the manager instead of payment. The joke, of course, is that the manager finds this offer abhorrent and not tempting in the slightest. As the audience, in order to laugh along, we have to agree that no one would ever want to touch a fat woman, a woman with cellulite or drooping breasts. Bubbles should be ashamed of her body – the fact that she is not and wants to take sexual pleasure in it makes her more alien, more grotesque and more repellent and, therefore, more funny. There is no reclamation of the type Rowe (1990) suggested we might find in *Roseanne*; no Jo Brand-esque acerbic put-down to male disgusted responses at the body, not even the type of brave face and pride exhibited by Dawn French. Rather, Bubbles and Desiree seem to have no understanding of the codes governing female appearance and (male) responses to it. Their overt sexuality is borne out of stupidity, not out of a desire to reclaim their bodies from these codes and gazes; therefore, it is no surprise that the constructed audience response is disgust, not empowerment.

The premise of the Emily Howard and Florence Rose sketch is the unconvincing nature of transvestites. The two characters' voices and their facial hair break through their poor disguises and spoil their attempts to 'be a lady'. Putting aside for a moment that their constructions of what 'being a lady' entails seem to be nothing more than talking in a high-pitched voice and ordering cake and wearing long skirts, this sketch is yet another example of an easy 'other' target. It is important to note here that trans issues were not at the forefront of alternative comedy's stereotype challenging. With the notable exception of Eddie Izzard, little has been done to challenge the 'bloke in a dress' stereotype or to admit trans identities as genuine, rather than just sites for mockery. Given this, the irony defence simply does not work. The premise would be flawed, If the defence is roughly described as the following: 'these social issues have been resolved, so it is now acceptable to go back to the old ways of talking about them, as long as we do it knowingly'. Transgender rights are trailing a long way behind work on gender and sexuality, in both law and popular consciousness. As such, the ridiculous images of this sketch might well be a mental port of call for ideas of trans for people who do not have any personal experience of these issues. This is especially pertinent given the popularity of *Little Britain* with children. The figure of the transvestite as presented by *Little Britain* is an easier one to call up than one of a person who easily 'passes' or simply has facets to his/her personality that are more interesting and diverse than the trans identity.

Matt Lucas and David Walliams as Figures

As *Little Britain* relies so heavily on the corporeality of its characters to tell us who they are and how we should feel about them, it is interesting to note the ways in which *Little Britain*'s creators themselves have been figured through their bodies.

A great deal of tabloid speculation and internet debate exists surrounding David Walliams' sexuality (Knight 2005; Maume 2005; *Mr Paparazzi* 2009). Not only does he 'play gay' but also seems pleased that his sexuality is seen as ambiguous, and he is often more open about Lucas's sexuality than Lucas himself. However, this seems more like a desire to keep speculation open and coverage ongoing – from a man who is so straight that he can do this with no threat to himself – than to infuse any genuine ambiguity. Walliams has a sort of hyper-masculinity about him, whether he is dressing up as James Bond (for the front cover of the *Radio Times*), swimming the Channel for Comic Relief, or being romantically linked with a string of blonde uber-babes, including

Abi Titmuss, Denise van Outen and Patsy Kensit. Given this heavily masculinised, almost superhero status, it seems totally safe for him to diverge from that identity in playing his characters in *Little Britain*. There is no risk when Walliams dresses up as a woman or plays the bitchy queen, because we 'know' he is nothing like that 'in real life'. One of the viewing pleasures taken in Walliams' characters is perhaps even in seeing a man who is absolutely coded as heterosexual in every other way playing gay.

Matt Lucas, on the other hand, is a very different, almost tragic figure. Newspaper profiles document his loss of hair through alopecia at the age of six, his struggles with his weight, and his difficulties in accepting his sexuality (see Phillips 2006). From his first well-known role, which was as the giant drumming baby (dressed in a pink romper suit), George Dawes, in *Shooting Stars* (BBC 1995–2002), to dressing up for his wedding in fancy dress, to dressing as Orville the duck, Lucas's body seems always presented to us as a site of comedy, as something to be laughed at. He does not have the position of power that Walliams' uber-heterosexuality and confidence afford him (although the association surely goes some way towards this) and thus it is easy to wonder whether Lucas's approach of laughing at himself and making people laugh *with* him is to avoid the probability that people will laugh *at* him.

Conclusion

There are moments when *Little Britain* challenges power and stereotypes. The characters Judy (Lucas) and Maggie (Walliams) are respectable members of the Women's Institute who enjoy activities as long as they perceive that everyone involved is just like them but vomit at the faintest hint of sexual or racial difference in their community ('Please! No more lesbian jam!', 2: 1). Slimming group leader Marjorie Dawes (Lucas) is shown up as ridiculous when she acts in a bigoted way towards an Asian member of her group, or when she insults her members for being fat and unattractive. However, although *Little Britain* might satirise racism, sexism, homophobia, ageism and classism from time to time, ultimately, it does far more to promote them. It's no wonder that it is so loved by the *Daily Mail* and that right-wing commentator Richard Littlejohn uses every opportunity to quote it.

Of course, there are serious problems with positioning the origins of alternative comedy as a golden age. Populated heavily by its white, middle-class comedians, who themselves were certainly not above critique, it lacked diversity and many issues were simply not addressed or challenged. However, there is no denying that there was a sense then that people were trying to shake things up, attempting to challenge prejudices and disrupt the status quo. Tony Allen once said, 'The entertainer gives the public what they want – the artist gives the public what they don't know they want' (quoted on the homepage of Allen's website, newagenda.demon.co.uk). It seems to me that *Little Britain* fulfils the former, rather than the latter, and has become the comedy equivalent of junk food. The comedy that challenges stereotypes has been pushed right back into the margins. As with the origins of alternative comedy, the male comedians need to speak out and start re-challenging those attitudes and presentations. Some have noticed the shift and the return to the old ways and have started to challenge it, in the way that Tony Allen once did. It may be too early to say that these challenges are the genesis of a turning tide, but there is some hope in this provocative quote from Richard Herring's 2007 show, 'Menage a Un', in which he pretends to support the BNP:

> Don't go thinking I'm the new Bernard Manning. I'm being post-modern and ironic. I understand that what I'm saying is unacceptable. But does that make me better than Bernard Manning, or much, much worse? (Armstrong 2007)

I get the joke, *Little Britain*, really I do. I just don't think it's anything to laugh at.

PART 3

Little Britain and Inter/national Audiences

'I'm Anti-*Little Britain*, and I'm Worried I Might Start Laughing': Audience Responses to *Little Britain*

Brett Mills

> Everybody mentions *Little Britain* in class, so I think it may be very important.
>
> —Discussion group participant response

Studies of audiences for comedy broadcasting are few and far between, with some notable exceptions (Fuller 1992; Jhally and Lewis 1992). This is odd, considering comedy encourages a more explicit response from its audience than many other kinds of television programming, often by including such responses in a laugh track. Furthermore, fan websites and the sales of DVDs suggest that comedy audiences build strong relationships with their desired programmes, with a range of fan communities built up around many series. For *Little Britain,* this can be seen in fan websites such as littlebritainonline.com and littlebritain.net. The fact that audiences for comedy programming have been so rarely explored is even odder considering that, for many, television comedy is a site of ideological struggle in which clichéd stereotypes are normalised and laughter at certain kinds of groups is encouraged (Grote 1983; Billig 2005a). Yet such positions have, on the whole, made many assumptions about what audiences do with comedy and how they make sense of it, perhaps ignoring the complex and mutable ways in which viewers gain pleasure from and respond to entertainment programming which is often academically and institutionally defined in terms of its 'unworthiness' (Attallah 2003: 93).

Little Britain is a useful case study for examining these concerns. The programme has moved through a variety of cultural forms (radio, television, theatre) and, in its television version, attracted a range of audiences as it moved from the more youthful, niche BBC3 to the more mainstream, populist BBC1, which is 'the BBC's most popular mixed-genre television service across the UK' with a 'focus on family viewing' (BBC 2008). As it has become more 'mainstream', the programme has also encountered resistance over its characters, jokes and representations. As other chapters in this book show, debates over the ways in which certain groups – especially those concerned with race, age, and disability – are represented inevitably arise when humour is connected to those topics. The concern over such programming makes assumptions about what audiences *do* with such representations and yet rarely engages with those audiences which are seen to be at risk.

In order to counteract this, then, this chapter recounts and explores the findings of an initial, small-scale focus group study into audience responses to *Little Britain*. The research is indeed small-scale: one focus group of six participants were shown one episode of the programme (series three, episode one) and then an hour's worth of discussion followed. The group is in no way representative of wider demographics; the six participants, all undergraduates in the School of Film and Television Studies at the University of East Anglia, volunteered to take part when all students in that school were asked if they would like to participate. Five of the participants were British who had seen the programme before; the sixth was from overseas for whom this was her first experience of *Little Britain*. Of course, there are problems in using Film and Television Studies students for such a discussion, especially as it took place in a room at the university, for their assumptions about what was required of them would inevitably be filtered through their academic experiences. In all, then, it's clear that this is intended only as an *initial* study whose findings are valuable not in representational terms but as a starting point for discussions about the ways in which audiences make sense of and think about comedy.

As will be shown, for all the participants *Little Britain* is a problematic series for a variety of reasons. This was discussed in terms of the programme's social role, its pleasure and displeasures, and its relationship to Britishness. Much of this discussion was tentative, perhaps highlighting recurring concerns of examining comedy too closely (Palmer 1994: 1). Yet it also demonstrated the recurring mismatch between the representational issues many participants had with the programme, and the obvious pleasures it gave others and themselves; as one of the participants said before viewing the chosen episode, 'I'm anti-*Little Britain*, and I'm worried I might start laughing'. As a statement *before* viewing, this is a valuable indication of the reflexive and active approach taken by many viewers towards the activity of watching comedy.

Social Role

> I don't particularly like it, but I still laugh. And I shockingly find myself quoting it, now and then.
>
> —Discussion group participant response

What was clear from the outset was that although participants may have had different views about *Little Britain*, they were very aware of its existence and the social impact it had had. Indeed, many participants stated that they had agreed to take part in the study precisely because of the mismatch between the phenomenal success of *Little Britain* and their (mainly negative) reading of the series, almost as if they wanted to meet someone who liked it and could explain its pleasures. The epigraph at the beginning of this chapter was from the overseas student, whose first viewing of the programme took place in the discussion group during the study. Her willingness to see it was motivated by a desire to engage in 'British culture', as this was a programme a number of British students had mentioned to her and she, therefore, felt she needed to engage with it in order to understand the country she was currently living in.

This widespread awareness of the programme is testament to television comedy's social nature, and a number of participants noted that their consumption of the programme was often a consequence of the desire of others to see it. As one participant noted, 'My mom really likes it, so I've only really watched it if she's got it on'. For others, the social nature of student house-sharing meant that *Little Britain* was a programme often viewed as a group activity, rather than as anyone's individual choice. As it has been argued that television comedy is a 'collective experience'

(Medhurst and Tuck 1982: 44), it's perhaps unsurprising that *Little Britain* should be viewed in this way. What it does demonstrate, however, is that the social and domestic nature of television entertainment can often result in viewers, if they wish to become part of a social group, consuming programmes they would actively avoid if alone.

These discourses are demonstrated by the merchandise which supports the programme, and the motivations behind their consumption. For example, one participant noted that he owned the *Little Britain* script-book but hadn't bought it himself and had instead received it as a Christmas present. As he was someone who didn't much like the programme, he had not asked for this present: 'So I think it was that *Little Britain* was popular at the time, I like comedy, so give him something from *Little Britain*'. This participant noted that it was an elderly relative who had bought this present, suggesting that an assumption had been made by that relative that everyone who belonged to this younger social group would be happy to receive something associated with *Little Britain*. The desire to use comedy for social and communal purposes was also demonstrated by another participant, who noted, 'My boyfriend has the script books...and he said it would be really good for when friends were around, they could all quote it together. But I don't think he's ever done it, which seems a bit pointless'. The intention of using the act of reciting comedy as a group activity not only shows how comedy has a communal purpose but also places *television* comedy – and *this* television comedy in particular – as a text assumed to be recognised by everyone.

Indeed, this awareness of the programme ran throughout the discussion, with all the British participants who never or rarely watched it admitting that they knew all the characters, catchphrases, and many of the specific jokes. Furthermore, *Little Britain*'s relationship to the ways in which they made sense of their everyday lives was apparent, as was their use of their real lives to make sense of the programme:

> I don't like the weeing one [Mrs Emery played by David Walliams], because I work in a pharmacy and there's an old woman who does come in and wees on the seats. Not very

often, but she's done it about three or four times since I've worked there for the last three years. And she doesn't seem to have any idea that she's doing it. She sits down and she talks to you, and she's quite nice but she's not all there, and she'll just go to the toilet, and then she'll get up and walk out again, and it's as if she doesn't know, like the woman on *Little Britain* acts as if she doesn't know. So I think because I've seen people do it, not as excessively, but still do it, I find it really uncomfortable to watch them making a joke out of it, ·when I have encountered people who are sort of similar to that.

In offering this reading of the programme, this participant acknowledged the personal and specific nature of her response. In arguing that she found such jokes uncomfortable because of her similar experiences, she was in no way suggesting that such comedy shouldn't exist on television. Instead this remained a resolutely personal reading, which was being communicated to others but not intended as evidence that such comedy was necessarily problematic. What this example and the others that preceded it show is that there is a complex relationship between the personal and the social within comedy. For many, readings were inflected through personal ideologies or experiences, which demonstrated the range of ways in which any television text can be read. However, there was also an awareness that such personal readings had to be subsumed within the programme's social position, which places it as a communal text for certain social groups. In that sense, these viewers were aware that *Little Britain* was a programme they *had* to have some knowledge of in order to engage with their peers; the active reading produced by their own experiences were, therefore, often minimised in order to maintain certain kinds of relationships.

This clearly feeds into debates about the social consequences of humour (Jenkins 1994; Billig 2005a), and whether it serves to normalise particular ideologies and certain ways of living. That is, if viewers feel their problematic responses to the programme must be kept private in order to maintain social cohesion, comedy can be seen to stifle debates about representation and acceptability. However, this concern must also be coupled with an acknowledgement that television comedy is one of the few places where such debates are active and recurrent. The battles over representation on television have often focussed on comedy, and it was such debates which led to the 'Alternative Comedy' movement in Britain in the 1980s (Wilmut and Rosengard 1989; Littlewood and Pickering 1998). Concerns over offence can be seen to have diminished the use of certain stereotypes often associated with British television comedy in the 1960s and the 1970s, especially those concerned with race, in series such as *Curry and Chips* (ITV 1969), *Love Thy Neighbour* (ITV 1972–76), and *Mind Your Language* (ITV 1977–99). Yet, in doing so, replacement comic representations are yet to be developed, resulting in a notable lack of non-white representations in television comedy as a whole (Small 1998; see also Sarita Malik's chapter).

Such concerns over representation are, therefore, now quite commonplace in discussions of television comedy and have moved away from certain pressure groups, becoming instead popular discourses about broadcasting. This was shown in this discussion group, which repeatedly worried about the consequences of the representations *Little Britain* offered. For one participant, *Little Britain* was a useful rejoinder to such debates:

> I think nowadays, in Britain, everything's trying to be too politically correct all the time, and I think they're just trying to make a joke out of that. They're just saying society is the way it is...But you just laugh at it, or I laugh at it, anyway. I understand that there are certain points where you've got to say that was a bit too much. But when I watch it I just think, okay, I can walk away from that, and I'm not going to be racist toward anyone, or sexist to anyone, it doesn't affect me to the point where I have to make a stand against it.

The use of the term 'politically correct' is notable here, as it is one which is vilified and justified in equal measure in contemporary British culture (Littlewood and Pickering 1998). It's clear that, for this viewer, there's a pleasure in mocking political correctness, even if you support the ideological intentions behind it. There's an insistence here on distinguishing between the comic sphere of humour and the 'realities' of everyday life – a distinction which not only notes the relationship between the two but also insists that 'to laugh' is to adopt a particular interpretive position which is more complex than simply to mock others. Also running throughout this statement is an awareness of the limits of the position being adopted, for the participant acknowledges that some things are 'too much'. Indeed, running throughout the discussion was a desire by the participants to make clear their concerns over some of *Little Britain's* content, while at the same time acknowledging the problem in insisting that certain kinds of jokes can't be made.

It may be for this reason that, very often, such concerns were placed onto others and that the participants, although clear about the programme not affecting them, couldn't be sure that it didn't have consequences for other audiences[1]. For example:

> I just think that because it's so popular with younger teenagers, and because you can buy so much merchandise, there's going to be people who aren't going to read it in that way, and it's going to be taken literally. I can imagine it coming out wrong in schools when people use catchphrases or take the mick out of fat people...And so I can see it having an effect on people who aren't reading it more sophisticatedly, or how the writers intend it. Because isn't it on at 9pm, and a lot of kids are still up at that sort of time, so the watershed doesn't stop them watching it. So I probably think it does have an effect on younger people, as they do see it as, 'It's funny; let's go round and do that ourselves'. Rather than seeing the social awkwardness of the situation, and rather than seeing the woman stepping away, they're going to see an old person weeing [Mrs Emery] and so make fun of old people in the street.

It's worthwhile noting that none of the participants stated they had seen such behaviour occur; instead, this was a pre-emptive concern which not only assumed the particular reading strategies of other audiences but also supposed that such strategies lead to certain kinds of behaviour. This might helpfully demonstrate how central concerns over comic representation now are, and how the debate about comic acceptability is an integral part of making sense of humour in contemporary Britain. For these viewers, interpreting whether such comedy was problematic was of primary concern (though it has to be acknowledged that these were all media students) and an activity which was integral to their decision of whether it was funny or not. This might give credence to the Relief Theory of humour, which suggests comedy is intricately linked to social repression and functions as a release of suppressed feelings and desires (Freud 1991 [1905]; Morreall 1983: 20–37; 1987: 90–126; Critchley 2002). Arguments about 'political correctness' often suggest that its repressive function may damage society by criminalising forms of communication which have been central to social interaction for centuries. What this discussion showed was how sensitive these viewers were to the social consequences comedy might have, and that any pleasures which might be taken from *Little Britain* were inflected through such critiques; for the Relief Theory, this is bound to have serious social consequences.

Before moving on to discuss these conflicts further, it should be noted that one participant did recount a story in which the content of *Little Britain* was used by someone in order to belittle. Though, considering the participants' fears over the ways in which children might be affected by the programme, it's surely significant that the person who used *Little Britain* as a tool to maintain dominance was a teacher, while the person who was mocked was a child:

> I think it gives adults an opportunity for adults to take the mick back. I remember when we were at school and someone came in late and they were giving all these excuses, and the teacher went, 'Yeah but no but yeah but'. And all of us burst out laughing because the teacher was getting one back. And the person who came in late just shut up and sat down.

If we should be concerned over comedy's social consequences, then, this suggests that those concerns should be directed more at those already in power, rather than at those whose jokes might have little social impact.

Pleasures/Displeasures

> It makes me think that Britain likes taking the piss out of other people and stereotypes and people who are different.
>
> —Discussion group participant response

Central to debates about comedy are issues of pleasure; although comedy is often usefully seen as having a social function which smoothes communication between parties (Radcliffe-Brown 1952; Davies 1990), its ability to give pleasure has also been a concern of comedy theorists (Aristotle 1925 [c350BC]; Billig 2005b). Comedy's categorisation under the rubric of 'entertainment' is paramount; although comedy may also valuably be seen as reflecting society and as having 'worthwhile' social messages, its ability to give audiences pleasure is paramount if it is to survive. Yet analysing such pleasure is complex, for the necessary critical vocabulary is yet to be developed. Saying 'it was funny' or 'it made me laugh' might be an accurate representation of the effects comedy can have (while usefully signalling the desire *not* to question or theorise those effects), but it doesn't get us very far if we are interested in thinking through why viewers enjoy certain kinds of comedy.

Running throughout the *Little Britain* discussion group was a debate over pleasure – or, to be more accurate, over displeasure. The majority of the participants found *Little Britain* to be a programme difficult to enjoy, for a variety of reasons. Some of these reasons were ideological, but others were to do with aesthetics and performance. Yet it was also clear that these viewers were aware that they were meant to enjoy the programme – that is, the sketch show clearly signalled itself as a piece of entertainment, rather than having an overriding educative or informative function. This demonstrates the ways in which audiences are capable of placing programmes generically, even if they find it hard to succumb to the pleasures associated with such genres. Being aware that something is 'funny' and finding it 'funny' are two different things, and that distinction belies the oft-repeated assumption that 'laughter is instinctive behaviour programmed by our genes, not by the vocal community in which we grow up' (Provine 2001: 1).

For many participants, *Little Britain*'s problem was its failure to conform to 'realism', as shown by this reaction to a Vicky Pollard (Matt Lucas) sketch;

> Well, because that one, when she's in the pool [1: 2], that could conceivably happen. And there was that recognisable character type. But now it's like she's just doing silly stuff for the sake of being funny. It's like she realises she's being ridiculous now, whereas before it was like she was a real character, and that was just what she happened to do. Whereas in this sketch she's getting her friends to pull her around as she's doing a break-dance, and it's completely non-naturalistic.

There are a number of aesthetic judgements within this response. For this viewer, the need to feel that a comic moment could 'conceivably happen' suggests an insistence on a link between comic representations and the real world, whether any particular text calls for this reading or not. There was some discussion about whether *Little Britain* asks to be understood in this realist sense, with some participants arguing that its name suggests it wants to be read as reflecting the nation, and others putting the generic argument that comedy is, by its very nature, non-realist.

Indeed, comedy has often been understood through its non-naturalist approaches, and it's clear that it has recourse to a range of representative strategies (such as comic coincidence, performers playing multiple roles, the laugh track, excessive performance) which are anathema to the traditions of British social realism (Lacey 1995, 2005). In a country with a comic tradition that includes programmes such as *The Goon Show* (BBC Home Service 1951–60), *Monty Python's Flying Circus* (BBC 1969–74), *The Young Ones* (BBC 1982–84), *Vic Reeves Big Night Out* (Channel 4 1990–91) and *The Mighty Boosh* (BBC 2004–present), it could be argued that a recurring absurdist strain is central to humorous representations. Yet it has been noted that, in the last decade or so, comedy aesthetics have started to change and, in some cases, have begun to adopt the representational tropes associated with other genres, such as drama and documentary (Mills 2004). Considering that comedy programmes such as *The Office* (BBC 2001–03), *Man Stroke Woman* (BBC 2005–present), *The Thick of It* (BBC 2005–present) and *Gavin and Stacey* (BBC 2007–present) have all abandoned the visual characteristics of 'traditional' comedy and instead offered themselves to be read within a 'realist' context, perhaps audience expectations for comedy as a whole are changing. The fact that viewers of *Little Britain* insist on reading it in terms of its 'realism', when the programme resolutely uses the traditional generic characteristics of comedy which have usually deliberately avoided such a reading, might say something about audience expectations for comedy as a whole. Furthermore, as debates about comic representation and its social consequences are now so mainstream, perhaps responding to the relationship between comedy programmes and the 'real world' is a much more prominent characteristic of reading strategies for sitcoms and sketch shows. This was certainly the case here, as the majority of participants repeatedly refused to accept the notion that *Little Britain* might be 'just' a comedy.

Another criticism made plain by the above quote is the ways in which comic representation changes as more and more series are made. It was agreed by the participants that Vicky Pollard was a funnier character in her earlier appearances because the joke was about the 'truth' of the character. The need to put her in increasingly ridiculous situations in order to continue finding humour in the character was seen not only as abandoning any social truth she may have once had, but also as indicative of the commercial need to keep reusing a character even after her comic mileage has been exhausted. Similar exhaustion was noted for Lou (David Walliams) and Andy (Matt Lucas), whose comic laziness was seen to be epitomised by the fact that 'those particular sketches don't even establish the fact that he [Andy] can't walk; it just plonks him in a situation, and it's only people who've watched it before that know something is going to happen in the background'.

Such aesthetic considerations recurred throughout the discussion. For example, one participant noted that their reading of the Ting Tong (Matt Lucas) sketches was marred because Matt Lucas's 'accent kept slipping'. For the participant, this not only indicated a failure of performative expertise but also raised complications in terms of deciding whether this representation was problematic or not. So, 'because his accent was consistent, you're not sure whether it's *supposed* to be Matt Lucas doing a bad accent'. For this viewer, the question of whether we're meant to be aware of the fact that we're watching Lucas perform a character, or whether we're meant to 'believe' the performance and, therefore, only 'see' the character caused confusion in terms of the comic meaning of the sketch. But it also raised a question of who we're being invited to laugh at, Lucas or Ting Tong. If it's the former, then the humour is 'comedian comedy' (Seidman 1981) resting on Lucas's 'star' quality and his ability to 'foreground' (Glick 2007: 292) comic intent, made more extreme by the absurdities of his make-up and the fact that he's a man playing a woman. However, if the joke is not one centred on Lucas's performance and is instead one inviting viewers to find the character of Ting Tong funny, then the representation becomes problematic at least partly because of its slapdash nature. That is, the fact that this sequence is quite 'badly' performed suggests that less care is being taken over its social truth and believability than is the case for British characters, and this has clear implications for debates about the ways in which comedy represents the 'other'.

This can also be seen in other sketches in which black and/or female characters are portrayed. This is perhaps most clearly seen in the sketches about Bubbles DeVere (Matt Lucas) and Desiree (David Walliams), where Lucas portrays a white woman while Walliams plays a black woman; the representational concerns are further multiplied as both characters are large and the sketches' punchlines often invite laughter at their physical excesses. For some in the discussion group, the problem was less that jokes mocked physical characteristics and more that white men were playing the characters under discussion. As one participant put it,

> I don't know how they're allowed to get away with it, because they don't even have any other black characters, played by black actors...so they're not counteracting this borderline racist representation with a positive representation of a black character. Obviously it's meant to be grotesque, he's [Walliams] wearing this body suit, but they might have got a

big fat black woman to do it, and that might have been a bit
more acceptable. It just seems too close to the bone.

However, another participant disagreed:

I don't know what would make it better, though. I don't even
think having a black woman as that person [Desiree] would
make it better, because then it would be making fun at her for
being fat and black.

In this discussion, the crux of the matter is originally the debate
about whether there is a problem in people from one social group
performing another and adopting the visual characteristics of that
group (Pickering and Lockyer 2005b: 180–97; Howells 2006).
In making such claims, the participant is placing the discussion
within debates about 'minstrel' and 'coon' (Bogle 1992; King
2002: 147) representations of black people, which have a long
and decidedly troubled heritage. Such performances have
caused outrage in Britain for some time – as in Spike Milligan's
'blacking-up' to play 'Paki Paddy' Kevin O'Grady in *Curry and
Chips* – though it wasn't until *The Black and White Minstrel Show*
(BBC 1958–78) was axed that they ceased to regularly appear
as part of mainstream broadcast entertainment. This is not to say
such 'blacking-up' has completely ceased, as can be seen by
the characters of Otis Redding and Marvin Gaye in *The Smell
of Reeves and Mortimer* (BBC 1993–95) and of Papa Lazarou
in *The League of Gentlemen* (BBC 1999–2002). The fact that,
as the participant notes, the representation is 'grotesque' and
that the comic intent of the sketch means there's no intention
for this performance to be seen as 'real', both show how such
representations can be placed within the comic mode (Neale and
Krutnik 1990: 19). Yet the call for a 'positive representation' clearly
insists that such performances are troubling, and their heritage
does not excuse them. But it's noticeable that this participant calls
this representation 'borderline racist', and this unwillingness to
definitively accuse the programme of inappropriate representation
was borne out of an awareness of the complexity of such
debates and the impossibility of 'proving' such an accusation.
Many participants in the discussion agreed with this reading of

Desiree; notably, however, they were wary of saying that such representations were worrying, troublesome or wrong. Instead, most said such a performance made them 'uncomfortable', which places such disquiet at the personal level, perhaps removing the social and ideological intent of many representational politics debates.

The second quote above shows the complexity in trying to solve the problem outlined by the first participant. In suggesting that a black performer might be less problematic because it offers visibility to under-represented groups on television, the first participant places the problem at the disjunction between the 'real' person and the performance. For the speaker of the second quote, however, a black actor performing Desiree would be more problematic, because it in some sense legitimises that representation. Indeed, the lack of realism which many discussants thought was a consequence of white men playing black women could, by this argument, be seen as making explicit the absurdities of the representation; to have a black woman playing this character might instead invite audiences to read the representation in terms of the real, inviting a less distanced interpretive strategy. The discussion group was unable to come to a conclusion about this problem, showing how 'a performance is a layered social experience, an interaction between audience and text, where meanings are contingent upon the interpretive schema placed upon the star performance by a particular audience' (Drake 2003: 188).

Perhaps what's more significant is that they signalled it as a problem at all. That is, the centrality of such debates to everyday conversations about culture seems to have resulted in creating awareness among viewers that they're meant to have such debates and should be sensitive to portrayals of a whole range of minority groups: at the same time, however, a lack of suggestions for alternative or progressive representations means that this becomes an issue which must be signalled but can't adequately be resolved. It may be unsurprising, then, that participants kept saying that such representations made them 'uncomfortable', for to have an awareness that something is wrong but to not have the conviction about what precisely is wrong or a certainty about how to fix it is likely to lead to discomfort. And, within this context, it's unsurprising that so many found the programme difficult to laugh at, for such discomfort is inevitably a bar to comic pleasure.

In order to try and explore these problems, the group discussed other representational issues. As noted above, another aspect of Bubbles DeVere which made some viewers uncomfortable was her size, and this is also a key comic component of the Marjorie Dawes (Matt Lucas) character, especially as she's commonly placed within her Fat Fighters club in the programme. Indeed, although his physical appearance in the programme offers up fat people for ridicule, it may unwittingly normalise such body shapes through their consistent display (Hole 2003). Marjorie Dawes spends much of her time ridiculing the members of her club for their size, which was read by some as jokes aimed at body size. Yet this was seen to be complicated by the fact that Dawes is herself fat (and so the joke rests on her inability to comprehend how she's seen by others) and that Matt Lucas, performing the character, is also fat (thus legitimising the joke as it is told by someone who would conventionally be the target of such humour). The question becomes, then, one of whether we're being invited by the programme to laugh *at* or *with* the character (and, by extension, which of these approaches is invited towards the relevant performer).

This problem of 'with/at' was outlined in the following comment:

> I don't like the bit in Fat Fighters, where she [Marjorie Dawes] doesn't understand the Indian woman. Because it's not as if she's speaking a different language, it's just making fun of the fact that she's foreign and has an accent. It's not as if she can't understand her, it's just that she's Indian, and that's not particularly funny. That's a bit...that's almost like...bordering on racist.

However, one discussant offered the following alternative reading:

> I thought the laugh track was indicating that we're supposed to be laughing *at* her [Marjorie Dawes] ignorance. That's how

I read it. I know it's not obviously clear, and that might be a problem because a lot of people who watch it might be laughing for the other reason. But I think we're supposed to be laughing *at* her, as opposed to *with* her.

This demonstrates the value placed on non-diegetic material, such as a laugh track. Because of their 'affiliative' (Wells and Bull 2007) purpose laugh tracks can be seen to suggest a particular reading intended by the programme and its makers, even if a participant acknowledged that viewers might read it in a different way. But the notion that we're 'supposed' to read it in a particular way has clear implications for debates about authorial and textual intention, and for the ways in which viewers might judge the appropriacy of any comic moment by trying to work out what its *intention* was. This may be unsurprising, considering that broadcasting regulations often adjudicate based on programme and programme-makers' intentions. Furthermore, this demonstrates the ways in which a kind of 'auteur' theory is at play here, with intention (and responsibility) placed at the feet of the programme-makers (in this instance, assumed to be the writers/performers Walliams and Lucas). The confusion over whether a representation is or isn't problematic may be a result of the difficulty in accurately demonstrating authorial intention in broadcasting as a whole and in comedy in particular. It also suggests that Structuralist and Post-Structuralist approaches, which have repeatedly attempted to question the appropriacy of examining any kind of text via its author, have had little impact on everyday interpretations of programmes.

Overall, then, the participants consistently raised concerns over the representations within *Little Britain* but found it very difficult to definitively adopt a position on this. There was clear surprise at some of the things the programme was allowed to 'get away with'; but the impression was that as the broadcasting institutions had seen such representations as being fit to broadcast, and as the programme has been gleefully consumed by mass audiences, such social acceptability outweighed any grievances a few individuals might have. Furthermore, such readings demonstrate the slippery nature of comedy and illustrate the ways in which it seems to invite a multiplicity of contradictory readings, sometimes giving pleasure at the same time as offending (Medhurst 2007: 20–25). Indeed, one of the reasons why these participants found the programme interesting (as opposed to enjoyable) was precisely its polysemic nature, and the difference between enjoying the programme and being made to feel uncomfortable by it seemed to rest on the ability to take pleasure in being outraged and amused simultaneously.

Britishness

> It's called *Little Britain*, so it's obviously making a connection to Britishness.
>
> —Discussion group participant response

A key concern running throughout the discussion was what *Little Britain* said about the nation which had produced it and enjoys it. Although all cultural forms can be examined for their insights into national identity, it's clear that comedy, because of its communal nature, is more often explored in these ways than other texts. Indeed, the notion of a national sense of humour is seen to be important in Britain, perhaps to a degree rare in other countries (Husband 1988; Richards 1997; Easthope 2000). This is exacerbated in this instance by the programme's title which, although not explicitly stating its intention as an examination of national mores, clearly encourages a reading related to geographical specificity, as the above comment shows. For the discussants, this concept could be thought about in two ways: first, what the programme says about the UK; and second, the consequences that it may have for other countries' understandings of Britain and Britishness.

Like many of the comments above, there was a contradiction within the discussants' views of this. All agreed that there was something 'British' about the programme, but also that this could be understood as a comment that was both negative and positive. For example,

> I can't imagine some other countries allowing it [*Little Britain*] to be on TV. Because I think it's quite liberal here, to some extent, with your opinions and broadcasting. And perhaps

> they're trying to make a point about Britain not being rude or racist, and it comes across as 'it doesn't matter who you are, we'll find a way to take the piss out of you, somehow'. Which isn't necessarily a good thing.

The statement that such programming might not be allowed in other countries is seen here both as a positive statement of free speech and as a negative one demonstrating that problematic representations are seen as acceptable; as Chiaro's chapter in this book shows, it's noteworthy that Italian viewers respond to the programme in precisely the same way. Similarly, the statement's latter half finds a positive aspect in *Little Britain*'s ability to make jokes about every social group, suggesting social cohesion and equality, adding that this fails to take into account communities' specificities or areas where humour might be problematic. Running throughout this statement is the notion that comedy can be a 'good' or 'bad' thing, and that if broadcasters get it 'right' then it will have beneficial social consequences; at the same time, there's an acknowledgement of the difficulties in definitively demonstrating how to judge such programming.

Yet one interviewee was reluctant to insist that comedy should have such a social significance:

> It's not pushing Britain to make a difference, or change how we are. It's just saying this is what we're like at the moment, and this is what they've seen when they've been doing their research.

This statement makes a distinction between representation as a strategy for depiction and as one for change. Indeed, although the latter was an area all participants found difficult to fully explicate, it was clear that they agreed that there was something about 'us' (and, by extension, about 'them') which was being shown in the programme and it, therefore, could be read in some way as 'British'.

Central to this was an understanding of the role of the reaction shot in the programme. For many, the humour in a number of the sketches was less in what the main characters were doing and more in the reactions of others. For example, interviewees' understanding of the Mrs Emery sketches was based not around her excessive and inappropriate urinating, but in the 'truthfulness' of the reactions of people around her. In these sketches, whoever Mrs Emery is talking to continues the conversation as if nothing is happening, embarrassedly ignoring the social indiscretion for fear of making a fuss. As one participant said:

> Everyone's had something like that where you've been with someone and you're not sure whether you should say something. And that is just Britain, really, isn't it, that's just a British sensibility.

It's certainly the case that embarrassment – or, more accurately, the *fear* of embarrassment – has been seen as a central part of British national identity for some time, and as working in tandem with national stereotypes such as the 'stiff upper lip' (Gray 2005; Ware 2007). The pleasure on offer here, then, is one which 'rings true', for it depicts an absurd social norm which the focus group could see themselves acting out in that situation. It's noticeable, though, that this is seen as a 'British sensibility', rather than as one based on other geographical factors or on other criteria such as age, class or background. Indeed, this response to the programme seems to demonstrate the national identities offered by broadcasting that have come to be accepted. That is, none of the participants suggested they saw this as a British sensibility because they knew it wasn't how people in other countries reacted; instead their notion of 'Britishness' appeared relatively unproblematic and consensual. Indeed, it is possible to gauge the success of *Little Britain* in depicting a sense of the nation only if viewers have an existing idea of what that nation is and how it works; the recognition which these participants acknowledge – as well as their pleasure in that recognition – suggests not only the surety with which national identities are maintained, but also the enjoyment to be garnered from acknowledging and mocking national specificities. This pleasure may come from an awareness of belonging to the correct 'shared culture' (Blake 2007: 22) for the programme, so that *Little Britain* is not only *about* us, but also *for* us.

This feeling that the programme required a specific 'humour competence' (Raskin 1985) and encouraged a reading which suggested the programme might say something about Britain led to concerns over what people from other nations might make from the programme. In the discussion group, there was one foreign participant and she had never seen *Little Britain* before. For her, the programme was not very funny, and this was down to cultural differences in humour. However, she also noted that she had difficulty with many British comedies, and so it wasn't something specific to *Little Britain*. Yet the concerns over the comic content were also apparent for this participant, who wondered what the programme might say about Britain:

> I think in general they make too many jokes about fat women, or gay people. After one or two, you think it's not good, you're making too much fun of these people...So first you laugh, and then you stop, because it seems inappropriate.

Clearly it's the accumulation of recurring comic targets which is the problem here, and this suggests that the worries outlined above are of a concern not solely to British audiences. This led to a discussion about the consequences *Little Britain* being broadcast abroad might have, and the assumptions about Britain overseas viewers might make from the programme. This could be seen to be of particular concern considering the UK's international reputation for producing television comedy and its success in selling such series abroad.

For the participants, this raised worries:

> The title, *Little Britain*, is almost ushering you towards thinking this is how some people are in certain sort of areas. And I don't think that in another country you'd look at it and see them taking the piss out of people who can't understand foreign people, and you'd make the more obvious reading, and not the subversive reading, and not get out of it what British people are meant to get out of it by living in that country. I think it could come out quite wrong as an interpretation of Britain in other countries.

Similarly:

> My watching of it is influenced by their [Lucas and Walliams]
> personas outside of the show. And I don't think that can
> translate necessarily to an international audience, not without
> quite large exposure. Matt Lucas is a gay man and he's married
> and I've seen him on *Shooting Stars* [BBC 1995–2002] and so
> I'm familiar with his characters, so I can more easily accept
> that he plays the gay Daffyd. And David Walliams is famous
> for having swum the Channel, and he deliberately puts
> across this ambiguous sexuality, and my knowledge of that
> heavily influences how I feel about watching the programme.
> That's why I'm more uncomfortable than I am offended by
> it, because I understand that they have groundings in, for
> example, homosexuality, so they're essentially making jokes
> about themselves. Whereas I don't think that would necessarily
> translate to other countries who are unfamiliar with them.

Here it is argued that the 'right' reading of the programme is
available only to those who have certain kinds of 'cultural
schemata' (see Julia Snell's chapter in this collection), which
justifies some of the humour because its targets are groups to
which Lucas and Walliams belong. In making such statements,
these participants are placing the programme within a social
context in which humour is made acceptable because of the
associations of the creative team behind it. While there are
debates about whether this does help legitimise comedy or
merely serves to render problematic representation acceptable
(Littlewood and Pickering 1998), what's most important is that
it's seen as necessary to have access to such information in order
to make an informed reading of the programme, and it's assumed
that overseas viewers won't be able to draw on such knowledge.
A distinction is, therefore, made between the 'obvious' reading
and the 'subversive' one, suggesting a complex polysemy to
the programme which helps legitimise its content. What this
certainly shows is a concern over readings made by overseas
viewers, who might take the programme at face value (whatever
that means). This suggests that it's assumed that overseas ideas
of 'Britishness' are fairly malleable, with centuries of historical

understanding liable to be changed, to a certain extent, by the content of comedy programming. This has clear consequences for the growth of international programming and for the increased access worldwide viewers have to broadcasts from round the globe. As the BBC's most recent charter requires the corporation to 'bring the UK to the world and the world to the UK' (BBC 2006), it could be expected that programming which might depict negative or problematic ideas of Britishness could cause institutional problems.

While concerns about overseas readings of the programme were evident, it was also clear that, for many participants, the series raised questions about the idea they had of Britishness. For example:

> All I keep thinking about is Daffyd, but I guess when I was younger there were gay people who came out, and thought they were the only gay person in the world, and we lived in a little rural community, so they were, 'Look at me, I'm gay. I'm the only gay one here; I'm better than you'. That's kind of rural and British.

Here the significant qualifier 'rural' is added to the term British, showing an awareness that Britishness is an 'umbrella category' (Crick 2008: 72) with many possible versions of it on offer. In requiring the term 'rural' to be added in order for the comment to be made comprehensible, it's clear that its opposite – 'urban' – is usually assumed and, therefore, redundant. This notion of the 'rural' may be significant for understandings of Daffyd, for the series suggests that it's only in such 'unsophisticated' locations (and, in this case, 'Wales' is also used to imply 'unsophisticated') that the character would assume his homosexuality was startling. What's noticeable here is that although participants were unable to define what Britishness was, they were keen to make sense of the programme through their own experiences and histories. In that way, they returned to ideas of realism discussed above, in which the programme's representations become justified if they can be related to personal experiences.

Overall, it was clear that the idea of Britishness was central to the pleasures on offer from *Little Britain*, not least because the programme's title encouraged such a reading. Yet this remained a problematic idea, with participants unable to define precisely what Britishness was, other than by relying on their personal experiences. For broadcasting, which functions nationally, this is of concern, requiring programming to construct an idea of Britishness for citizenry for whom it is only through such institutions that national identity is made explicit. Of course, this may be made even more manifest by the comedic intent of the programme, considering humour is often seen as having a communal inflexion (Davis 1993). Yet perhaps the overriding factor in this discussion was, once again, the lack of surety within many statements in which the participants were unwilling to make certain, definitive comments about national identity, its relationship to broadcasting, or the effects of such programming on overseas ideas of 'us'. As one participant noted, 'I just feel unsure how much I want to say, "Yes, this is Britain".'

Conclusion

As was noted at the beginning, this chapter is a small-scale, initial research whose intention is to begin thinking through the ways in which audiences for comedy in general and *Little Britain* in particular might be explored. The inability for the participants to come to definitive conclusions might be seen as a drawback in such debates, but I think it can perhaps more usefully be seen as demonstrating the difficulties in definitively stating what comedy is 'about' or what it 'says'. Clearly there is something within many moments of *Little Britain* which the majority of these participants found troubling, even though, as they acknowledged, they often found it funny and were aware of the pleasures it gave to other viewers. This could be seen as indicative of the effects of higher education on them, in which they are encouraged to be open to alternative voices and debates. Yet I think it can also be read as a fear of the consequences of definitively stating that a programme is 'wrong' and should not be broadcast. Such statements clearly contradict the notions of tolerance and free speech which all participants espoused, and which are themselves often seen as central to ideas of Britishness (Crick 2008: 77). The assumption here seemed to be that, if the programme gives pleasure to *someone* then its value is evident, which may be as heartening a version of liberal values as can be imagined.

But what does this say about debates about comedy in general? First, it certainly suggests that audiences are active viewers of such programmes, able to both enjoy and be offended by comedy simultaneously. Second, it demonstrates the social role comedy as a whole and specific series in particular can come to play, bringing together disparate viewers and occupying a central position within certain social groups where it's assumed everyone has knowledge of things such as specific characters, catchphrases and jokes. But perhaps more importantly, it shows the complex ways in which comedy is required to be understood, with even quite 'simple' moments capable of being interpreted in a variety of ways. That has extremely far-reaching consequences for debates about the social consequences of humour.

Acknowledgements

Thanks to those who agreed to participate in this research. The tea and biscuits at the discussion group were funded by the School of Film and Television Studies, University of East Anglia.

Note

1. This may sound like a criticism, but it should be noted that this is no different from the position adopted by regulators and academics, who not only often valorise their own complex reading positions but also similarly agonise over how others might be affected by media (see Gauntlett 1998).

Chapter NINE

Little Britain: An American Perspective

Arthur Asa Berger

Little Britain moved from a 'cult' to a 'mainstream' hit in Britain, and its catchphrases are now part of everyday speech. *Little Britain* is a remarkable tour de force of comedic acting by its two writers, Matt Lucas and David Walliams. Thanks to some wonderful wig-makers and make-up artists, they play all the main roles in the show and do so brilliantly.

Little Britain and American Comic Strips

Why is it that when I watched *Little Britain* I kept thinking about how it was similar, in many ways, to certain classic American comics strips such as *Krazy Kat, Li'l Abner, Peanuts* and *Dilbert?* *Little Britain* is a sketch show made of short segments of varying lengths, each of which is complete in itself. In this respect, it is similar to comic strips such as *Krazy Kat, Li'l Abner, Peanuts, Doonesbury* and *Dilbert* (see Berger 1973). The show is full of grotesques – bizarre comedic types, often with monomaniacal fixations and obsessions of one sort or another – and in this respect too it reminds me of the American comic strips mentioned above and American underground comics. Think, for example, about Ignatz Mouse, the hero of *Krazy Kat*, who spent decades figuring out how to crease Krazy Kat's head with a brick; or of Charlie Brown, never able to kick a football held by Lucy; or of the marvellous zanies in *Li'l Abner* such as Fatback Roaringham, who pursued their crazy passions with boundless energy.

Contemporary humorous comic strips can be defined as having continuing characters, a narrative thrust that generally ends each day with a gag or some kind of humorous twist, and with dialogue in balloons. As I see *Little Britain*, it is very much like a comic strip, except that it is acted out on television. The same kinds of zanies that populate *Dilbert* can be seen on *Little Britain*; in fact, some of the characters found in *Dilbert* are even more bizarre than those found in *Little Britain*. The show is also close to American underground comics in terms of their extreme characterisations; one thinks of 'Mr. Natural', 'The Fabulous Furry Freak Brothers' and other characters from underground strips that are as bizarre as the characters in *Little Britain*. But the characters in the American underground comics are heterosexual unlike many of the characters in *Little Britain*.

The American Comedic Sensibility

I watched only the first series of the television show, so I can't comment on how it evolved, but watching the first year of *Little Britain* made me think about how different it is from American televised comedy shows. American television humour, in general, isn't as crude, low-brow and vulgar as *Little Britain* and other low-brow British television shows from the past such as *The Benny Hill Show* (BBC/ITV 1955–89). *Little Britain,* in its sketch structure, resembles *Monty Python's Flying Circus* (BBC 1969–74) and American shows from years ago such as *Rowan and Martin's Laugh In* (NBC 1968–73). American comedic television is essentially made up of situation comedies, and none of our situation comedies is as imaginative, bold or tasteless as *Little Britain*.

When my wife saw the show she was turned off by it and described it as infantile. In a sense, all the characters in the show are like infants/children, unable to break away from their childish behaviour. The title of the show, *Little Britain,* can be taken literally. The humour is also often very low-brow: the way the gardeners trim the hedges in the Dame Sally Markham skits, as penises and breasts, for example, strikes me as both crude and not particularly funny. Americans do not, as a rule, find men dressing up as women hilarious while it would seem British audiences really enjoy that kind of thing. And while we have gays in some of our comedies, we don't have gays like Daffyd (Matt Lucas), the 'committed homosexualist' who takes pride in being the only gay in his small Welsh village, even though he's mistaken about this assertion. Daffyd, like many of the characters in *Little Britain*, refuses to face reality – and this takes on a comic turn since in episode after episode he has to deal with other gays and lesbians living in the village (e.g., the barmaid, Myfanwy (Ruth Jones), turns out to be lesbian) or gays and lesbians who come to visit the village for one reason or another. Repetition, with variations, is a basic element in comedy and in the show.

Consider, by way of contrast, the two great American situation comedies of recent years: *Seinfeld* (NBC 1989–98) and *Frasier* (NBC 1993–2004). Both of those shows also had characters with numerous fixations and obsessions, but the humour in these shows was much more sophisticated than we find in *Little Britain*. Kramer (played by Michael Richards), 'the weirdo' in *Seinfeld,* probably comes closest to the kind of characters we find in *Little Britain,* which pushes its characterisations to extreme lengths and seems to revel in bad taste.

Most of the comedy found on contemporary American television comes either from films that are being broadcast or from situation comedies. Shows such as *Little Britain* are not popular now and earlier comedy shows, such as Sid Caesar's *Your Show of Shows* (NBC 1950–54), made in the early 1950s, no longer are being made. We do have comedy in our late night shows, which are basically interview shows that star comedians or spoofs of news shows by comedians. In part, situation comedies are popular because they are a formulaic narrative genre and are, relatively speaking, easier to produce than other genres of comedy shows. It has been said 'Death is easy, comedy is hard' and that applies to all kinds of comedy. It is much easier to make people cry than it is to make them laugh. It isn't difficult to make bad or mediocre situation comedies, but it is very difficult to make great ones.

Another reason is that the financial payoff from a successful situation comedy is so great that even though most situation comedies fail and many successful ones do not last very long, a great situation comedy such as *Seinfeld* or *Frasier* makes an enormous amount of money, both in terms of the revenue through commercials on these shows and because of the hundreds of millions of dollars to be made on their reruns.

On the Techniques of Humour

A number of years ago, I made a content analysis of the techniques of humour found in humorous texts of all kinds, such as comic strips, jokes, plays and movies – not only in works that were contemporary but also in some texts from the near and distant past (see Berger 1995). My focus was on the techniques the creators of these texts used to generate mirthful laughter. I found 45 techniques which I claim are comprehensive and different from one another. Table 1.1 lists these techniques. After examining the techniques, I found that they could be fit into four categories: humour that was essentially based on language, based on logic, based on identity and based on action.

In order to make these techniques more precise and easier to use in analysing humorous texts, I decided to list them in alphabetical order and number them. Thus, it would be possible for anyone using these techniques to deconstruct a humorous text in any genre or media by listing the number of each of the techniques operating in a text. There is a problem we face in using the techniques: in some cases it is difficult to determine which technique is basic to understanding how a joke, a passage in a

Table 1.1 Techniques of Humour According to Category

LANGUAGE	LOGIC	IDENTITY	ACTION
Allusion	Absurdity	Before/After	Chase
Bombast	Accident	Burlesque	Slapstick
Definition	Analogy	Caricature	Speed
Exaggeration	Catalogue	Eccentricity	
Facetiousness	Coincidence	Embarrassment	
Insults	Comparison	Exposure	
Infantilism	Disappointment	Grotesque	
Irony	Ignorance	Imitation	
Misunderstanding	Mistakes	Impersonation	
Over literalness	Repetition	Mimicry	
Puns/Wordplay	Reversal	Parody	
Repartee	Rigidity	Scale	
Ridicule	Theme/Variation	Stereotype	
Sarcasm	Unmasking		
Satire			

text, or a scene in a TV show/movie generates mirthful laughter. But, despite these problems, I would suggest that having these techniques enables us to understand how writers and performers make us laugh. Table 1.2 is my list of techniques that are numbered and in alphabetical order. I should add that it is not unusual to find three or four different techniques at work in a simple text such as a joke or some dialogue in a television comedy.

I will use these techniques to make some generalisations about the humour used in the first series of *Little Britain* and then say something about several of the main characters in the show. We must keep in mind that in many cases a technique of humour uses other 'secondary' techniques to achieve its effects. Thus satire might use insults, exaggeration, imitation, ridicule and reversal as 'secondary' techniques.

Humorous Techniques in *Little Britain*

The show, as its title suggests, is a satire on British culture and society, a show about the 'little people' in Britain or the ordinary folk – though a Prime Minister wouldn't, generally speaking, be considered an ordinary or typical British person. Technically

Table 1.2 Techniques of Humour Numbered and in Alphabetical Order

1. Absurdity	16. Embarrassment	31. Parody
2. Accident	17. Exaggeration	32. Puns
3. Allusion	18. Exposure	33. Repartee
4. Analogy	19. Facetiousness	34. Repetition
5. Before/After	20. Grotesque	35. Reversal
6. Bombast	21. Ignorance	36. Ridicule
7. Burlesque	22. Imitation	37. Rigidity
8. Caricature	23. Impersonation	38. Sarcasm
9. Catalogue	24. Infantilism	39. Satire
10. Chase Scene	25. Insults	40. Scale, Size
11. Coincidence	26. Irony	41. Slapstick
12. Comparison	27. Literalness	42. Speed
13. Definition	28. Mimicry	43. Stereotypes
14. Disappointment	29. Mistakes	44. Theme/Variation
15. Eccentricity	30. Misunderstanding	45. Unmasking

speaking, it would seem to be a *Menippean* satire, which Northrop Frye, in his *Anatomy of Criticism,* has described as one that:

> deals less with people as such than with mental attitudes. Pedants, bigots, cranks, parvenus, virtuosi, enthusiasts, rapacious and incompetent professional men or all kinds are handled in terms of their occupational approach to life as distinct from their social behavior. (1957: 224)

I would modify Frye's' notion about occupational approach to life and suggest that this kind of satire has much to say about social behaviour – though we could say that the behaviours of the characters in the show are their occupations.

Satire generally attacks the status quo, though sometimes it is used to reinforce power relationships in a society. In *Little Britain,* there is a certain ambiguity about who is being ridiculed – the eccentrics and grotesques in the show or the British society that produces them. There seems to be a correlation between class-bound hierarchical societies such as we find in Britain and eccentric behaviour. In hierarchical societies, where everyone knows his or her place, it is easy to be an eccentric since you don't have to worry about your status. This isn't the case in egalitarian societies such as the United States, though its egalitarian ethos is actually more myth than reality and doesn't adequately recognise the class-based nature of American society. Social mobility is higher in a number of countries than in the United States but the myth of the self-made man and woman still survives. Our aristocracy is based to a considerable degree on achievement, not heredity.

Generally speaking, most of the techniques employed in *Little Britain* come under the category of identity humour. It is a show about people with all kinds of identity problems such as Daffyd (Matt Lucas), the homophobic 'only gay in the village'; Andy Pipkin (Matt Lucas), who pretends he can't walk so Lou Todd (David Walliams) will do all kinds of things for him; Marjorie Dawes (Matt Lucas), an overweight leader of a fat-fighter group who doesn't or refuses to recognise that she's overweight; and Emily Howard (David Walliams), the transvestite who doesn't seem to be aware that most others can see through 'her' performance.

We see theme and variation in the skits that always end series one episodes, in which the characters are seeking to set a world record of one kind or another, always attempting something absurd and silly and always being frustrated and miscalculating one way or another so their efforts come to naught.

The Dame Sally Markham (Matt Lucas) skits involve caricature and imitation. Caricature traditionally involves comic drawings that exaggerate a person's features, but it can also be used for portraying types of individuals and professions. Dame Sally is a romance novelist who resembles a famous writer who allegedly can dictate three or four different novels at the same time to her secretaries. Dame Sally lies on her sofa, with her lap dog, and dictates novels, but she's always asking how many pages she's written and finding ways to pad her books because she doesn't want to do the work of dictating a complete novel. In the 'Radio' sketch (1: 8), lacking ideas and looking for filler material, Dame Sally turns on the radio and has her faithful secretary, Miss Grace (played by David Walliams), type what she hears.

In the case of Andy Pipkin and Lou Todd, we have 'discrepant awareness' operating. This involves a situation in which the members of the audience know something that one of the characters doesn't know – namely that Andy can walk. He often walks, jumps off swimming pool diving platforms and so on, but Lou never sees him doing this. In my typology, discrepant awareness is classified as a form of ignorance. Another example of discrepant awareness would be the 'Pub' sketch (1: 1) in which a man at the bar is attracted to Emily Howard and offers to buy her a drink. When she goes to the bathroom, he says, to the barkeeper 'she's gorgeous'. He is shocked and confused a few moments later when he goes to the men's bathroom and finds Emily there.

In addition to the use of discrepant awareness, we also have theme and variation in the Pipkin-Todd skits. We know that Andy will always choose something he won't like, such as a greeting card ('Birthday Card', 1: 6) or a colour to paint his room ('Painting Andy's Room', 1: 7). He always chooses something that Lou knows Andy doesn't like but Andy insists on getting what he picks. So Lou will buy a greeting card or paint a room the colour Andy chose, and, a second later, Andy will change his mind and say, 'I don't like it', or indicate that he wants something different.

Members of the audience know that Andy will always change his mind and will want something different from what he has purchased. The variations involve the different things Andy wants to buy or have Lou do for him. Lou is continually being disappointed; he always hopes that just this one time Andy will like what he says he wants – a technique I call 'defeated expectations'. And, of course, Andy never does. Lou never learns, which is what makes the routines so funny to audiences who are all waiting for the moment when Andy changes his mind (see Margaret Montgomerie's chapter for more on Lou and Andy). In a sense, viewers of the show have been 'conditioned' to respond to Andy's behaviour – a kind of comedic conditioning that is not too far removed from Pavlov's experiments. The use of catchphrases is an important element in this conditioning – analogous to Pavlov's ringing a bell when he fed his dogs. When we hear these catchphrases uttered by the characters in the show, we don't salivate but we laugh.

Identity Humour and the British Psyche

What *Little Britain* relies upon is its audience having a familiarity with the various characters and their obsessions as well as an appreciation of the way the show satirises a number of different aspects of British culture such as grammar schools, prime ministers, Welsh small-town life, and Scottish hotels. It is the continual repetition of scenarios related to British culture, in which characters act out their obsessions in numerous variations, that generates much of the humour, so the show is probably much funnier to people in Britain than it is to Americans – who probably don't get many of the allusions – and it is funnier, possibly, to those who have watched it over a period of time than it is to someone seeing an episode for the first time. The same applies to American comic strips such as *Little Abner, Krazy Kat, Peanuts, Doonesbury* and *Dilbert*. The longer you follow these comics, the funnier the characters become.

Little Britain can be thought of as a 'gay' show and one that reflects attitudes (problems?) about sexual identity in British society. Daffyd is gay, Emily Howard is a transvestite and the aptly named Sebastian Love (played by David Walliams) has a crush on the Prime Minister (played by Anthony Head). Some critics have suggested that *Frasier* should be considered to be a gay show, but in America many gay television shows tend to disguise their true nature whereas in England that doesn't seem to be the case. Having gay characters in a show isn't the same thing as having a gay show. Perhaps the attitudes towards sexuality in Little Britain are a reflection of the fact that England is much less puritanical than the United States and much more open about sexuality.

There is an element of the theatre of the absurd in Little Britain. Some of the sketches have a touch of Ionesco's *Bald Soprano* in them – in their subversion of logic and language. There's also a bit of *Waiting for Godot* in the endless repetition and meaningless chatter in the show as the characters endlessly wait for a resolution – Godot's arrival.

One problem with extreme characters such as the ones we follow in Little Britain is that although we find them amusing and may laugh watching the program, I would suggest that we don't identity with them and don't become emotionally involved with any of them. So while the show is, to my mind, brilliant and extremely clever, it is curiously empty and doesn't move me at all. That may be because I'm an American and can't empathise with the characters, but I tend to think it is because the characters are all so one-dimensional and hollow.

That wasn't the case with the best episodes of *Frasier* or *Seinfeld,* for example, where viewers not only laughed at what went on but also were often moved. We laugh at the zanies in Little Britain but we don't laugh with them. We see them over and over again, so we do get to know them, but they never grow and are very much like comic strip characters that we find amusing but recognise that they aren't 'real'.

Theories of Humour and *Little Britain*

Aristotle said that comedy involved making people ridiculous, and Matt Lucas and David Walliams have certainly done a wonderful job of doing that with their bizarre characters. Aristotle is a proponent of the *superiority* theory of humour, which states that we laugh at others because we feel superior to them. In Britain, which is a class-ridden stratified society, with its lords, ladies, royals and so on, this kind of humour finds a natural home. In an egalitarian society such as America, it would be more difficult for this kind of show to succeed. How the Americanised version of the show will do when it is shown in the United States is hard to predict (see Postscript).

A second group of humour theorists suggests that it is *incongruity* that is basic to humour – we are amused by incongruous resolutions that we don't expect, such as the punchlines in jokes. Bergson's (1911/1999) theory of types would be an example of incongruity theory. He wrote about the mechanical being encrusted upon the living and said that when characters resemble machines and are automaton-like, in that they exhibit 'mechanical inelasticity', we have humour. Bergson's notions about comedic types helps explain the humour in *Little Britain* which is full of invariant character types and it is their invariability and inability to adapt to different situations that we find amusing.

A third group of humour theorists argue that humour is based upon *masked aggression,* a theory promulgated by Freud (1991) and a number of other humour scholars who have adapted his ideas. If you examine the humour in *Little Britain,* you can see that there is a great deal of aggression in the show, such as the way that various kinds of people (gays, cross-dressers) and various professions (the Prime Minister, professors, hotel keepers and psychiatrists) are ridiculed. Psychological studies of comedians reveal that most of them are very hostile and that they deal with their hostility and aggressive feelings by making people laugh – or by trying to do so. And members of the audiences of comedies get rid of their aggressive feelings by laughing at others.

What the creators of *Little Britain* have done, I would suggest, is create a collection (I am tempted to use the term 'bestiary') of bizarre and zany characters who never change. Once the mould is cast, the characters will all play their parts with only mild variations in the events that will transpire. This rigidity is humorous at first, but after a while for some audiences, particularly those without British cultural knowledge and/or experience, it will become tedious. What Lucas and Walliams haven't done, as I see things, is made their characters human, given them souls.

Chapter TEN

'In English Please!' Lost in Translation: *Little Britain* and Italian Audiences

Delia Chiaro

Although 'British humour' is a notion which exists within the Italian collective imagination, it is unlikely that individuals would be capable of exemplifying it through its sketch shows and sitcoms. Italian audiences, in fact, are fundamentally unfamiliar with British sketch shows and sitcoms because very few television products are imported from the UK and they, therefore, simply do not get the chance to see them.

Following a discussion of the possible reasons for the absence of British comic products from Italian television, this chapter sets out to examine the issue of the culture-specificity of British humour – especially the role that the language barrier, and hence translation, plays in the export of audiovisual comedy to non-English-speaking countries such as Italy. After discussing the specific problems involved in translating and subtitling *Little Britain*, the opinions and attitudes of a group of Italian students on a number of sketches from the series will be reported.

British Humour on Italian TV

It is a commonplace that humour does not travel well. Indeed, judging by the choice of programmes offered by British television channels, it would appear that much audiovisual comedy is destined to remain within the geographic boundaries in which it was produced. Significantly, since the arrival of television in Britain in the 1950s, no sitcoms or stand-up comedy shows from any other European country have ever been broadcast. In fact, apart from autochthonous products, British TV imports comedy, and indeed TV programmes in general, almost exclusively from the USA. Of course, importing from the USA is an opportune choice. Language has traditionally been an insurmountable barrier for the British public that appears to be averse both to subtitles – which are strongly associated with art house cinemas and educated, elitist audiences – and to dubbing, often linked to the poor quality dubs of oriental and South American products. But perhaps the true reason for a preference for US products, over and above the language factor, lies in the fact that Britain has always felt both culturally and politically closer to the US, than to its 'continental' neighbours. Yet this feeling of proximity appears to be somewhat unreciprocated if we consider that British sitcoms often tend to be localised for the US market rather than accepted in their original form. Classics such as *Till Death Us Do Part* (BBC 1965–75), *Absolutely Fabulous* (BBC 1992–96, 2001–05), *Queer as Folk* (Channel 4 1999–2000) and *The Office* (BBC 2001–03) are just a few of the sitcoms that have been completely reworked for the US market, not only in terms of adjusting dialogues from British to American English, but also with regard to aspects such as location and cast. Notably, at the time of writing, *Little Britain* itself was being modified for US television.

Similarly, sitcoms and comedy shows broadcast across Europe are also mainly imported from the USA rather than from nearby neighbours – and this *despite* the language barrier. In fact, foreign languages do not present a problem as the non-English speakers of continental Europe are used to audiovisual products that are either subtitled in the so called 'subtitling block' (Benelux countries, Scandinavia and Portugal) or else dubbed in the 'dubbing block' (Austria, France, Germany, Italy and Spain).[1] Yet here too, it is mainly US rather than British sitcoms that are translated, dubbed and/or subtitled for non-English speakers. Terrestrial TV in Italy, for example, screens little or no British products; although privately owned Mediaset's *ITALIA UNO* specialises in broadcasting sitcoms in the late afternoon and early evening for younger audiences, these tend to be exclusively of North American origin, for example, *The Simpsons* (FOX 1989–present), *Malcolm in the Middle* (FOX 2000–06) and *Veronica Mars* (FOX 2004–07). In fact, the only UK comedies screened in Italy since the early

1980s have been sporadic re-runs of *Mr Bean* (ITV 1990–95), which replaced slots previously occupied by *The Benny Hill Show* (BBC/ITV 1955–89). Needless to say both Rowan Atkinson and Benny Hill make or made little or no use of verbal language and are thus easily exportable and cost-effective as they require no translation. Nonetheless, apart from these two shows, the only other British sitcoms on Italian terrestrial TV have been *Man about the House* ('*Un uomo in* casa', ITV 1973–76), screened in 1978 on state-owned RAI Due, and *George and Mildred* (ITV 1976–79), broadcast first on RAI and later repeated on *ITALIA UNO* (1979–81). It is, however, worth noting that these programmes were neither especially British-culture specific nor heavily based on linguistic ambiguity and, therefore, easily exportable. George (played by Brian Murphy), the stereotypically hen-pecked husband, and Mildred (Yootha Joyce), his undersexed wife, can be considered fairly universal subjects of comedy which presumably Italian audiences would immediately recognise. Nowadays, however, in order to watch British comedy other than *Mr Bean,* Italian viewers need to turn to cable networks such as *BBC Prime* and *JIMMY,* while countless US sitcoms such as *Friends* (NBC 1994–2004) and *Ally McBeal* (FOX 1997–2000) continue to be regularly broadcast on terrestrial TV and to enjoy widespread popularity.

Little Britain on Italian TV

The rights to broadcast *Little Britain* in Italy were acquired by Digicast in 2004 who chose to screen the programme on JIMMY, a pay TV channel which is part of the *SKY Italia* package. JIMMY broadcasts several British sitcoms such as *The League of Gentlemen* (BBC 1999–2002), and *Green Wing* (Channel 4 2004–07) and dramadies such as *Shameless* (Channel 4 2004–present) as well as products such as *Bodies* (BBC 2004–06) and *Torchwood* (BBC 2006–present). Such products are likely to be considered too cutting-edge for mainstream, terrestrial Italian TV, especially for state-owned *RAI* channels (Chiaro 2008a), and are thus destined to be screened on cable channels, if at all. However, despite this restriction, JIMMY does have its audiences, and niche audiences to boot. The first series of *Little Britain* was broadcast by JIMMY in August and September 2004 in the afternoons and the second series from February to March 2006 in the early evenings. From September to October 2007, the series were repeated for the first time on terrestrial TV (MTV), in the clearly post-watershed time-slot of 11.30 pm. Furthermore, re-runs of the series continue (worldwide) at frequent intervals on *BBC Prime*, where they can be accessed with Italian subtitles. Thus, apart from never having been screened during prime time and mainly on cable channels, the programmes have been subtitled as opposed to being dubbed. The choice of the latter translational modality is likely to have reduced potential audiences even further as many Italians, being more used to dubbing, would be unlikely to want to make the extra effort of reading subtitles. Sabrina Ceci, responsible for subtitling at Digicast claims that subtitles are chosen for programmes that the company considers to be niche products. Owing to the fact that dubbing a product costs eight to ten times more than subtitling (the dubbing process involves more operators and is technically more complex than subtitling – see Whitman-Linsen 1993), TV channels are unwilling to invest in dubbing a series that might not attract a large audience and consequently generate less income in terms of takings from advertising. According to Ceci, *Little Britain* falls into the category of a series that would not be followed by many viewers and would thus not justify the cost of dubbing.[2]

Until *Little Britain* was screened on MTV, the series was practically unheard of in Italy. However, as soon as it went out on terrestrial, the attention of critics began to focus on the social undertones of the programme, rather than on its comic features:

> Two young actors Matt Lucas and David Walliams [...] through their various characters convey a strong social criticism of today's world. But will such a politically incorrect series be able to make its point or has it simply gone too far? (*Corriere della Sera* [my translation])[3]

Notably, this critic from Italy's top newspaper makes no mention of humour, but only of its being politically incorrect.[4] Nevertheless, the shift to mainstream TV was welcomed by the nation's bloggers who posted positive comments about *Little Britain*'s outlandish humour as well as its portrayal of British society:

> Politically incorrect, fierce, totally over the top and full of British humour; in a word, brilliant. The self-righteous stay clear.[5] (www.blimunda.net [my translation])

> ... How can anyone resist *Little Britain*'s ugly characters in this raunchy-sociological gem broadcast on Jimmy and needless to say, made in Britain? Just two actors on scene (Matt Lucas and David Walliams) playing both sexes and a thousand characters in the best Shakespearian tradition. A slice of present day British society, which in many ways is eternal and unchanged, is portrayed in all its squalor and with such captivating cynicism that at the end of the day, what emerges is the actors' love of the nation. Unlikely Weight Watchers' meetings, white, flaccid bodies, accents ranging from polished BBC English to the glottal-stop-English of pub-talk; beer, racism and homophobia in an all-embracing landscape stretching from Downing Street to council estates; from Scottish valleys to grammar schools. (www.tvblog.it [my translation])[6]

Translating Verbally Expressed Humour

The issue of humour and translation has been largely limited to discussions of equivalence and/or (un)translatability (e.g., Laurian and Nilsen 1989; Pisek 1996), with much literature verging upon the anecdotal rather than on scholarly research. And until recently the little research that existed on the subject tended to be confined to the translation of literary humour. Despite the fact that worldwide audiences are consuming vast quantities of translated humour in films and sitcoms, mostly translated from English, only recently have researchers turned to the area of audiovisual humour. Moreover, since the birth and subsequent growth of the discipline of Humour Studies in the mid-1970s, humour itself has begun to be taken seriously in academia, especially within the sub-disciplines of health, psychology and linguistics, yet in the latter field too, matters concerning verbal humour in translation have tended to be widely ignored. One reason for this could be the very complexity of translating humour (Chiaro 2005). But then, of course, the need arises to distinguish the difficulty of actually translating humour from that connected with examining the result of its translation (Vandaele 2004). In other words, although formal equivalence is indeed impossible and, in a sense, humour is untranslatable, it *is*, nevertheless, translated all the time. What we really mean when we say that humour is untranslatable is that it is very complicated to translate and keep it funny at the same time. This is because non-native recipients are unlikely to know the infinite details of the source culture upon which much humour pivots; in addition, the fact that linguistic duplicity (i.e., puns, spoonerisms etc.) rarely corresponds in different languages further compounds the difficulty (Chiaro 1992).

There are several factors to consider with regard to the complexity of translating comic audiovisual products. How, for example, are accent and regional variety upon which so much British sitcom and sketch show humour depends to be conveyed? Are they to be replaced with a local variety in the target language dub and/or subtitles? Are socio-cultural references (i.e., mention of specific places, institutions, foods, holidays etc.) to be translated or left as in the original? If they are left as in the original, audiences may not understand them, if they are translated verbatim, the humorous connotation may be lost. Of course, these problems apply to the translation of written comedic texts too, but in the case of audiovisual products they are multiplied several times over because of the added likelihood that the verbal gag may be totally dependant on the combination of the verbal code with the visual code. Furthermore, if the product is subtitled, the sub by default will involve a drastic reduction of the original spoken dialogue. Viewers need time to read the subtitles while watching the action and there is only so much that a person can read from a single screen shot before reading the next group of captions. In other words, subtitles try to keep up with the spoken words, but they simply cannot do so because the speed of spoken discourse is faster than viewers' hypothetical reading speeds. Thus subtitles are severely restricted in quantitative terms (Dries 1995). In the case of *Little Britain*, a clear example of the necessity to condense subtitles can be found Vicky Pollard's (Matt Lucas) utterances that are packed with dozens of words uttered at breakneck speed.

The norms of subtitling are such that Vicky's speech needs to be condensed into two rows of 35 characters (at the most) that will remain on screen for about four seconds and then disappear to be replaced by other subtitles (Ivarsson 1992). Undoubtedly, a large part of the character's comic effect will be lost, even if, we can safely presume that some of it can be recuperated by the visual impact 'she' makes. In the case of Vicky Pollard, it could be argued that audiences will find the way 'she' speaks funny even if they do not understand a single word 'she' is saying (see the 'Negative but Funny' section below), but arguably, the character will be even funnier if people understand everything 'she' says.

Linguistic theories of humour offer us the Semantic Script Theory (Raskin 1985: 99) based upon the hypothesis that verbal humour occurs when one single verbal script contains two separate semantic scripts which both simultaneously oppose and overlap each other. This theory was to be reformulated and refined to become the General Theory of Verbal Humour (GTVH Attardo and Raskin 1991) which, over and above the requirement of two overlapping scripts, adds the proviso that Verbally Expressed Humour (VEH) involves the principle that the recipient of such a script is in possession of a complex set of Knowledge Resources (KRs) necessary to decipher it. Naturally the primary KR required for understanding VEH is a shared linguistic code between sender and recipient (Attardo 1994). It thus follows that VEH is confined within a number of inter- and intra-cultural boundaries which include regional and national origin, ethnicity, social class, education, religion, gender, sexual orientation as well as special interests which can span from knitting to nuclear science, thus showing that 'there is a sense in which all communication is cross-cultural' (Romaine 1994: 29). And certainly VEH is one of the most extreme examples of highly culture-specific discourse, which, once understood by a certain group of people, is then also dependent on a wide variety of other variables linked to individual personality and mood for the humorous message to be felicitous (Ruch 1998). Now, although on the one hand the GTVH is convincing, it presents significant shortcomings when applied to translation, especially the translation of audiovisual products. Not always will translators find a parallel overlapping and opposing script in the target language which simultaneously coalesces perfectly with the visual code. And not all translators have the ability to create one.

Interlingual translation[7] modifies the verbal code of an audiovisual product, but it acts upon only one part of a larger polysemiotic message, namely, the words. The visual code remains intact. Thus translating for the screen (and for stage) is an extremely constricted type of translation as much dialogue in a filmic or theatrical product will be based upon actors' actions, movements, gestures, physical appearance and so on. In the case of comedy, translators have little room for manoeuvre if a gag depends on the action on screen. This is most unlike a joke which is simply spoken. Chiaro (1992: 86) quotes an example of the difficulty of translating VEH on screen in the Italian dubbed version of Lawrence Kasdan's *The Big Chill* (USA 1983) in which Meg (Mary Kay Place) who wants to get pregnant asks Sam (Tom Berenger) to father her child:

Sam: 'You're giving me a mass headache.'
Meg: 'You're not gonna use that old excuse, are you? You've got genes.'
[Sam looks down and rubs his jeans with a puzzled expression on his face.]

In the Italian version Sam's gesture is incongruous because the translation provided is literal and, unlike English, the words 'genes' and 'jeans' are not homophonous.

The *Little Britain Comic Relief* (2007) interview 'Sir Elton John', featuring Daffyd Thomas (Matt Lucas) and Elton John, provides a similar example of the type of visual-verbal constraint that inevitably complicates screen translation. At a certain point, the interview is interrupted by the entrance of an extremely camp Spanish waiter (Walliams) who brings tea and cakes. Upon recognising Elton John, the waiter gets excited and starts singing the first lines of some of the singer's hits. As the waiter slowly chants the first bars of *Your Song* – 'It's a little bit funny, this feeling inside' – he visibly bends over and patently points a finger towards his rectum. The subtitles do provide a literal translation of the lyrics – *E' abbastanza piacevole questa sensazione dentro di me* – but the effect will be odd unless audiences recognise the word for word translation and link it to the original. This would require a sophisticated knowledge of both English and the lyrics of the song. Although audiences can recover the comic effect by just looking at the waiter prancing about, the visual-verbal joke is lost. We no longer have a script opposition, but a single Italian script, with the only trace of the original gag being the tune of *Your Song*.

However, visual-verbal constraints are only the tip of the screen-translational iceberg. When linguistic ambiguity is combined with cultural-specificity, translation is even more problematic. In the same interview, Daffyd refers to the 'Llandewei Breffi Gazzette' and to 'old Mann Evans who works at the post office'. Again, although the name of the newspaper is provided in the subtitles, the comic dimension attached to Welshness in British humour is not conveyed and, therefore, audiences cannot hope to 'get' the joke which gets lost together with references to the local postmaster in particular and to Welsh village life in general. Similarly, in the many Sir Norman Fry (David Walliams) press statements, the politician typically refers to having to use public lavatories in Hampstead Heath in the middle of the night – 'On Monday night, following a long meeting with the Chancellor, I needed to go to the toilet. So I went to one that I knew would be open at three in the morning, on Hampstead Heath' ('Hampstead Heath', 3: 3) – or to going 'for a relaxing drive in the Kings Cross area' ('Rastafarian', 1: 1)'. These are all connotations which even if they are kept in the subs, Italians are unlikely to recognise.

Research demonstrates that Italian audiences simply misunderstand much of the verbally expressed humour (VEH) which occurs in imported films and sitcoms (Antonini, Bucaria and Senzani 2003; Chiaro 2007a). This raises the question of how far the success of audiovisual comedy depends on culture-specificity or whether VEH – and, in fact, humour *tout court* – in such products might not be getting across because the concept of 'sense of humour' is culture-specific. On the other hand, many imported comedies (especially from the USA, e.g., *Friends* and *The Simpsons*) are indeed successful beyond the boundaries of their country of origin. How far does their success depend on the quality of their translations and how far on good marketing?

Translating and Subtitling *Little Britain*

But what do non-English-speaking audiences really understand of *Little Britain* if they are watching it with the help of subtitles? Will they get the point of the gags? Is the visual code sufficient to keep audiences amused? Is *Little Britain* to remain confined to niche audiences because of its high culture specificity? After all, the series is most unlike the typical US sitcoms broadcast on terrestrial TV in Italy. The latter are indeed 'situational' and playing very much on farcical circumstances and 'good lines' which are linguistically straightforward and unproblematic in translational terms (i.e., rarely based on puns or straight language play [Chiaro 2005]). Again, unlike North American products, much of *Little Britain,* like so many British sitcoms, is centred on humour based upon class differences (Wagg 1998a; see also Sharon Lockyer's chapter in this collection). Can mainstream Italian audiences who are not au fait with the British class system appreciate the underlying humour? Each time they speak, the characters in *Little Britain* portray a facet of class not only through their accents but also through their lexico-grammatical choices. For example, the Italian subtitles need to deal with the complexity of Vicky Pollard's (apparently simple) 'No but yeah but no but yeah but...' and Bubbles DeVere's (Matt Lucas) impeccable yet phoney command of Queen's English and Received Pronunciation.[8] Typical US series such as *Friends* do not appear to present similar problems. Gags tend to be based upon a more general global culture, rather than on high culture-specificity. But again, *The Simpsons* is similar to *Little Britain* in many ways because it is extremely US referential. Could it simply be that US culture-specificity is more global than UK culture-specificity? If that is the case then marketing is playing a huge part in how humour travels.

What follows are some considerations regarding the translational choices made in the Italian version of *Little Britain* and how they impinge on the humorous effect of the sketches.

Translating Culture-specificity in *Little Britain*

As we have seen, *Little Britain* contains many examples of culture-specific items that are often the basis of gags and innuendos.

Without a reference for these items, Italians are unlikely to understand and appreciate the jokes. There is no easy solution to translating lines such as 'Even *The Guardian* was positive' (cfr. writing about the shadow minister) or 'I have an interview with Paxman' (cfr. The Shadow Minister), when audiences will have no notion of the political tendencies of the *The Guardian* and TV personalities ('Philip', 2: 1). Again references to 'mini-chipolatas' and 'banoffee pie' during the Marjorie Dawes/Fat Fighters (Matt Lucas) sketch left intact in the subtitles will be equally meaningless ('Engagement Party', 2: 6). In a sketch featuring Lou (David Walliams) and Andy (Matt Lucas), the off-screen narrator tells us that Lou has just been spending a 'busy morning taking all the K's out of Andy's Alphabetti Spaghetti' ('Feeding the Ducks', 2: 1). The Italian subtitles supply a word for word translation:... *una mattinata passata a rimuovere tutte le 'K' dall'Alphabetti Spaghetti di Andy*. However, Alphabetti Spaghetti is not available in Italy, making the subtitles futile. Yet, the translators did not need to look very far for a more feasible translation as alphabet-shaped pasta does exist in Italy but has a different name. It is likely that the translators themselves had no idea what Alphabetti Spaghetti actually is.

Again, in the absence of a similar idiom in Italian, the gag 'Yes Prime Minister, No Prime Minister, Three Bags Full, Prime Minister', uttered by Sebastian Love (David Walliams), was translated as *Sì Onorevole, no Onorevole, le faccio anche il bidet onorevole*– literally: 'Yes Prime Minister, No Prime Minister, I'll give you a bidet too Prime Minister', thus capturing the essence of the original quip ('Philip', 2: 1). Yet, in the same sketch Love offers the leader of the opposition a 'chocolate finger', adding 'I like to dunk mine and suck off the chocolate', but the translators display less creativity than in the previous example (or maybe they didn't look at the screen in which the biscuits could be clearly seen) and translated the item literally instead of with the Italian name for the same product (i.e., *Togo*). Thus in Italian, Love offers the shadow minister a (real) finger covered in chocolate and not a biscuit. The finger of a hand, combined with the words 'dunk' and 'suck off', could indeed be considered a sexual innuendo, but without the duplicity of the chocolate finger/biscuit, and hence the humour, of the semantic overlap and opposition of a chocolate biscuit called a finger, the joke falls flat (*Dito di cioccolato?...Mi piace inzuppare il mio e succhiare il cioccolato*).

The problem with translating such references is that (a) the translator needs to recognise the reference in question in the first place and (b) have the skill to translate it, not *mot à mot* as was the case with the examples above, but creatively so as to retain their humorous effect.

Translating Language Variation in *Little Britain*

In his discussion of the translation of regional variation in literary texts, Sternberg refers to the 'homogenising convention' in which all deviation from the norm is flattened to a single standard variety (1981). When faced with linguistic variation, in a sense, translators have few options. In the opening pages of *Great Expectations*, for example, translators are faced with the question of whether to transform the marshland accents into Neapolitan, Viennese or Parisian. Such a choice would give a very different connotation to the one which Dickens had intended, so usually translators opt for the homogenising convention and opt for the national and literary variety. Thus, in a suspension of disbelief, the reader is led to believe that all the characters in a literary text speak in a single national standard variety. Both in dubbing and subtitling, the translational norm is also that of flattening and homogenising any deviation from the standard norm in the original product (Chiaro 2008b), although, in the case of dubbing comedy, it is not uncommon to find varieties in the source product replaced with a variety belonging to the target language (Heiss 2004; Chiaro 2008b). Subtitling leaves little choice other than homogenising, as asking audiences to read non-standard varieties (and quickly) would be tantamount to asking them to read in a foreign language. Therefore, the tendency is to ignore variation and replace it with the standard language.

Thus Italian viewers are unaware of Vicky Pollard's West Country twang, Daffyd's Welsh accent or Tom Baker's refined Received Pronunciation as what they read in the subs will not (and probably cannot) connote phonological variation. For example, in the Elton John interview, judging by the amount and intensity of laughter, the studio audience in Britain appeared to be especially amused by Daffyd's pronunciation of 'Billy Eliot' in which the 'o' sound was lengthened and highlighted in a stereotypically Welsh manner. Italian audiences would be unlikely to pick that up as there is no way in which it can be carried across into the subs.

Again, the translation of a simple utterance such as Vicky Pollard's 'No but yeah but no but yeah but...', which has been subtitled almost word for word as *Sì ma no ma sì,* totally loses its comic effect when read. The same thing goes for other catchphrases such as Carol Beer's (David Walliams) 'Computer says no' – *Il computer dice no.* In order to 'get' the joke, an Italian viewer would need to be (a) familiar with English and (b) versatile enough with the subtitles to look away from them and concentrate on the characters so as to catch the humour in the actor's paralinguistic features. A number of characters in *Little Britain* are phonetically and phonologically connoted for their class. Unfortunately, all the connotations connected to their way of speaking (inevitably) vanish in Italian.

Translating Taboo

Both dubbed and subtitled Italian versions of series and sitcoms tend to be severely censored in Italy even though operators involved in their translations generally deny the fact.[9] Sabrina Ceci (responsible for subtitling *Little Britain*) likewise claims that products translated by her company are never censured. Yet, in examining the subtitles, several examples of censorship clearly emerge. In the classic sketch in which Daffyd Thomas comes out to his parents ('Coming Out', 2: 1) and declares that he would like to invite the family so as to inform them all of his outing, his mother says it is out of the question, suggesting that as all his relations are involved in clearly homosexual activities, that is, his Uncle Gareth would be in San Francisco and his cousin Bryn at a Shirley Bassey concert – two allusions that would be lost on Italians. In particular, however, we are told that Daffyd's Auntie Sioned 'stays in on a Sunday and eats *minge.*' Now, the Italian subtitle tells us that his aunt stays in on a Sunday and *mangia patate,* that is, literally 'eats potatoes'. In several regions of Italy, *patata* is a word used by mothers in their communication with small children to refer to female genitalia, thus this is a clear example of toning down the original allusion by replacing it with a euphemism. However, this euphemism is bound to go unnoticed because in Italian, 'eating potato' means just that and has absolutely nothing to do with cunnilingus. Significantly, an important fansub site on the internet provides a different translation, that is, 'leccare l'erbetta' – literally 'licking weed'[10]. Fansubs are created by fans of series who are dissatisfied with the way they are subtitled and thus provide their own, improved translations. It is a pity that, in this case, the translator provides another non-existent euphemism for cunnilingus.

Again, in the same scene, Daffyd's father tries to fix his son up with 'a right 'ansom lad that works down the mine, *he takes it up the chuff*!' which is toned down to *prenderlo nel fumaiolo,* literally meaning 'up the chimney', which is not an Italian euphemism for engaging in anal sex. Once more, either the translator did not understand the original or, what is more likely, it is just another example of censorship. In the same episode, in the 'Jam' sketch (2: 1), while Maggie (David Walliams) and Judy (Matt Lucas) are tasting homemade jams at a garden fete, Maggie vomits when she discovers that it was made by a woman who had run off with a headmistress. In Italian, the female head is neutralised into *preside* which can be either male or female.

Several striking examples of censorship also occur in the Elton John interview. For example when the musician is asked, 'Could you say you have a theatrical bent?', the subs read, *Direbbe che ha un inclinazione teatrale,* literally meaning 'Could you say you have a theatrical inclination?' Admittedly, the word 'bent' does not have the same polysemy in Italian than it does in English, but, all the same, the translators make no attempt at replacing the gag with a fitting (sexual) allusion in Italian. Similarly, 'Do you like splashing out on David' becomes *Le piace sperperare per David?* The verb *sperperare* is monosemous and only means 'spending money', again with no other sexual innuendo.

Translation and Personality

Unlike translating anything else, translating humour requires a translator to have a sense of humour – or to at least recognise the intent to amuse in what he or she is translating. After which, he or she needs the humorous ability to recreate the comic effect required. Now, if having a sense of humour is regarded as a virtue, a positive personality trait (Ruch 1998), there appears to be an underlying suggestion that it is something innate and something which cannot be learnt. In fact, some people are more open to humour than others, are more easily amused and generally tend to see the funny side to life's ups and downs. We can safely presume that a translator equipped with such a personality is likely to recognise instances of humorous discourse. But again, according to personality, some people are averse to certain types of humour – the terrible three being religion, politics and sex, not to mention the most politically incorrect forms of humour of all, sick humour and humour which jokes about disasters and disabilities. Some of these elements are the backbone of *Little Britain*. What is the translator to do if he/she is loath to the topic of the humour he/she is to translate? If it is particularly malicious and aimed at a peripheral group to which he/she belongs? Is he/she to grit his/her teeth and get on with the job? And even if we have a perfectly well-balanced translator who recognises humour and is unaffected by the tasteless and the crass, it is one thing to recognise humour, but quite another to appreciate it and still another to produce it. Such a person would surely resemble Ruch's (2002) hypothetical computer programme, which, apart from being able to generate humour, would be capable of perceiving, understanding and responding to it. After all, how many people do we know who are actually able to deliberately create VEH? Not many, otherwise there would be a world surplus of comedians. Faced with a humorous text, a translator would presumably be expected to nevertheless tackle it in the same way as he/she would produce an interlingual rendition of a legal agreement or an academic paper. Yet instinctively these are two very different tasks. And it isn't simply a question of the language of highly referential technical texts. We know that they are infinite and extensive yet restricted by default by a number of finite rules and conventions which the translator can indeed learn, as opposed to VEH, which is anarchic, somewhat unrestricted by rules and, I would argue, possibly un-learnable.

Thus it is uncertain whether our hypothetical translator can be trained to consistently find the right solution to the unrestrained behaviour of VEH. Interestingly, poetry and song, the two other notorious areas of untranslatability, behave in the opposite way of humorous texts as they are restrained by rhyme, metre, stanzaic forms, genre-bound rules and conventions. It could be argued, at least partly, that these constraints make translation difficult. Yet along a cline of translatable complexity, humour easily wins first prize. The thing is that there is the added element of dexterity in the creation of VEH which exists in no other text type. Let us put ourselves in the translator's shoes. As we have said, the translator needs to recognise the humorous quality of the text. There is no need to appreciate it; to just identify it as such is indispensable to a professional translator. And whatever the quintessential element in the text which renders it humorous may be, what the translator needs to do is to adopt the very ingredient which its creator adopts in order to trigger off a similar emotion of exhilaration in the recipient which is created by the recognition of humour. However, this ingredient has nothing to do with formal equivalence – maybe functional equivalence, but certainly not formal equivalence. Furthermore, it is the very fact that the translator must provoke exhilaration in the recipients of the translation which renders the interlingual solution to the transposition of humorous discourse more complex than the straight language switch of a technical text or even of serious literary prose. Humour does indeed fulfil Jakobson's poetic function of consciously foregrounding and estranging language and meaning against a background of referential language (1959), but at the same time it also accomplishes an emotive feat in the real sense of the word. The translator of VEH must transform him/herself into a temporary wit and, however professional he/she may be, is almost bound to fall short if he/she does not possess special prerequisites which are more typical of a comic actor than a linguist. In fact, I would like to suggest that translating an orator's single witticism calls for more resourcefulness than an entire treatise on the world economy. And if you don't have much of a sense of humour or you're not an especially funny person by nature, that single quip really does become untranslatable.

How Italians Perceive *Little Britain*

In order to explore the opinions of young Italians towards *Little Britain*, a group of volunteers were asked to watch a number of selected sketches from the series and subsequently jot down their thoughts, first, about British humour in general and, second, about each sketch.

The Respondents

The informants in this study were a group of students in the third and final year of a degree course in translation and liaison interpreting at the University of Bologna's *Scuola Superiore in Lingue Moderne per Interpereti e Traduttori* (Advanced School in Modern Languages for Interpreters and Translators), one of the most prestigious translation and interpreting faculties in Europe. All the volunteers were majoring in English, had spent long periods in an English-speaking country and could thus be considered as being highly proficient speakers of English, with a fairly good knowledge of British culture. A total of 36 respondents volunteered to take part in the study.

The sample consisted of twenty-seven females and nine males, which closely reflects the gender ratio of the faculty. They were aged between 20 and 40 and were all Italian except one male Spanish and two female Russian students, one of whom had lived in Israel most of her life. The feedback from the latter respondents has nevertheless been included in the study. Most of the respondents claimed that they had a good sense of humour and all of them said that they were in a reasonably good mood before watching the clips. Moreover, although several respondents had heard of *Little Britain*, only two had actually watched the programme a few times and, therefore, could not be considered especially familiar with it.

The Sketches

The informants were shown a total of eleven sketches chosen randomly from series one–three as well as from the *Comic Relief DVD* and *Little Britain Abroad DVD*. The clips featured the following characters: Vicky Pollard, Sir Norman Fry, Harvey (David Walliams) and Jane (Samantha Power), Maggie and Judy, Lou and Andy, Daffyd and Emily Howard (David Walliams) and

Florence Rose (Matt Lucas). Thus, although they did not get to see all the characters in the programme, they were exposed to a fairly wide range of them.

The volunteers were randomly divided into two groups; the groups then watched the clips together in two one-hour and a half-hour sessions.

Before watching the clips, the respondents were asked to note down five adjectives which in their opinion most closely described British humour. Interestingly, the students produced a total of 58 different adjectives, but with a common core of adjectives upon which many agreed. Respondents were subsequently asked to jot down, in a few sentences, what they understood by the concept of British humour. They were then shown the 11 clips and were allowed three minutes after each to write down their responses.

What follows is a discussion of respondents' perception of British humour and then of the *Little Britain* sketches.

The Lexis of British Humour

Respondents' thoughts on the notion of British humour were elicited prior to watching the clips. The aim behind this was to identify the words which were most recurrent in their responses and thus gain a vague idea of how they perceived British humour. These recurring items have been labelled 'humour words' and will form a basis for our discussion of how the notion of British humour and the sketches which the informants watched were perceived.

The words were classified according to frequency into 'high consensus humour words' and 'average to low consensus humour words'. The labels 'high', 'low' and 'average' were chosen so as to show the degree of agreement among individuals in the sample. None of the words were prompted by the researcher.

Perceiving British Humour

1) High consensus humour words
When asked to give five adjectives to describe British humour, 'subtle', 'witty' and 'sarcastic' were the adjectives which gained most consensus amongst the respondents. In fact, 13 of them consider British humour to be subtle; 11 find it witty and 10 sarcastic.

'...Italian humour tends to be direct, British humour tends to be more *subtle*...' (Giovanni, age 21)[11]

'English humour is somehow '*peculiar*', as sometimes it can be *witty* and quite difficult to understand...' (Maria, age 21)

'English humour crosses the border between what is proper and what is not, and for someone who doesn't know it, it might come across as rude or 'too much'. Some people might not even get the humour because the *sarcasm* is too *subtly* hidden'. (Carla, 21)

The issue of subtlety and the perceived difficulty in understanding humour is not uncommon in cross-cultural communication. Reporting on the occurrence of what Coates calls 'humour talk' (2007) in a sample of 59 bilingual, cross-cultural couples in stable relationships, Chiaro (2009) found that attempts at humour by speakers of English were often misconstrued and taken as rudeness. However, in the responses regarding what they understood by British humour, although 'subtlety' was often highlighted, it was the adjectives 'difficult' and 'peculiar' as well as the concept of impenetrability which occurred most often when watching the clips.

'...I guess it [British humour] has its *peculiarities* otherwise people wouldn't talk about it so much'. (Antonio, 25)

'British humour is *particular* in a way that even if it might make you laugh...' (Miriam, 27 from Israel)

'British humour is somehow '*peculiar*', as sometimes it can be witty, respectful and quite *difficult to understand* especially if culture related...' (Giulia, 21)

And several respondents used Mr Bean as an example of British humour:

'...it [British humour] can also be quite *stupid* like Mr. Bean...' (Giulia)

'...I have watched some Mr Bean episodes and I found them *really funny*...' (Claudia, 20)

'Mr Bean is *cool*...' (Antonio)

2) Average and low-consensus humour words

Clusters of between four to six respondents came up with the following adjectives: clever (six informants); cold, cynical, funny and ironic, (five); culture-specific, eccentric, and weird (four). Furthermore, only two or three respondents came up with each of the following adjectives: grotesque, polite and politically incorrect (three); allusive, astonishing, difficult, dry, hilarious, nonsensical, physical, silly and unfunny (two).

Other adjectives produced by single informants were the following: absurd, bitter, black, blunt, caustic, dark, different, dry, elegant, elitist, insular, irreverent, inoffensive, naïve, non-conformist, old-fashioned, pointless, puzzling, sharp, stylish, unsophisticated and weak. Some of these adjectives have negative connotations (e.g., pointless, weak etc.), thus probably reflecting an individual's opinion rather than an objective description of British humour:

> British humour is *particular* in a way that even if it might make you laugh, you might be deeply disgusted as well. It's based mostly on stereotypes. It's very *strong*. Too *physical*. Why does everything have to be about sex? (Miriam, 27 Russian from Israel)

Perceiving Little Britain

Responses displayed mixed feelings about the clips. Often the responses were couched in terms of 'negative adjective + funny' or 'negative adjective + not funny'.

1) Negative but funny

One thing that clearly emerges from respondents' comments is what I have labelled the 'naughty but I liked it' factor.

The two clips featuring Vicky Pollard – one in which she stubs out her cigarette in swimming pool water and then urinates in the swimming pool ('Swimming Pool', 1: 2) and another in which she talks about her career with her ex-school friends ('Reformed Character', 1: 8) – evoked such opposing feelings amongst many respondents. Comments from females included 'disgusting but funny', 'dramatic but funny', 'scary but funny', 'weird but really funny' and 'shocking but funny'.

Similar mixed reactions emerged from the sketches in which Harvey is breastfed. The students appeared to be amused but at the same time disgusted. Comments included the following: 'Very funny and grotesque', 'Very funny but shocking and disgusting at the same time.' Furthermore, several respondents linked the sketches to the Italian habit of offspring well into their thirties living at home with parents. One student even perceived Harvey as an 'English version of an Italian mummy's boy'.

Several respondents commented on the difficulty in understanding Vicky's speech but added that they still found her funny: 'Couldn't understand what she was saying but she was so cool!', 'Funny even though I couldn't understand!' and simply 'Funny speech'.

Maggie and Judy in the 'Vomiting Lady in Italy' sketch (series three – *Little Britain Abroad*), despite being funny, were defined as 'ugly' and 'over the top' by several respondents. Comments included the following: 'A conservative lesbian is funny in itself, the way they acted was great.', 'Vomit is disgusting but in a sense it makes me laugh', 'Excellent' and 'ROTFL jokes about fascists and lesbians are hilarious', 'allusions went too far for an Italian public even though I enjoyed it a lot!' and 'Hilarious!!! Simply great...I think that in British humour there's a lot of sex, sexual innuendos...and they joke on prejudices'.

2) Negative but not funny

Not everyone was amused by Vicky's grossness: 'Not funny. The man dressed up as a woman is grotesque' and 'Offensive. I didn't laugh' as well as 'Scary and disturbing'.

Another clip which disturbed several respondents was one featuring Harvey being breastfed by his mother. One respondent said, 'Depressing and disgusting', while another considered the vomiting Maggie to be 'gross'.

Again some general negative comments included 'Sex is the *fil rouge* of the clips and not very refined, the homosexual theme becomes obsessive'; 'Elton John is too explicit, I really think they went too far' and 'They went too far (cfr. Daffyd Thomas and Elton John), I think in Italy they would be censored'; 'George Michael was offensive' (cfr. *Comic Relief* sketch with Lou and Andy).

3) Realistic and funny

Several students commented on the realistic aspect of Vicky Pollard's character:

> 'It's the portrait of a typical English girl or teenager. Got pregnant young. Got arrested. Very funny.' (Silvia, 21)

Again, some were surprised by the 'Italianness' of the 'breastfeeding' sketch in which they generally found the man to be 'very Italian':

> I thought that Italian men were supposed to be tied to their mother's apron strings, not British, they didn't expect an English man to act that way. (Daniela, 21)

Moreover, even Maggie and Judy were perceived as realistic. One student claimed that they gave a 'wonderful rendition of the English versus Italian stereotype and English superiority'.

The Norman Fry sketches certainly struck a chord presumably because of similar Italian politicians who have also been involved in sex scandals: 'The funniest clip of all because they remind me of Italian politicians' and 'Understandable even in Italy'.

4) Italian censorship

The students generally thought that Italian television is less permissive about subjects joked about in the series: 'No chance of getting to see anything like that in Italy'. Specifically with regard to the Sir Norman Fry sketches, comments read, 'You would never find such explicit situations on Italian TV' and 'Hilarious. Good satire, we don't have it in Italy'; 'Far too strong for Italian public. Funny use of word "accidentally"' (cfr. 'a part of my body *accidentally* entered his'). And it would appear that in terms of censorship, Italy is not alone: 'Shocking! I don't think I've ever seen anything like that on Israeli TV'.

Translational Issues

What is especially interesting about *Little Britain* from a translational viewpoint is the fact that traditional wordplay (e.g., punning), although present in the series, is not its most prominent feature. As we have seen, there are indeed instances of linguistic ambiguity where translators are hard put to find a solution, but mostly the humour in the series relies on a mixture of visuals and irony. Irony is not difficult to translate, but it is hard to understand for recipients lacking in adequate socio-cultural knowledge. But more significantly perhaps, the voice quality of the characters and their movements, gesture and paralinguistic features that are beyond translation are sufficient to carry over a lot of the humorous intent. Several students actually claimed that although they didn't understand what Vicky Pollard actually said, they found her funny all the same. They knew she was meant to be funny. The concept of exaggeration and ugliness, reminiscent of Aristotle's 'comic mask', seem to ring true.

However, with much of the comic intent being of the politically incorrect variety, it is perhaps understandable why the series was subtitled, rather than dubbed, in a dubbing stronghold such as Italy. Dubbing would have required a greater effort in terms of translation in order to bypass the enormous challenge posed by linguistic variation and up-to-the-minute culture-specific references. The choice of subtitling may well have been a political choice. Dubbing is more expensive than subtitling as it involves more operators and complex technology. It is perfectly feasible for a translator to provide a translation and then physically subtitle a single episode of *Little Britain* from his or her workstation in under 24 hours, whereas dubbing would require three days from script to finished dubbed reel and several operators: translator, technicians, voice-actors and the like. However, it does appear that all sitcoms from the USA are dubbed on Italian TV; why an exception should be made for a British product seems rather unfair and possibly short-sighted in terms of audience ratings.

Conclusion

Had *Little Britain* been dubbed, rather than subtitled, had it been broadcast on a terrestrial channel at prime time and had it been provided with the right marketing, there is no reason to believe that it would not have been as successful as North American products such as *Friends*.

Admittedly, *Little Britain* is a 'difficult' product for some people to accept in terms of political correctness, thus those who dislike it, whatever the language they speak, may do so because they abhor scatological, sick and sexually based humour, while others, like many of the Italian students interviewed, dare to laugh at the disgusting/shocking/scary/grotesque funniness of the product. However, subtitling does not do the series justice. If Italians watching it know English well, then subtitles can be useful to clarify linguistic aspects they may miss, but if they don't, reading the subs will simply distract them from the many visual clues that are necessary to catch the humour.

Translating the cultural-specific has never stopped the USA from exporting its products with the result that typically North American features of life such as high school culture, Halloween and the world of lawyers have become totally global. Who is to say that more exposure to Welsh villages and British beauty farms might not do the same for British culture? As one student stated:

> English humour is based on a perception of reality seen with cynicism. Its greatest merit is that people tell the truth with nonchalance, like someone sipping a cup of tea. (Anna, age 31)

Notes

1. Both dubbing and subtitling present advantages and disadvantages, not only of a practical nature but also of a sociolinguistic and political kind. Countries which originally favoured dubbing tended to do so for protectionist reasons, thus the 1930s saw the birth of dubbing in Italy and Germany both to inhibit English and to exalt national languages. Conversely, the preference to subtitling in other countries is not simply a question of a more open attitude towards other languages (viz. English) but an inexpensive form of translation for a relatively restricted number of spectators.
2. Interview carried out by Nicole Rampone and reported in *Inchiesta sulla percezione e ricezione di un programma sottotitolato: 'Little Britain', una case study;* unpublished degree dissertation, University of Bologna's Advanced School in Modern Languages for Interpreters and Translators, March 2006, pp. 63–68.

3. '*Due giovani autori-attori Matt Lucas e David Walliams sfornano gags a ripetizione, spulciando dalla varia umanità e società inglese, colpendo con estrema derisione anche disabili, gay, casi umani, facendo pure leva su razzismo, omofobia e sessismo, per fare una forte "critica sociale" del mondo contemporaneo attraverso l'interpretazione di personaggi diversi. Riuscirà una serie così politicamente scorretta a colpire nel segno o stavolta si è andati un po' troppo oltre con le provocazioni?*'

4. Certainly, nothing similar to *Little Britain* exists in Italy and attempts at strong (political) satire have often resulted not only with the exclusion of comic actors from TV (e.g., Sabrina Guzzanti and Daniele Luzzanti) but also with targeted politicians actually complaining about being joked about in the press.

5. '*Politicamente scorrettissima, feroce, intrisa di British humour, in una parola, geniale. Astenersi buonisti.*'

6. '*Ma come resistere ai bruttissimi personaggi di Little Britain, chicca cattivistico-sociologica trasmessa sul satellitare Jimmy e, manco a dirlo, made in Britain? Due soli attori in scena (Matt Lucas and David Walliams) e mille personaggi: ovviamente, come da tradizione Shakespeariana, di ambo i sessi. Una certa società inglese contemporanea e, per certi versi, eterna e immutabile, è raffigurata in tutto il suo squallore, con quel cinismo così disarmanete che alla fine, paradossalmente, è quasi una manifestazione d'affetto. Improbabili sedute di Weight Watchers, carni bianchissime e flaccide, accenti che variano dalla più smaltata pronuncia BBC ai più gutturali suoni da pub, birra, razzismo e omofobia in uno sguardo che abbraccia, si fa per dire, tutto quanto: da Downing Street ai quartieri popolari, dalle vallate scozzesi alle grammar school. Un altro di quei programmi deliranti, sull'onda di Smack the Pony e Ali G, in cui chi ama le sottoculture o ha il feticcio della comicità inglese più sboccata dovrebbe provare a curiosare*' (Blog accessed 14 January 2008).

7. An interlingual translation refers to the translation of a text from Language A to Language B (e.g., English to Italian).

8. Vicky Pollard's 'No but yeah but no but yeah but...' is part of the character's way of speaking and is uttered in most of her appearances. Similarly, excessive RP is typical of Bubbles DeVere whenever she speaks.

9. For detailed studies on how Italy censors through dubbing, see Bianchi's study of *Buffy the Vampire Slayer* (2008) and Chiaro's study of *Sex and the City* (2007b).

10. www.italiansubs.net

11. In order to maintain anonymity, all names are invented.

Postscript: *Little Britain USA* ·············

Kim Akass

I had many reservations about writing this postscript on the latest outing of Matt Lucas and David Walliams. As a fan of *Little Britain,* I have, over the past few years, bored people rigid with my 'yeah but, no but' impressions and embarrassed many a friend by telling them 'I want that one'. In fact, the computer nearly did say 'no' as I worried that I could not be objective enough to write sensibly about *Little Britain USA* (HBO 2008; BBC 2008). Despite being aware of gendered power relations within joking relationships (Freud 1991: 142–44) and knowing that stereotypes are 'usually directed against the powerless – the politically ineffective and economically deprived' (Dorinson and Boskin 1988: 164) – I still find myself chortling at Vicky Pollard and defending the right of middle-class men such as Lucas and Walliams to lampoon young and uneducated working-class women. After all, and agreeing with Andy Medhurst, just as comedy is often used as 'a weapon of the powerful,...a way of selling us bigotry in the name of entertainment', it can also be 'unifying, inclusive, a weapon against prejudice, a voice for the marginalised, a way of exposing discrimination through highlighting its absurdities' (2007: 19). A feat that *Little Britain* arguably achieved in its British incarnation.

What a Kerfuffle!

Much hype accompanied the arrival of *Little Britain USA* on US and UK screens, with Lucas and Walliams' ubiquitous interviews and media appearances promising new characters written specifically for the American context. The most lauded of these were Mark (Matt Lucas) and Tom (David Walliams), two muscle-bound gym buddies, Bing Gordyn (David Walliams), the eighth man on the moon, and Ellie Grace (Matt Lucas) and her mom (David Walliams), 'a typical American mother and daughter with a loving relationship' (HBO 2008). Of course, these would be interspersed with old favourites such as Lou and Andy, Vicky Pollard, Daffyd and Marjorie Dawes (to name but a few) and, with such a tried and tested formula, it seemed that nothing could go wrong. Especially considering *Little Britain*'s new home – HBO: a cable channel known for its boundary-pushing comedies such as *Curb Your Enthusiasm* (HBO 2000–07) and earlier British import *Da Ali G Show* (HBO 2003).

Advance reviews were a mixed bag, however. Some applauded the new venture, with Robert Bianco saying that the series was proof 'that while sketch comedy may be on its last legs in America – and getting lamer with each outing of *Saturday Night Live* –...it's clearly thriving in Britain' (2008). An opinion shared by many who predictably compared *Little Britain USA* to other successful UK imports such as *Monty Python's Flying Circus* (PBS 1974, 2006) and *The Tracey Ullman Show* (FOX 1987–90). But there were others who thought HBO had missed the mark. Glenn Garvin in particular bemoaned the fact that HBO had descended from 'can't-miss to can't-watch', replacing 'Gourmet dishes like *The Sopranos*, *Sex and the City*, *Deadwood* and *Rome*' with the 'video equivalents of E. coli'. *Little Britain USA* was, for him at least, a good example of how HBO comedies still had 'a long way to go' (2008). It is fair to say that for every critic who argued for *Little Britain USA* as British humour at its best, another missed the joke entirely, confirming Brian Lowry's point that 'nothing could be more subjective than this brand of comedy' (2008).

Yeah but, No but ...

Watching *Little Britain USA* was not a happy experience. To be honest I had not found series three of *Little Britain* particularly amusing and I knew it would take a lot to convince me that Lucas and Walliams had regained their comedy form. By season's end, my worst fears had been confirmed. To be sure there were moments in *Little Britain USA* that made me chuckle – Andy Pipkin, lying slug-like on the floor of a Mississippi church toilet after his miraculous 'cure' (4) and Vicky Pollard's spell in boot camp (2–5) – sketches that hinted at the former brilliance of Lucas and Walliams. There were also squirm-inducing newcomers Sandra (Matt Lucas) and George (David Walliams), reminiscent of the more nuanced comedy of early *Little Britain*. But, regrettably, for the most part, I have to agree with critic Matthew Gilbert who said, 'I was glad to learn that it's only a six-episode series' because 'it's always best to leave us wanting more, rather than overdosing viewers into exhaustion' (2008). Except that, after five years, three television series of *Little Britain*, and the first *Little Britain USA* series, it may already be too late for this exhausted viewer.

But if this is the case, why can I still find much to please in *Little Britain*'s earlier outings, despite my lack of amusement over series three and the new American version? The 2006 Christmas specials that had Lou and Andy 'stranded' *Lost*-like on a desert island and Vicky Pollard's mum (Dawn French) appearing in a Thai Court made me laugh out loud all over again, even while reviewing them as research for this article. Revisiting the first two series of *Little Britain* found me gasping anew at how far Lucas and Walliams dared to go with characters such as Jason and Nan and Maggie and Judy, and Mrs Emery. And yet none of this made sense as I watched sketches that I (and many others) had found distinctly unfunny in series three as adapted for an American audience. It reminded me of how *Little Britain*'s move from digital channel BBC3 to mainstream BBC1 in 2004 had raised fears over whether the show would lose its edge (McLean 2004). Four years on, after an even bigger move from the BBC to HBO, and Lucas and Walliams are again accused of relying upon old catchphrases and inventing new characters that lack the nuance of earlier creations (Phillips 2005). *Little Britain* may have originally given us 'a vision of ourselves through fairground mirrors, through a glass darkly' (McLean 2004) but unfortunately *Little Britain*'s journey from the UK to the USA seems to have fatally compromised what remained of its original taboo-busting comedy that both 'amuse[d] and terrify[ied]' (McLean 2004).

... And Don't Go Giving Me No Evils

It would not be fair to expect *Little Britain USA* to match the shock-value of early *Little Britain*s, especially as the format was already showing signs of wear and tear in 2005, but I did expect more. In the past, *Little Britain* has been happy to rummage around in that Pandora's box of taboos, equally poking fun at attitudes towards race, class, age, gender and sexuality. Their move to the USA, however, has spawned an uneasy comedy where the only taboos that Lucas and Walliams seem confident to lampoon are those of gender and sexuality. New characters Tom and Mark who revel in their homophobia and misogyny (while engaging in a very homoerotic relationship) are representative here; as are Phyllis (David Walliams) and Mr Doggy whose humour, although marginally more subtle than the gym buddies, is entirely dependent on scatological and sexual behaviour. Saccharine-sweet Ellie Grace shocks her mom with knowledge of vibrators learned from the Internet, and kindly grandmother Mildred (Matt Lucas) regales grandson Connor (David Walliams) with tales of her daring sexual exploits from the past. For critic Mary Mcnamara at least, *Little Britain* has lost its edge: 'Where once its wildly diverse sketches were politically incorrect glimpses into different facets of British life...now they are firmly rooted in genital humor, an endless fascination with homosexuality and fat jokes, often in the same sketch' (2008). The result is that, for some, *Little Britain USA* is 'mostly just crude...reveling in mock condescension toward American stereotypes' (Lowry 2008) – a charge that seems impossible for British-born Lucas and Walliams to defend.

What happened to the comic derring-do of *Little Britain*'s creators in their transition to America? And is their loss of 'edge' just an inevitable consequence of exporting comedy from one culture to another? Boskin and Dorinson's study on ethnic humour and subversion is useful here as they argue that comic stereotypes can only ever successfully be brought into play when used by the victims of stereotyping themselves in 'mocking self-description...as a means of revenge against their more powerful detractors' (1985: 80), arguably a position held by Lucas and Walliams in class-based Britain but lost once they crossed the Atlantic and moved outside their milieu. Which leads to another problem for the series: who is laughing at whom in *Little Britain USA*? Lawrence E. Mintz argues that successful stand-up comedy (including television comedy partnerships) depends upon a sense of cultural community between audience and comedian, where he/she acts as a 'mediator, an "articulator" of our culture, and as our contemporary *anthropologist*' (1985: 75; emphasis in original). While Walliams and Lucas are amply equipped for this role in Britain, they can only act as contemporary observers of American life and, as they lack familiar cultural references, their characters seem two-dimensional, too dependent upon anachronistic attitudes towards gender and sexuality for British tastes. For once Lucas and Walliams seem uncharacteristically reluctant to go where others fear to tread, relying instead on lacklustre characters and occupying safe comedy ground.

There are plans for Lucas and Walliams to return to HBO with 'specials', even though the first series managed only an average audience of 500,000, significantly less than the 3 million that *Little Britain* originally got on BBC1. And it may be that HBO knows best in this case. But in my opinion at least, *Little Britain* should have been retired, in the best *Fawlty Towers* tradition, after two series leaving us with a 'warped version of this green and pleasant land' that, for me, had 'real resonance' (McLean 2004). Instead there is a real danger that, for many, *Little Britain* will be remembered as merely 'crude burlesque' (Gilbert 2008), past its prime and just '*a load of old fuss about somefink or nuffin. Right?*'

Film, TV and Radio Guide ···················

Film

Angel at My Table, An (1990)
Big Chill, The (1983)
Birthday Girl (2001)
Cabinet of Dr Caligari, The (1920)
Carry on Films (1958–78, 1992, 2008)
Copy Cat (1995)
Hannibal (2001)
Hannibal Rising (2007)
Manhunter (1986)
One Flew over the Cuckoo's Nest (1975)
Red Dragon (2002)
Silence of the Lambs, The (1991)
Titanic (1997)

TV

10 Years Younger (Channel 4 2004–present)
11 O'clock Show, The (Channel 4 1998–2000)
3 Non-Blondes (BBC 2003)
Absolutely Fabulous (BBC 1992–96, 2001–05)
'Allo 'Allo (BBC 1982–92)
Ally McBeal (FOX 1997–2000)
Army Game, The (ITV 1957–61)
Attachments (BBC 2001–02)
Balamory (BBC 2002–05)
Barking (Channel 4 1998)
Benny Hill Show, The (BBC/ITV 1955–89)
Black and White Minstrel Show, The (BBC 1958–78)
Blackadder (BBC 1983–89)
Bodies (BBC 2004–06)

Bremner, Bird and Fortune (Channel 4 1999–present)

Catherine Tate Show, The (BBC 2004–07)

Clarence (BBC 1988)

Cracker (ITV 1993–96, 2006)

Crouches, The (BBC 2003–04)

Curb Your Enthusiasm (HBO 2000–07)

Curry and Chips (ITV 1969)

Da Ali G Show (Channel 4 2000)

Da Ali G Show (HBO 2003)

Dad's Army (BBC 1968–77)

Desperate Housewives (ABC 2004–present)

Dick Emery Show, The (BBC 1963–81)

Dr Who (BBC 1963–89, 2005–present)

Eastenders (BBC 1985–present)

ER (NBC 1994–present)

Fall and Rise of Reggie Perrin, The (BBC 1976–79)

Fast Show, The (BBC 1994–97)

Father Ted (Channel 4 1995–98)

Fawlty Towers (BBC 1975–79)

Frasier (NBC 1993–2004)

French and Saunders (BBC 1987–2007)

Friends (NBC 1994–2004)

Frost Report, The (BBC 1966–67)

Games World (Sky One 1993–98)

Gavin and Stacey (BBC 2007–present)

George and Mildred (ITV 1976–79)

Good Life, The (BBC 1975–78)

Goodness Gracious Me (BBC 1996–2001)

Green Wing (Channel 4 2004 –07)

Harry Enfield and Chums (BBC 1990–92, 1994–97)

Hell's Kitchen (ITV 2004–present)

How Clean Is Your House? (Channel 4 2003–present)

I Claudius! (BBC 1976)

I'm a Celebrity, Get Me Out of Here (ITV 2002–present)

Incredible Games (BBC 1994–95)

It'll Be All Right on the Night (ITV 1977–present)

Jim Davidson Show, The (ITV 1979–82)

Kath and Kim (ABC TV 2002–04, 2007)

Keeping Up Appearances (BBC 1990–95)

Kenny Everett Video Show, The (ITV/BBC 1978–87)
Kumars at No 42, The (BBC 2001–07)
Ladette to Lady (ITV 2005–08)
League of Gentlemen, The (BBC 1999–2002)
Life Laundry, The (BBC 2002–04)
Little Miss Jocelyn (BBC 2006–)
Love Thy Neighbour (ITV 1972–76)
Malcolm in the Middle (FOX 2000–06)
Man about the House (ITV 1973–76)
Man Stroke Woman (BBC 2005–present)
Mighty Boosh, The (BBC 2004–present)
Mind Your Language (ITV 1977–79)
Monty Python's Flying Circus (BBC 1969–74)
Monty Python's Flying Circus (PBS 1974, 2006)
Morecambe and Wise (ITV 1961–68, BBC 1968–78, ITV 1978–83)
Mr Bean (ITV 1990–95)
My Family (BBC 2000–present)
My Name Is Earl (NBC 2005–present)
New Heroes of Comedy (Channel 4 2008)
Newman and Baddiel in Pieces (BBC 1993)
No Problem! (Channel 4 1983–85)
Not Only...But Also (BBC 1965–70)
Not the Nine O' Clock News (BBC 1979–82)
Office, The (BBC 2001–03)
On Big Women (ITV 1994)
One Foot in the Grave (BBC 1990–2000)
Only Fools and Horses (BBC 1981–2003)
Open All Hours (BBC 1973, 1976, 1981–85)
Phoenix Nights (Channel 4 2001–02)
Queer as Folk (Channel 4 1999–2000)
Real McCoy, The (BBC 1992–96)
Rising Damp (ITV 1974–78)
Robin's Nest (ITV 1977–81)
Rock Profiles (UK Play 1999–2000)
Roseanne (ABC 1988–97)
Rowan and Martin's Laugh In (NBC 1968–73)
Royle Family, The (BBC 1998–2000, 2006; 2008)
Saturday Night Live (NBC 1975– present)
Seinfeld (NBC 1989–98)

Sez Les (ITV 1969–76)
Shameless (Channel 4 2004–present)
Shooting Stars (BBC 1995–2002)
Simpsons, The (FOX 1989–present)
Sir Bernard's Stately Homes (BBC 1998)
Smack the Pony (Channel 4 1999–2003)
Smell of Reeves and Mortimer, The (BBC 1993–95)
Some Mothers Do 'Ave 'Em (BBC 1973–78)
South Park (Comedy Central 1997–present)
Spaced (Channel 4 1999–2001)
Spitting Image (ITV 1984–96)
Spoofavision (Paramount Comedy 1996)
Steptoe and Son (BBC 1962–65, 1970–74)
Sweeney, The (ITV 1975–78)
Tandoori Nights (Channel 4 1985–87)
Terry and Julian (Channel 4 1992)
That Was the Week that Was (BBC 1962–63)
Thick of It, The (BBC 2005–present)
Till Death Us Do Part (BBC 1965–75)
Tittybangbang (BBC 2006–present)
Torchwood (BBC 2006–present).
Tracey Ullman Show, The (FOX 1987–90)
Two Ronnies, The (BBC 1971–87)
Veronica Mars (FOX 2004–07)
Vic Reeves Big Night Out (Channel 4 1990–91)
Vicar of Dibley, The (BBC 1994–2007)
Victoria Wood as Seen on TV (BBC 1985–87)
What Not to Wear (BBC 2001–07)
Wind in The Willows, The (BBC 2007)
X-Factor, The (ITV 2004–present)
Young Ones, The (BBC 1982–84)
Your Show of Shows (NBC 1950–54)

Radio

Bandwaggon (BBC Radio 1938–39)
It's That Man Again (BBC Radio 1939–49)
Star Vaudeville (BBC Radio 1932)
Take It from Here (BBC Light Programme 1948–60)
The Goon Show (BBC Home Service 1951–60)

Bibliography ⋯⋯⋯⋯⋯⋯⋯⋯⋯⋯⋯⋯⋯

Ahmed, Sara. *Strange Encounters: Embodied Others in Post-coloniality*. London: Routledge, 2000.

Albrecht, Gary L. 'Disability Humour: What's in a Joke?'. *Body and Society*. 5 (1999): 67–74.

Antonini, Rachele, Chiara Bucaria and Alessandra Senzani. ' "It's a Priest's Thing, You Wouldn't Understand": *Father Ted* Goes to Italy'. *Antares Umorul – O Noua Stiinta*. VI (2003): 26–30.

Aristotle. *Ethica Nicomachea*. Translated by W.D. Ross. London: Humphrey Milford, 1925 [c350BC].

Armstrong, Stephen. 'Middle England Has Fallen Head over Heels for Outrageous *Little Britain*. Yeah, but No, but Why?' *Sunday Times*. 30 October 2005: 16.

Attallah, Paul. 'The Unworthy Discourse: Situation Comedy in Television'. In Joanne Morreale, ed. *Critiquing the Sitcom: A Reader*. New York: Syracuse University Press, 2003. 91–115.

Attardo, Salvatore. *Linguistic Theories of Humor*. Berlin: Mouton de Gruyter, 1994.

Attardo, Salvatore. *Humorous Texts: A Semantic and Pragmatic Analysis*. Berlin: Mouton de Gruyter, 2001.

Attardo, Salvatore and Victor Raskin. 'Script Theory Revis(it)ed: Joke Similarity and Joke Representation Model'. *Humor, International Journal of Humor Research*. 4: 3 (1991): 293–347.

Auslander, Philip. *Liveness: Performance in a Mediatized Culture*. London, New York: Routledge, 1999.

Barnes, Colin. *Disability Imagery and the Media*. Krumlin and Halifax: Ryburn Publishing, 1992.

BBC. *BBC Royal Charter*. London: HMSO, 2006.

BBC. *BBC Statements of Programme Policy 2007/2008*. London: BBC, 2008.

Berger, Arthur Asa. *The Comic-stripped American:* What Dick Tracy, Blondie, Daddy Warbucks and Charlie Brown Tell Us about Ourselves. New York: Walker & Co, 1973.

Berger, Arthur Asa. *Blind Men and Elephants: Perspectives on Humor.* New Brunswick, NJ: Transaction, 1995.

Bergson, Henri. *Laughter: An Essay on the Meaning of the Comic. Translated by Cloudesley Brereton and Fred Rothwell.* Copenhagen and Los Angeles: Green Integer, 1911/1999.

Bianchi, Diana. 'Taming Teen-language: The Adaptation of 'Buffyspeak' into Italian'. In Delia Chiaro, Chiara Bucaria and Christine Heiss, eds. *Updating Research in Screen Translation.* Amsterdam: John Benjamins. 2008. 153–162.

Billig, Michael. 'Humour and Hatred: The Racist Jokes of the Ku Klux Klan'. *Discourse & Society.* 12: 3 (2001): 267–289.

Billig, Michael. *Laughter and Ridicule: Towards a Social Critique of Humour.* London: Sage, 2005a.

Billig, Michael. 'Comic Racism and Violence'. In Sharon Lockyer and Michael Pickering, eds. *Beyond a Joke: The Limits of Humour.* Basingstoke: Palgrave Macmillan, 2005b. 25–44.

Blake, Barry. *Playing with Words: Humour in the English Language.* London: Equinox, 2007.

Blanden, Jo, Paul Gregg and Stephen Machin. 'Social Mobility in Britain: Low and Falling'. *CentrePiece* (2005): 18–20.

Bogle, Donald. *Toms, Coons, Mulattoes, Mammies and Bucks: An Interpretive History of Blacks in American Films.* New York: Continuum, 1992.

Bok, Lee. *The Little Book of Chav Jokes.* Bath: Crombie Jardine Publishers, 2006.

Bolter, Jay David and Richard Grusin. *Remediation: Understanding New Media* Cambridge, MA: MIT, 2000.

Boskin, Joseph and Joseph Dorinson. 'Ethnic Humor: Subversion and Survival'. *American Quarterly.* 37 (1985): 80–97.

Bourdieu, Pierre. *Distinction: A Social Critique of the Judgement of Taste.* London: Routledge and Kegan Paul, 1984.

Bourdieu, Pierre. 'The Aristocracy of Culture'. In Pierre Bourdieu and Richard Nice, eds. *Distinctions: A Social Critique in the Judgement of Taste.* London, New York: Routledge, 1992.

Brown, Maggie. 'Why the *Little Britain* Boys Need to Heed History: Media View'. *The Stage.* 8 December 2005: 14.

Burchill, Julie. 'Yeah but, No but, Why I'm Proud to Be a Chav'. *The Times 2.* 18 February 2005: 4.

Butsch, Richard 'Ralph', Fred, Archie and Homer: Why Television Keeps Re-creating the White Male Working-class Buffoon'. In Gail Dines and Jean McMahon Humez, eds. *Gender, Race and Class in*

Media: A Text-reader, 2ⁿᵈ ed. Thousand Oaks and London: Sage, 2003. 575–582.

Cameron, Deborah, Fiona McAlinden and Kathy O'Leary. 'Lakoff in Context: The Social Linguistic Functions of Tag Questions'. In Jennifer Coates and Deborah Cameron, eds. *Women in Their Speech Communities.* London: Longman, 1989. 74–93.

Castaneda, Claudia. *Figurations: Child, Bodies, Worlds.* Durham, NC: Duke University Press, 2002.

Cavendish, Dominic. 2005. 'Big Laughs at *Little Britain*: Lucas and Walliam's Grotesque Characters Shocked and Awed Comedy Lovers'. *The Daily Telegraph,* 24 December 2005: 16.

Chambers, Deborah. 'Comedies of Sexual Morality and Female Singlehood'. In Sharon Lockyer and Michael Pickering, eds. *Beyond a Joke: The Limits of Humour.* Basingstoke: Palgrave, 2005. 162–179.

Chiaro, Delia. *The Language of Jokes: Analyzing Verbal Play.* London: Routledge, 1992.

Chiaro, Delia. 'Verbally Expressed Humour and Translation: An Overview of a Neglected Field'. *Humor, International Journal of Humor Research.* Special Issue 'Humor and Translation'. 18: 2 (2005): 135–145.

Chiaro, Delia. 'The Effect of Translation on the Humour Response: The Case of Dubbed Comedy in Italy'. In Yves Gambier, Miriam Shlesinger and Radigundis Stolze, eds. *Translation Studies: Doubts and Directions.* Amsterdam: John Benjamins, 2007a. 137–152.

Chiaro, Delia. 'Not in Front of the Children? An Analysis of Sex on Screen in Italy'. *Linguistica Antverpiensia.* 6 (2007b): 255–279.

Chiaro, Delia. 'Issues of Quality in Screen Translation: Problems and Solutions'. In Delia Chiaro , Chiara Bucaria and Christine Heiss, eds. *Updating Research in Screen Translation.* Amsterdam: John Benjamins, 2008a. 198–210.

Chiaro, Delia. 'Where Have All the Varieties Gone?: The Vicious Circle of the Disappearance Act in Screen Translations'. In Irmeli Helin, ed. *Dialects for All Seasons: Cultural Diversity as a Tool and Directive for Dialect Researchers and Translators.* Münster: Nodus Verlag, 2008b. 9–26.

Chiaro, Delia. 'Cultural Divide or Unifying Factor?: Humorous Talk in the Interaction of Bilingual, Cross-cultural Couples. In Neal R. Norrick and Delia Chiaro, eds. *Humor in Interaction.* Amsterdam: John Benjamins, 2009.

Clark, Terry Nichols and Seymour Martin Lipset. 'Are Social Classes Dying?'. *International Sociology.* 6: 4 (1991): 397–410.

Coates, Jennifer. *Women Talk: Conversation between Women Friends*. Oxford: Blackwell, 1996.

Coates, Jennifer. 'Talk in a Play Frame: More on Laughter and Intimacy'. *Journal of Pragmatics*. 39 (2007): 29–49.

Cook, Guy. *Discourse and Literature*. Oxford: Oxford University Press, 1994.

Cook, William. *Ha Bloody Ha: Comedians Talking*. London: Fourth Estate, 1994.

Cook, William. *The Comedy Store: The Club That Changed British Comedy*. London: Little, Brown & Co, 2001.

Crick, Bernard. 'The Four Nations: Interrelations'. *The Political Quarterly*. 79: 1 (2008): 71–79.

Critchley, Simon. *On Humour*. London: Routledge, 2002.

Crompton, Rosemary. *Class and Stratification: An Introduction to Current Debates* 2nd ed. Cambridge: Polity Press, 1998.

Crowther, Bruce and Mike Pinfold. *Bring Me Laughter: Four Decades of TV Comedy*. London: Columbus Books, 1987.

Culpeper, Jonathan. *Language and Characterisation*. Harlow: Pearson, 2001.

Culpeper, Jonathan. 'A Cognitive Stylistic Approach to Characterisation'. In Elena Semino and Jonathan Culpeper, eds. *Cognitive Stylistics: Language and Cognition in Text Analysis*. Amsterdam: John Benjamins, 2002. 251–277.

The Daily Mail. *Little Britain* blasted by Father Ted. 12 January 2006: 33.

Darke, Paul. 'Understanding Cinematic Representations of Disability'. In Tom Shakespeare, ed. *The Disability Reader: Social Science Perspectives* London and New York: Continuum, 2003: 181–201.

Davies, Christie. *Ethnic Humor around the World: A Comparative Analysis*. Bloomington: Indiana University Press, 1990.

Davies, Dan. 'Not Likely Lads'. *The Mail on Sunday*. 18 December 2005: 16.

Davis, Lennard. J, ed. *The Disability Reader*. New York and London: Routledge, 1997.

Davis, Murray S. *What's So Funny? The Comic Conception of Culture and Society*. Chicago: University of Chicago Press, 1993.

Delingpole, James. '*Little Britain*. It Is Are You?' *Sunday Telegraph*. 5 December 2004: 3.

Dent, Susie. *Larpers and Shroomers: The Language Report*. Oxford: Oxford University Press, 2004.

Devereux, Eoin. *Understanding the Media*. 2nd ed. London and Thousand Oaks: Sage, 2007.

Dickson, Sandra. *Sex in the City: Mapping Commercial Sex across London*. The POPPY Project, 2004.

Dodd, Kathryn and Philip Dodd. 'From the East End to East Enders: Representations of the Working Class, 1890–1990'. In Dominic Strinati and Stephen Wagg, eds. *Come on Down?: Popular Media Culture in Post-war Britain*. London and New York: Routledge, 1992. 116–132.

Dorinson, Joseph and Joseph Boskin. 'Racial and Ethnic Humor'. In Lawrence E. Mintz, ed. *Humor in America: A Research Guide to Genres and Topics*. Westport, CT: Greenwood Press, 1988. 163–193.

Dorling, Daniel, Jan Rigby, Ben Wheeler, Dimitris Ballas, Bethan Thomas, Eldin Fahmy, David Gordon and Ruth Lupton. *Poverty, Wealth and Place in Britain, 1968 to 2005*. Bristol: Policy Press, 2007.

Double, Oliver, *Stand-up: On Being a Comedian*. London: Methuen, 1997.

Drake, Philip. 'Low Blows? Theorizing Performance in Post-Classical Comedian Comedy'. In Frank Krutnik, ed. *Hollywood Comedians: The Film Reader*. London: Routledge, 2003. 187–198.

Draper, Rob. 'Winning Olympics "Can Stop Britain Becoming a Nation of Vicky Pollards"'. *Mail on Sunday*. 20 February 2005: 15.

Dries, Josephine. *Dubbing and Subtitling: Guidelines for Production and Distribution*. Dusseldorf: European Institute for the Media Eurobarometro, 1995.

Easthope, Antony. 'The English Sense of Humor'. *Humor: International Journal of Humor Studies*. 13: 1 (2000): 59–75.

Farley, Anna. 'BBC Removes "WI" Logo from *Little Britain* Sketches'. *Press Association*. 30 December 2004.

Fine, Gary Alan. 'Sociological Approaches to the Study of Humor'. In Paul E. McGhee and Jeffrey H. Goldstein, eds. *Handbook of Humor Research: Volume 1 Basic Issues*. New York and Berlin: Springer-Verlag, 1983. 159–181.

Freud, Sigmund. *Jokes and Their Relation to the Unconscious*. New York: W.W. Norton, 1963.

Freud, Sigmund. *Jokes and Their Relation to the Unconscious*. Translated by James Strachey. London: Penguin, 1991 [1905].

Frye, Northrop. *Anatomy of Criticism*. Princeton, NJ: Princeton University Press, 1957.

Fuller, Linda K. *The Cosby Show: Audiences, Impact and Implications*. Westport: Greenwood Press, 1992.

Garland Thomson, Rosemarie, ed. *Freakery: Cultural Spectacles of the Extraordinary Body*. New York and London: New York University Press, 1996.

Gauntlett, David. 'Ten Things Wrong with the Effects Model'. In Roger Dickinson, Ramaswami Harindranath and Olga Linne, eds. *Approaches to Audiences*. London: Arnold, 1998, 120–130.

Gill, Rosalind. *Gender and the Media*. Cambridge: Polity Press, 2007.

Gill, Rosalind. 'Empowerment/Sexism: Figuring Female Sexual Agency in Contemporary Advertising'. *Feminism and Psychology*. 18: 1 (2008): 35–60.

Gillespie, Marie. 'From Comic Asians to Asian Comics: *Goodness Gracious Me*, British Television Comedy and representations of Ethnicity'. In Michael Scriven and Emily Roberts, eds. *Group Identities on French and British Television*. Oxford: Berghahn, 2003. 93–108.

Givanni, June, ed. *Remote Control: Dilemmas of Black Intervention in British Film and T.V.* London: BFI Publishing, 1995.

Glick, Douglas J. 'Some Performative Techniques of Stand-up Comedy: An Exercise in the Textuality of Temporalization'. *Language & Communication* 27: 1 (2007): 291–306.

Gray, Frances. 'Privacy, Embarrassment and Social Power: British Sitcom'. In Sharon Lockyer and Michael Pickering, eds. *Beyond a Joke: The Limits of Humour*. Basingstoke: Palgrave Macmillan, 2005. 146–161.

Grice, H. P. 'Logic and Conversation'. In Peter Cole and Jerry Morgan, eds. *Syntax and Semantics, Vol. III*. New York: Academic Press, 1975. 41–58.

Grote, David. *The End of Comedy: The Sit-com and the Comedic Tradition*. Hamden: Archon, 1983.

Hall, Julian. *The Rough Guide to British Cult Comedy*. London: Rough Guides, 2006.

Hanna, Laurie. '£22m Little British Empire'. *Daily Mirror*. 27 October 2005: 6.

Harding, Robert. Historical Representations of Aboriginal People in Canadian News Media. *Discourse & Society*. 17: 2 (2006): 205–235.

Hayward, Keith and Majid Yar. 'The "Chav" Phenomenon: Consumption, Media and the Construction of a New Underclass'. *Crime, Media, Culture*. 2: 1 (2006): 9–28.

Heiss, Christine. 'Dubbing Multilingual Films: A New Challenge?'. *Meta*. 49: 1 (2004): 208–220.

Hills, Matt. *Fan Cultures*. London, New York: Routledge, 2002.

Hole, Anne. 'Performing Identity: Dawn French and the Funny Fat Female Body'. *Feminist Media Studies*. 3: 3 (2003): 316–328.

Holmes, Janet. *Women, Men and Politeness*. London: Longman, 1995.

Holton, R. J. and Bryan S. Turner. *Max Weber on Economy and Society*. London: Routledge, 1989.

Howells, Richard. 'Is It Because I Is Black? Race, Humour and the Polysemiology of Ali G'. *Historical Journal of Film, Radio and Television*. 26: 2 (2006): 155–177.

Husband, Charles. 'Racist Humour and Racist Ideology in British Television, or Laughed till You Cried. In Chris Powell and George E. C. Paton, eds. *Humour in Society: Resistance and Control.* Hampshire and London: Macmillan, 1988. 149–178.

Hynes, William. J. and William. G. Doty, eds. *Mythical Trickster Figures: Contours, Contexts, and Criticisms.* Tuscaloosa: University of Alabama Press, 1993.

Ivarsson, Jan. *Subtitling for the Media.* Stockholm: Ljunglöfs Offset AB, 1992.

Jakobson, Roman. 'On Linguistic Aspects of Translation'. In Reuben A. Brower, ed. *On Translation.* Cambridge, MA: Harvard University Press, 1959. 232–239.

Jenkins, Ron. *Subversive Laughter: The Liberating Power of Comedy.* New York: Free Press, 1994.

Jespersen, Otto. *Language: Its Nature, Development and Origin.* London: Allen & Unwin, 1922.

Jhally, Sut and Justin Lewis. *Enlightened Racism: The Cosby Show, Audiences, and the Myth of the American Dream.* Boulder: Westview Press, 1992.

King, Geoff. *Film Comedy.* London: Wallflower, 2002.

Koblas, Lauri. E. *Disability Drama in Television and Film.* Jefferson, NC: McFarland, 1988.

Koestler, Arthur. *The Act of Creation.* London: Hutchinson, 1964.

Kumar, Krishan. *The Making of English National Identity.* Cambridge: Cambridge University Press, 2003.

Lacey, Stephen. *British Realist Theatre: The New Wave in its Context, 1956–65.* London: Routledge, 1995.

Lacey, Stephen. 'Becoming Popular: Some Reflections on the Relationship between Television and Theatre'. In Jonathan Bignell and Stephen Lacey, eds. *Popular Television Drama: Critical Perspectives.* Manchester: Manchester University Press, 2005. 198–214.

Lakoff, Robin. *Language and Woman's Place.* New York: Harper and Row, 1975.

Laurian Anne-Marie and Don L.F. Nilsen, eds. *Humour et Traduction: Humor and Translation.* Special issue: *Meta.* 34: 1 (1989).

Lawler, Stephanie. 'Introduction: Class, Culture and Identity'. *Sociology.* 39: 5 (2005): 797–806.

Leapman, Michael. Littler Britain: Once Scathingly Witty, Why Has the Gloriously un-PC *Little Britain* Suddenly Lost Its Way? *The Daily Mail,* 13 December 2005: 15.

Lewisohn, Mark. *The Radio Times Guide to TV Comedy.* London: BBC Books, 1998.

Littlewood, Jane and Michael Pickering. 'Heard the One about the White, Middle Class, Heterosexual Father-in-law?'. In Stephen Wagg, ed. *Because I Tell a Joke or Two: Comedy, Politics and Social Difference.* Routledge: London and New York, 1998. 291–312.

Longmore, Paul, K. 'Screening Stereotypes: Images of Disabled People in Television and Motion Pictures'. In Alan Gartner and Tom Joe, eds. *Images of the Disabled, Disabling Images.* New York: Praeger, 1987: 65–87.

Longmore, Paul, K. *Why I Burned My Book and Other Essays on Disability.* Philadelphia: Temple University Press, 2003.

Lucas, Matt. 'Radio 5 Live Interview'. Little Britain: *The Complete First Series.* DVD. BBC Worldwide Ltd. 2005.

Lucas, Matt and David Walliams. Little Britain: *The Complete Scripts and That: Series One.* London: Harper Collins, 2004.

Lucas, Matt and David Walliams. *Little Britain Live* (tour brochure). London: Granada Ventures, 2005 (This is also included in a miniature form in the special edition of the DVD).

Lucas, Matt and David Walliams, 'Making the Tour' in 'Extras' on *Little Britain Live* (DVD), 2 Entertain, 2006a.

Lucas, Matt and David Walliams. Little Britain: *The Complete Scripts And Stuff: Series Three.* London: Harper Collins, 2006b.

Lucas, Matt, David Walliams and Boyd Hilton. *Inside* Little Britain. London: Ebury Press, 2007.

MacKinnon, Catherine. *Only Words.* London: HarperCollins, 1994.

Malik, Sarita. *Representing Black Britain: Black and Asian Images on Television.* London: Sage, 2002.

McLean, Gareth. 'Don't Be Cruel'. *The Guardian.* 16 October 2004: 50.

McRobbie, Angela. 'Notes on "What Not to Wear" and Post-feminist Symbolic Violence'. *The Sociological Review.* 52: s2 (2004): 97–109.

Medhurst, Andy. *A National Joke: Popular Comedy and English Cultural Identities.* London and New York: Routledge, 2007.

Medhurst, Andy and Lucy Tuck. 'The Gender Game'. In Jim Cook, ed. *BFI Dossier 17: Television Sitcom.* London: British Film Institute, 1982. 43–55.

Mills, Brett. 'Comedy Verite: Contemporary Sitcom Form'. *Screen.* 45: 1 (2004): 63–78.

Mintz, Lawrence E. 'Stand-up Comedy as Social and Cultural Mediation'. *American Quarterly.* 37 (1985): 71–80.

Morreall, John. *Taking Laughter Seriously.* Albany: State University of New York Press, 1983.

Morreall, John. *The Philosophy of Laughter and Humour.* Albany: State University of New York Press, 1987.

Mount, Ferdinand. *Mind the Gap: The New Class Divide in Britain*. London: Short Books, 2004.

Muir, Frank. *A Kentish Lad*. London: Bantam Press, 1997.

Mulkay, Michael. *On Humour: Its Nature and Place in Modern Society*. London: Basil Blackwell, 1988.

Nayak, Anoop. 'Displaced Masculinities: Chavs, Youth and Class in the Post-industrial City'. *Sociology*. 40: 5 (2006): 813–831.

Neale, Steve and Frank Krutnik. *Popular Film and Television Comedy*. London: Routledge, 1990.

Norden, Martin F. *The Cinema of Isolation. A History of Physical Disability in the Movies*. Brunswick: Rutgers University Press, 1994.

Norrick, Neal R. 'Non-verbal Humor and Joke Performance'. *Humor*. 17:4 (2004): 401–409.

Ochs, Elinor. 'Indexing Gender'. In Alessandro Duranti and Charles Goodwin, eds. *Rethinking Context*. Cambridge: Cambridge University Press, 1992. 335–358.

Orwell, George. 'The Art of Donald McGill' in *The Penguin Essays of George Orwell*. London: Penguin Books, 1941/1994. 193–203.

Pakulski, Jan and Malcolm Waters. *The Death of Class*. London: Sage, 1996.

Palin, Michael. *Diaries 1969–1979: The Python Years*. London: Weidenfeld and Nicolson, 2006.

Palmer, Jerry. *Taking Humour Seriously*. London: Routledge, 1994.

Peters, Lloyd and Sue Becker. New Comedy: Back to Little England? Yeahbutnobutyeahbutnobutyeah. Paper presented at Playing for Laughs Symposium, De Montfort University, Leicester, 9–10 February 2008.

Phelan, Peggy. *Unmarked: The Politics of Performance*. London, New York: Routledge, 1993.

Pickering, Michael and Sharon Lockyer. 'Introduction: The Ethics and Aesthetics of Humour and Comedy'. In Sharon Lockyer and Michael Pickering, eds. *Beyond a Joke: The Limits of Humour*. Basingstoke: Palgrave, 2005a. 1–24.

Pickering, Michael and Sharon Lockyer. 'The Ambiguities of Comic Impersonation'. In Sharon Lockyer and Michael Pickering, eds. *Beyond a Joke: The Limits of Humour*. Basingstoke: Palgrave, 2005b. 180–197.

Pisek, Gerhard. 'Wordplay and the Dubbing/subtitler'. *Arbeiten aus Anglistik und Amerikanistik*. 22: 1 (1996): 37–51.

Podesva, Robert J. 'Intonational Variation and Social Meaning: Categorical and Phonetic Aspects'. *U. Penn Working Papers in Linguistics* 12: 2 (2006): 189–202.

Provine, Robert R. *Laughter: A Scientific Investigation*. London: Penguin, 2001.

Radcliffe-Brown, Arnold. *Structure and Function in Primitive Society*. London: Cohen and West. 1952.

Rampone, Nicole. *Inchiesta sulla percezione e ricezione di un programma sottotitolato:* 'Little Britain', *una case study*. Unpublished Degree Dissertation. University of Bologna's Advanced School in Modern Languages for Interpreters and Translators. March 2006.

Rampton, James. 'Little Treasures: *Little Britain* Is Back for a Third Series, and the Characters Are as Grotesque as Ever'. *The Independent*. 16 November 2005: 50–51.

Raskin, Victor. *Semantic Mechanisms of Humour*. Dordrecht: Reidel, 1985.

Richards, Jeffrey. *Films and British National Identity: From Dickens to Dad's Army*. Manchester: Manchester University Press, 1997.

Robertson, Cameron. 'Handbagged: Women's Institute Force BBC to Change *Little Britain* Sketch'. *The Mirror*. 30 December 2004: 7.

Romaine, Suzanne. *Language in Society. An Introduction to Sociolinguistics*. Oxford: Oxford University Press, 1994.

Ross, Karen. *Black and White Media: Black Images in Popular Film and Television*. Cambridge: Polity Press, 1996.

Rowe, Kathleen. 'Roseanne: Unruly Woman and Domestic Goddess'. *Screen*. 31: 4 (1990): 408–419.

Rowe, Kathleen. *The Unruly Woman: Gender and the Genres of Laughter*. Austin, Texas: University of Texas Press, 1995.

Ruch, Willibald, ed. *The Sense of Humor: Explorations of a Personality Characteristic*. Berlin: Mouton de Gruyter, 1998.

Ruch, Willibald. 'Computers with a Personality? Lessons to Be Learnt from Studies on the Psychology of Humour'. In Oliviero Stock, Carlo Strappavara and Anton Nijhold, eds. *Proceedings of the International Workshop on Computational Humor* (TWLT4). University of Twente, Enschede, NL, 2002. 57–70.

Rudden, Liam. '*Little Britain* Pair Test Comic Boundaries'. *Evening News*. 10 November 2006: 12.

Sapsted, David. 'Headmistress Calls for *Little Britain* Ban'. *The Daily Telegraph*. 17 December 2005; 11.

Schank, Roger C. and Robert P. Abelson. *Scripts, Plans, Goals and Understanding*. Hillsdale, NJ: Lawrence Erlbaum, 1977.

Seidman, Steve. *Comedian Comedy: A Tradition in Hollywood Film*. Ann Arbor: UMI Research Press, 1981.

Semino, Elena. *Language and World Creation in Poems and Other Texts*. London: Longman, 1997.

Shakespeare, Tom. 'Joking a Part'. *Body and Society*. 5 (1999): 47–52.

Shakespeare, Tom, ed. *The Disability Reader: Social Science Perspectives*. London and New York: Continuum, 2003.

Shakespeare, Tom. *Disability Rights and Wrongs*. New York and London: Routledge, 2006.

Shepherd, Jessica. 'Breaking Free'. *The Guardian*. 23 October 2007: 1.

Sherwin, Adam. 'Middle England Calls Foul on *Little Britain*'s WI Skits'. *The Times*. 30 December 2004: 13.

Shohat, Ella 'Ethnicities-in-relation'. In Lester Friedman, ed. *Unspeakable Images: Ethnicity and the American Cinema*. Urbana: University of Illinois, 1991: 220–247.

Simpson, Mark. 'The Straight Men of Comedy'. In Stephen Wagg, ed. *Because I Tell a Joke or Two: Comedy, Politics and Social Difference*. Routledge: London and New York, 1998. 291–312.

Simpson, Paul. *Stylistics: A Resource Book for Students*. London: Routledge, 2004.

Skeggs, Bev. *Formations of Class and Gender: Becoming Respectable*. London: Sage, 1997.

Skeggs, Bev. *Class, Self, Culture*. London and New York: Routledge, 2004.

Skeggs, Bev. 'The Making of Class and Gender Through Visualizing Moral Subject Formation'. *Sociology*. 39: 5 (2005): 965–982.

Small, Stephen. 'Serious T'Ing: The Black Comedy Circuit in England'. In Stephen Wagg, ed. *Because I Tell a Joke or Two: Comedy, Politics and Social Difference*. London: Routledge. 1998. 221–243.

Smith, Jeanne R. *Writing Tricksters: Mythic Gambols in American Ethnic Literature*. Berkeley: University of California Press, 1997.

Snell, Julia. 'Schema Theory and the Humour of *Little Britain*'. *English Today*. 22: 1 (2006): 59–64.

Sternberg, Meir. 'Polylingualism as Reality and Mimesis as Mimesis' .*Poetics Today*. 2: 4 (1981): 221–239.

Stockwell, Peter. *Cognitive Poetics: An Introduction*. London: Routledge, 2002.

Thorpe, Vanessa. 'The Observer Profile: *Little Britain*'. *The Observer*. 2 January 2005: 23.

Tyler, Imogen. 'Welcome to Britain: The Cultural Politics of Asylum'. *European Journal of Cultural Studies*. 9: 2 (2006): 185–202.

Tyler, Imogen. ' "Chav Mum Chav Scum": Class Disgust in Contemporary Britain'. *Feminist Media Studies*. 8: 1 (2008): 7–34.

Vandaele, Jeroen, ed. *The Translator*. Special Issue 'Translating Humour'. 8: 2 (2004).

Wagg, Stephen. 'Everything Else Is Propaganda: The Politics of Alternative Comedy'. In George Paton, Chris Powell and Stephen Wagg, eds. *The Social Faces of Humour: Practices and Issues*. Aldershot: Arena/Ashgate, 1996. 321–347.

Wagg, Stephen. 'At Ease, Corporal': Social Class and the Situation Comedy in British Television, from the 1950s to the 1990s. In Stephen Wagg, ed. *Because I Tell a Joke or Two: Comedy, Politics and Social Difference*. London and New York: Routledge, 1998a. 1–31.

Wagg, Stephen. 'Punching Your Weight: Conversations with Jo Brand'. In Stepehen Wagg, ed. *Because I Tell a Joke or Two: Comedy, Politics and Social Difference*. London and New York: Routledge, 1998b. 111–136.

Wallis, Sarah. 'Schools Where Girls Can Pick Up the Pill'. *The Mirror*. 3 May 2007: 24.

Ware, Vron. *Who Cares about Britishness? A Global View of the National Identity Debate*. London: Arcadia, 2007.

Weeks, Jeffrey. *Sex, Politics and Society: The Regulation of Sexuality Since 1800*. Harlow: Longman, 1981.

Wells, Pam and Peter Bull. 'From Politics to Comedy: A Comparative Analysis of Affiliative Audience Responses'. *Journal of Language and Social Psychology*. 26: 4 (2007): 321–342.

Whelehan, Imelda. *Overloaded: Popular Culture and the Future of Feminism*. London: Women's Press, 2000.

Whitman-Linsen, Candance. *Through the Dubbing Glass. The Synchronization of American Motion Pictures into German, French and Spanish*. Frankfurt am Main: Peter Lang, 1993.

Wilmut, Roger and Peter Rosengard. *Didn't You Kill My Mother-in-law?: The Story of Alternative Comedy in Britain from the Comedy Store to Saturday Live*. London: Methuen, 1989.

Wodak, Ruth. 'Critical Discourse Analysis and the Study of Doctor–Patient Interaction'. In Michael Toolan, ed. *Critical Discourse Analysis: Critical Concepts in Linguistics*. London: Routledge, 2002 (originally published 1997). 340–364.

Wood, Helen and Bev Skeggs. 'Notes on Ethical Scenarios of Self on British Reality TV'. *Feminist Media Studies*. 4: 2 (2004): 205–208.

Yeap, Sue. 'Big Laughs with *Little Britain*'. *Metro*. 3 March 2007: 14.

Web Citations

Allen, Graham. 'Intertextuality'. *The Literary encyclopaedia*. 24 January 2005. http://www.litencyc.com/php/stopics.php?rec=true&UID=1229.

Alton Towers. www.altontowers.com/

Andersen, Gisle. 'Pragmatic Markers in Teenage and Adult Conversation'. Paper presented at the 18th ICAME Conference. Chester, May 1997. gandalf.aksis.uib.no/~gisle/pdf/CHESTER.pdf

Anon. 'Forms of Variety Theatre', American Variety Stage: Vaudeville and Popular Entertainment 1870–1920. 31 October 1996. http://memory.loc.gov/ammem/vshtml/vsforms.html

Anon. Fringe Archive: Comedy at the Fringe. 11 October 2005. http://www.edfringe.com/story.html?id=124

Armstrong, Stephen. 'On the Offensive'. *The Guardian.* 20 June 2007. http://www.guardian.co.uk/britain/article/0,,2107009,00.html

Barrell, Tony. 'The Battle of *Little Britain*'. *Times Online.* 6 November 2006. http://www.timesonline.co.uk/tol/life_and_style/article621516.ece

Barrow, Andrew. 'Matt Lucas and David Walliams: The Odd Couple'. *The Independent.* 28 November 2004. http://www.independent.co.uk/news/people/profiles/matt-lucas-and-david-walliams-the-odd-couple-535012.html

BBC Guide to Comedy: Little Britain. 2007. http://www.bbc.co.uk/comedy/guide/articles/l/littlebritain_1299003526.shtml

BBC Guide to Comedy: *Rock Profile.* 2008. http://www.bbc.co.uk/comedy/rockprofile/index.shtml

BBC. *Little Britain* Character Guide: *Anne. 2007.* http://www.bbc.co.uk/comedy/littlebritain/cahracters/anne.shtml.

BBC. Little Britain Character Guide: Lou and Andy. 2007. http://www.bbc.co.uk/comedy/littlebritain/characters/louandy.shtml

BBC News. '*Little Britain* Two Top Comic List'. 10 January 2005a. http://news.bbc.co.uk/1/hi/entertainment/tv_and_radio/4161579.stm

BBC News. '*Little Britain* Tops Sketch Poll'. 3 April 2005b. http://www.channel4.com/entertainment/tv/microsites/G/greatest/comedy_sketches/

BBC News. 'Head Calls for *Little Britain* Ban'. 16 December 2005c. http://news.bbc.co.uk/1/hi/england/kent/4534064.stm

BBC News. '*Little Britain* Sketch Criticised'. 23 November 2005d. http://news.bbc.co.uk/1/hi/health/4460876.stm

BBC News. '*Little Britain* Draws Child Fans'. 8 November 2005e. http://news.bbc.co.uk/1/hi/entertainment/tv_and_radio/4416920.stm

BBC Radio 4. Should We Be Laughing? 17 February 2004. http://www.nasty-girls.co.uk/Interviews.htlm

Bennett, Steve. '*Little Britain*, Large Audience'. *BBC Comedy Blog.* 21 November 2005. http://www.bbc.co.uk/comedy/news/2005/11/21/27421.shtml

Bianco, Robert. 'HBO's *"Little Britain USA"* Lends Us Lots of Laughs'. *USA Today*. 29 September 2008. http://www.usatoday.com/life/television/reviews/2008–09-25-little-britain-usa_N.htm?csp=34

Blimunda. www.blimunda.net

The British Sitcom Guide. 'About *Little Britain*'. 2008. http://www.sitcom.co.uk/little_britain/about.shtml

Calvi, Nuala. 'A Healthy Dose of Disability': An Interview with Paul Henshall. 2005. http://www.bbc.co.uk/print/ouch/features/paulhenshall.shtml

Channel 4. 'Britain's Favourite Celebrity Chav'. http://www.channel4.com/entertainment/tv/microsites/G/greatest/chavs/resultstml

Clark, Laurence. 'Disabling Comedy: "Only When We Laugh"'. Paper presented at the *Finding the Spotlight* Conference, Liverpool Institute for the Performing Arts, 2003 http://www.leeds.ac.uk/disability-studies/archiveuk/Clark,%20Laurence/Clark%on%20comedy.pdf

Cooke, Rachel. 'Big Briton: The Interview, David Walliams'. *The Observer*. 11 November 2007. http://arts.guardian.co.uk/theatre/comedy/story/0,,2208914,00.html

Denton, Andrew. '*Little Britain* – Matt Lucas and David Walliams'. *Enough Rope*. 16 October 2006. http://www.abc.net.au/tv/enoughrope/transcripts/s1763999.htm.

Dugan, Emily. '*Little Britain* Enters Record Books with £3m DVD. *The Independent Online*. 27 September 2007. http://www.independent.co.uk/news/media/little-britain-enters-record-books-with-pound3m-dvd-403665.html

Ellen, Barbara. '*Little Britain* May Be the Toast of the Post-pub, Non-PC Crowd. But Its Punchlines Are Way below the Belt...'. *The Observer*. 12 December 2004. http://www.guardian.co.uk/theobserver/2004/dec/12/features.magazine27

The Fabian Society. 'Stop Using Chav: It's Deeply Offensive'. July 2008. http://fabians.org.uk/publications/extracts/chav-offensive.

Finding, Deborah. '"I Can't Believe You Just Said That": Figuring Gender and Sexuality in *Little Britain*'. *MEDIA@LSE Electronic Working Papers*. 13 (2008). http://www.lse.ac.uk/collections/media@lse/mediaWorkingPapers/ewpNumber13.htm

Garvin, Glenn. 'It's Not Funny – It's HBO'. *The Miami Herald*. 28 September 2008. http://www.miamiherald.com/entertainment/tv/story/702854.html

Gilbert, Matthew. 'HBO's Humor Is Hit and Miss'. *The Boston Globe*. 27 September 2008. http://www.boston.com/ae/tv/articles/2008/09/27/hbos_humor_is_hit_and_miss/

The Guardian Online. 'The Only Catchphrase in the Village'. 11 January 2005. http://www.guardian.co.uk/media/2005/jan/11/broadcasting. uknewsFarouky, Jumana. 'Mother-in-law Problems: They're Worse for Women'. 4 December 2008. www.time.com.

Hari, Johann. 'Why I Hate *Little Britain*.' *The Independent Online.* 22 November 2005. http://comment.independent.co.uk/columnists_a_l/ johann_hari/article328516.ece

HBO official site. http://www.hbo.com/littlebritainusa/characters/ellie-grace.html

Italian Subs. www.italiansubs.net

Knight, Kathryn. 'The Lothario of *Little Britain*'. *The Mail Online.* 3 March 2005. http://www.dailymail.co.uk/tvshowbiz/article-339946/ The-lothario-Little-Britain.html

Levy, Andrew. 'Why Women Don't See the Funny Side of Their Mothers-in-law.' *The Mail Online.* 3 December 2008. www.dailymail.co.uk.

Lowry, Brian. '*Little Britain USA*'. *Variety.* 24 September 2008. http://www. variety.com/review/VE1117938494.html?categoryid=32&cs=1

Lucas, Matt and David Walliams. 'Matt Lucas and David Walliams Discuss...'. No date(a). www.bbc.co.uk/comedy/littlebritain/interviews/ interview3.shtml

Lucas, Matt and David Walliams. 'Matt Lucas and David Walliams Discuss...'. No date(b). www.bbc.co.uk/comedy/littlebritain/interviews/ interview1.shtml

Maume, Chris. 'David Walliams: Not So Little'. *The Independent.* 29 October 2005. http://www.independent.co.uk/news/people/profiles/ david-walliams-not-so-little-513076.html

McCalmont, Jonathan. 'Phatic Discourse and the Death of British Comedy'. *Diplomat.* 22 December 2006. http://www.sfdiplomat. net/sf_diplomat/2006/12/phatic_discours.html

McCarthy, Anna. 'Benny Hill and Reviving British Comedy'. *Flow TV.* 10 June 2005. http://flowtv.org/?p=587.

McLean, Gareth. 'Don't Be Cruel'. *The Guardian.* 16 October 2004. http:// arts.guardian.co.uk/features/story/0,,1328578,00.html#article_ continue

Mcnamara, Mary. 'An Ill-advised Crossing for "*Little Britain USA*"'. *L.A. Times.* 26 September 2008. http://articles.latimes.com/2008/sep/26/ entertainment/et-littlebritain26

Mr Paparazzi. 'David Walliams Isn't Ready to Settle Down'. 13 January 2009. http://www.mrpaparazzi.com/blog/post/5369/David-Walliams-Isnt-Ready-To-Settle-Down.aspx

Newagenda. http://www.newagenda.demon.co.uk/

Ofcom. 'The Representation and Portrayal of People with Disabilities on Analogue and Terrestrial Television'. 2005. http://www.ofcom.org/research/tv/reports/portrayal/portrayal.pdf

Ofcom. 'Ofcom Broadcast Bulletin', Issue No 92. 10 September 2007. http://www.ofcom.org.uk/tv/obb/prog_cb/obb92/issue92.pdf.

Open University/BBC. 'Just a Bit of Fun: A Survey of British Jokes'. 2007. http://www.open2.net/lennysbritain/bitoffun.html.

Ouch. 'TV's Most Popular Disabled Character on our TV Screens'. 2005a. http://www.bbc.co.uk/print/ouch/yourspace/tvvote/vote_analysis.shtml

Ouch. 'Voters Comments on Disabled TV Characters'. 2005b. http://www.bbc.co.uk/ouch/yourspace/tvvote/andy.shtml

Oxford English Dictionary. 2nd ed. 1989 (ed. J. A. Simpson and E. S. C. Weiner), Additions 1993–1997 (ed. John Simpson and Edmund Weiner; Michael Proffitt), and 3rd ed. (in progress) Mar. 2000– (ed. John Simpson). OED Online. Oxford University Press. http://oed.com.

Phillips, John. '*Little Britain* Review'. *offthetelly.co.uk*. 17 November 2005. http://www.offthetelly.co.uk/reviews/2005/littlebritain.htm

Phillips, Martin. 'Warts 'n All: Matt Lucas'. *The Sun*. 5 September 2006. http://www.thesun.co.uk/article/0,,2001320029–2006410208,00.html

Pool, Hannah. 'Return to the Dark Ages'. *The Guardian*. 22 September 2006. http://www.guardian.co.uk/media/2006/sep/22/pressandpublishing.raceintheuk

Rampton, James. 'Matt Lucas: *Little Britain*'. *The Independent*. 1 January 2007. http://www.independent.co.uk/news/people/matt-lucas-littler-britain-430385.html

Russell, W.M.S. 'Ethnic Humour around the World: A Comparative Analysis'. Book Review. *Reviewing Sociology*. 9:2 (1996). http://www.rdg.ac.uk/RevSoc/home.htm.

Shelley, Jim. 'Jim Shelley's *Little Britain* Verdict'. *The Mirror*. 18 November 2005. http://www.mirror.co.uk/celebs/news/2005/11/18/jim-shelley-s-little-britain-verdict-115875–16383983/

Sheppard, Fergus. '*Little Britain*'s in Trouble...no buts about it'. *Scotsman. Com News*. 1 December 2005. http://news.scotsman.com/littlebritain/Little-Britains-in-trouble-no.2682800.jp

Sherwin, Adam. '*Little Britain* Aiming for Huge Remake in America', *Times Online*. 25 August 2006. Available at http://www.timesonline.co.uk/article/0,,11069–2327749,00.html

Smith, David. 'Nobody Neets This Lazy Lot Any More'. *The Times Online*. 7 January 2007. http://www.timesonline.co.uk/tol/news/article1290102.ece.

ThaiFarang. '*Little Britain* – Racism in Sheep's Clothing?'. http://articles.
thaifarang.co.uk/10.html.

TV Blog It. www.tvblog.it

Urban Dictionary. 1999–2008. *Urban Dictionary*. www.urbandictionary.
com.

Wardrop, Murray. 'Wives Find Mothers-in-law Hardest to Deal With'.
The Telegraph. 30 November 2008. www.telegraph.co.uk.

Index ....

abject body 124
aggression, masked 180
Albrecht, Gary L. 117
Ali G 101
Allen, Graham 25
'Allo 'Allo 37, 38
alternative comedy 128–30
America 171–81
  audiences 14
  importing and exporting comedy
    programmes 184
  Little Britain USA 209–13
  radio comedy 22
  sketch shows 20
Anatomy of Criticism (Frye) 176
Andersen, Gisle 62, 63
Anne 48, 111, 112, 117, 121–2
Apter, Terri 105
aquarium sketch 117
Aristotle 179, 180
Atkinson, Rowan 185
audiences 13–15, 147–70
  engagement strategies 46–52
  Italian 199–205
  participation 46–52
audiovisual humour and
    translation 187–91
Auslander, Philip 35
authorial intention 162
awards 2–3
awareness, discrepant 177

Baker, Tom 2, 32
Bandwaggon 22–3
Barnes, Colin 121
Barr, Roseanne 102
Bathroom sketch 119
Beagrie, Dr 121, 122
Bennett, Steve 92–3

Bergen Corpus of London Teenage
    Language 62, 63
Bergson, Henri 180
Bianco, Robert 210
Big Chill, The 190
Billig, Michael 130–1
black characters 84, 86, 90, 158–60
blacking up 86, 87, 159
bladder control, lack 7, 124, 150–1
bodies, singular 123–5
Boskin, Joseph 212
Bourdieu, Pierre 47, 48
breastfeeding 104, 105, 106,
    203, 204
Breasts sketch 120
brides, mail order 135–8
British National Corpus (BNC) 63
Britishness 79, 163–9
  see also Englishness
broadcast comedy 22–5
Butsch, Richard 99

Call Centre sketch 98
Cambridge Footlights Society 21
canned laughter 89–90, 162
caricature 177
catchphrases 8, 9, 23, 69, 107
  in translation 195
categorical salience 58–9
Ceci, Sabrina 186, 195
censorship 195–6
chav (chavette) 11, 61–2, 64, 69,
    96–100
chav-nots 103–7
cheats 111, 116–17, 118–19
'The Cheese Shop' sketch (Python) 29
children
  affect 6
  as viewers 31

Christmas Decorations sketch 112
Chumley, Sir Bernard 4
Clark, Laurence 112, 114
Clary, Julian 139
class 11, 95–109
Coates, Jennifer 201
COLT 62, 63
comedy
  aesthetics 156–8
  alternative 128–30
  American 172–3
  complexity 101
  radio 22–4
  techniques 8, 9, 20, 174–8
comedy chavs 97–100
comedy schema 68–70
comic strips 171–2
Coming Out sketch 195–6
Connor 212
context 64–7
continuity sequences 2, 32
Cooperative Principle 65–6
criticism 5–7, 11, 32, 86, 157
cross-dressing 26–7, 29–30, 59,
  140–1
Culpeper, Jonathan 54–5, 64–5, 81
culture
  British 178
  differences 67–8, 84
  knowledge 213
culture-specificity 192–4

Dad's Army 37, 38
Daffyd 138–9, 172–3, 191, 195
Daily Mail 6
Darke, Paul 114
Davies, Christie 68, 81–2
Dawes, Marjorie 4, 49, 161–2
Delingpole, James 2
Dent, Susie 61
DeVere, Bubbles 90–1, 124–5,
  140, 161
DeVere, Desiree 86, 89, 90–1, 140,
  158–60
Dining Room sketch 122
disability 11–12, 111–25
discrepant awareness 177
displeasures 155–63
'Diving Board' sketch 70–1
Doctor sketch 124

doctors 56–7, 65, 121, 122–3, 124
Doggy, Mr 212
Dorinson, Joseph 212
Doty, William G. 117
drag 26–7, 29–30, 59, 140–1
dubbing 186, 194, 205
Dudley 88–9, 136
DVDs, sales 3

Edinburgh Festival 21
Ellen, Barbara 11
Ellie Grace 212
Elton John interview sketch 190–1,
  194–5
embarrassment, fear 165
Emery, Mrs 124, 140, 165
end-of-pier comedy 24–5, 80–1
Englishness 79, 82, 83
  see also Britishness
Ethnic Humor around the World
  (Davies) 68
ethnic humour 76–8, 80, 81–2, 92
exports, TV programmes 184–5

Fabian Society 97
fakery 111, 116–17, 118–19
fans 3, 51–2, 147, 196
The Fast Show 37
'Fat Fighters' Club 49
Fat Fighters sketch 193
fat people 49, 123–4, 161–2
Feeding the Ducks sketch 193
femininity 27
figurative analysis 134–5
fish 117
focus groups 148–56, 157–69,
  199–205
Frasier 173
freak show 123–5
French, Dawn 129
Fringe, Edinburgh Festival 21
The Frost Report 108
Fry, Sir Norman 103, 191, 204
Frye, Northrop 176

Garden sketch 121–2
Garnett, Alf 101
Garvin, Glenn 210
gays 12, 26, 29, 48–9, 138–9,
  168, 179

gender   12, 13, 135–42, 212
General Theory of Verbal Humour
     (GTVH)   189–90
genres   20–1, 22–5, 26–8, 32
George and Mildred   185
Gilbert, Matthew   211
Gill, Rosalind   132, 134
graduates, comedic   21
*Greatest Disabled TV Character
     poll*   113–14, 116, 118
Grice, H. P.   65, 66

Hampstead Heath sketch   191
Hari, Johann   5, 84–5, 100
hatred and humour   130–3
Henshaw, Paul   112
Hill, Benny   27, 185
Hills, Matt   51
history of sketch comedy   8, 22–5
Hole, Anne   129–30
Holiday sketch   119–20
homogenising   194
homosexuals   12, 26, 29, 48–9,
     138–9, 168, 179
Howard, Emily   55–9, 65, 140–1, 177
humiliation of audience   49–50
humour
     American   172–3
     British   200–2
     and disability   111–14, 117–22,
          123–6
     ethnic   76–8, 80, 81–2, 92
     and hatred   130–3
     non-verbal interplay with
          verbal   70–1
     sense of   196–8
     techniques   174–8
     theories   180
     and translation   187–91
Hynes, William J.   117

identity   10–13
     Britishness   79, 165
     class   95–7, 107, 108
     fan   51–2
     humour   176–7
     national   79
     race   84–9
     sexual   179
imports, TV programmes   184–5

improvisation   44–6, 50
incongruity   54, 180
incontinence   7, 124, 150–1
in-jokes   8
in-law relationships   106
intention, authorial and textual   162
international audiences   13–15,
     199–205
intertextuality   8, 25–30
irony   133, 139, 205
Italy   14–15, 183–207
It's That Man Again (ITMA)   23
Ivanka   137

Jam sketch   196
James sketch   90
Jason   19
JIMMY   185–6
jokes   8, 92, 193–4
Judy   203, 204

Kasdan, Lawrence   190
Kaye, Des   48–9
Kenarbum, Stevie   113
Krutnik, Frank   20

lady   40, 55–9, 66, 140–1
language   9, 65–6, 67, 203
     of a lady   58–9
     teenagers   62–4
     translating variation   194–5
*Larpers and Shroomers: Language
     Report, The* (Dent)   61
laughter track   89–90, 162
Lawler, Stephanie   96
Lawrence, Dr   121, 122–3
The League of Gentlemen   37
learning difficulties   120–1
Lewisohn, Mark   27–8
Library sketch   121
literary schema   68
live performance   35, 36–52
Love, Sebastian   193
Lowry, Brian   212
Lucas, Matt   2, 8, 38–9
     and cross-dressing   30
     as Daffyd   138–9
     as figure   142
     and improvisation   45
     influences   26

Lucas, Matt – *continued*
  on *Little Britain Live*   43
  partnership with David
    Walliams   3–5
  and Ting Tong   157–8
  on Vicky Pollard   102

Macadangdang, Ting Tong   85–6, 88,
    89, 135–6, 137, 157–8
Maggie   90, 203, 204
Magistrates' Court sketch   59–61,
    66–7
mail order brides   135–8
Malcolm in the Middle   113
Mann, Mr   19
Manning, Bernard   77–8
Margaret   19
Mark   212
markers, pragmatic   62–4
Markham, Dame Sally   177
Martinez, Francesca   120
masked aggression   180
McCalmont, Jonathan   32
McCarthy, Anna   27
McCooney, Ray   19
McDonald, Sir Trevor   77–8
McGill, Donald   25
McLean, Gareth   211, 213
Mcnamara, Mary   212
McRobbie, Angela   131–2
Mead, Mrs   117–18
Meet the Parents sketch   104, 105
Menippean satire   176
mental illness   32, 120–3
merchandising   3, 150
middle classes   102, 103, 106, 108
Mildred   212
minstrels   20, 87–8, 159
Mintz, Lawrence E.   213
Monty Python's Flying Circus   27–8, 37
Moore, Myfanwy   5
mothers   84–5, 104, 105, 106,
    203, 210
Mr Bean   185, 201
Muir, Frank   24
music-hall comedy   24–5

narrative construction   30, 31–2
national audiences   13–14
national identity   79

Neale, Steve   20
New Laddism   133
non-verbal humour, interplay with
    verbal   70–1
Norden, Denis   24
Norrick, Neal R.   70
Nuts   133

obesity   49, 123–4, 161
Ofcom   77, 78
*Ofcom Report: The Representation
    and Portrayal of People with
    Disabilities on Analogue
    Television* (2005) 114–15
On Big Women   129
oppositions, script   59, 66
originality   19
Orwell, George   25
Other   76, 141
Ouch   113–14, 116, 118, 119
overweight people   49, 123–4, 161

paedophilia   48–9
Palin, Michael   28
pantomime   40
participation, audience   46–52
pathology   115–16
Patio sketch   111–12
performance techniques,
    theatre   44–6, 47–50
personality, affect on
    translation   196–8
Peter Sellers Is Dead   77
Philip sketch   193–4
Phyllis   212
physicians   56–7, 65, 121, 122–3, 124
Pincher, Harvey   19, 103–7, 203
Pipkin, Andy   39–40, 70–1, 111,
    120, 124, 177–8
  and comic exhaustion   157
  and shape shifting   117, 118, 119
pleasure   155–63, 168–9
Pollard, Vicky   11, 19, 59–61, 107,
    108, 202, 204
  as chav   69–70, 97–100
  language   62–4, 203
  in Magistrates' Court sketch   66–7
  and realism   156, 157
  and subtitles   188–9
  as 'unruly woman'   102–3

Pool, Hannah 86
popularity poll 113–14, 116, 118
postcards 25
Potter, Gillie 22
pragmatic markers 62–4
Provine, Robert R. 155
Pub sketch 177
public service broadcasting
      (PSB) 77, 78, 92
punch-lines 90

quickies 20–1

race 75–94
racialisation 10, 75–6, 81, 84–7
radio comedy 22–4
Radio sketch 177
Rastafarian sketch 191
ratings 3, 7
realism 156–7
Reformed Character sketch 202
Reith, John 22
Relief Theory of humour 154
remediation 35
repetition 69
representation 152, 168
    and Ali G 101
    of black characters 158–9
    class 107
    comic 156, 158
    of disability 114–15
    of doctors 122–3
    of fat people 161–2
    racial 81, 84, 92, 93
    of women 158–60
    of working classes 99–100
Restaurant sketch 105–6
ridicule 104–6
ritual 51–2
Rock Profiles 4–5
Rose, Florence 140–1
Roseanne 102, 128
Rowe, Kathleen 102, 128
Roy 19
Russell, Bill 82
Russell, Ken 5

salience, categorical 58–9
satire 79, 176
schema theory 9–10, 53–4, 67

schemata 53, 54–5, 67–8, 69,
      70, 81
script oppositions 59, 66
scripts 54, 57–8, 61–2, 66–7, 70–1
Seaside sketch 117
Sebastian 139
Seinfeld 173
Semantic Script Theory 189
Semino, Elena 67
sexuality 12, 13, 98–9, 135–42,
      179, 212
Shakespeare, Tom 112, 118
shape shifting 117–19
Shelley, Jim 86
Shohat, Ella 81
Should We Be Laughing? 120, 121
Simpson, Mark 139
single mothers 84–5
singular bodies 123–5
Sir Bernard Chumley and Friends
      shows 4
situation comedies 101, 172, 173
sketch shows 19–33
social categories 54–5
social class 11, 95–109
social role 149–54
social schema 58, 59, 61–2, 81
Social Worker sketch 98
society, portrayal 187
speech 65–6, 67
    teenagers 62–4
    see also language
Speight, Johnny 101
Spitting Image 21
stereotypes 58, 64
Sternberg, Meir 194
Stockwell, Peter 68
subject-matter of sketch shows 21
subtitles 14, 186, 188–9, 194,
      205, 206
    and censorship 195–6
subtlety 201
superiority theory of humour 180
Supermarket sketch 99
surrealism 23
swimming pool sketches 2, 70, 202

Take It from Here (TIFH) 24
Tatchell, Peter 12
teenagers 62–4

television
  importing and exporting
    programmes 184–5
  as medium 35–6
teratology 123–5
Terry and Julian 139
Thai-UK.org survey 137–8
theatre 35, 38, 39–52, 44–6, 47–50
Thomas, Garland 125
Till Death Us Do Part 101
Ting Tong Macadangdang 85–6, 88,
    89, 135–6, 137, 157–8
Todd, Lou 39–40, 70–1, 119–20,
    157, 177–8
Tom 212
translation 187–98, 204–5
transvestism 26–7, 29–30, 59, 140–1
tricksters 111, 116–17, 118–19
Tyler, Imogen 100, 134, 135

UK, importing and exporting TV
    programmes 184–5
United States 171–81
  audiences 14
  importing and exporting comedy
    programmes 184
  Little Britain USA 209–13
  radio comedy 22
  sketch shows 20
upper classes 103–6, 108
Urban Dictionary 62, 69

Vaudeville 20
Verbally Expressed Humour
    (VEH) 189, 190, 191, 197–8
  interplay with non-verbal 70–1

Video sketch 120
viewers
  children 31
  figures 3, 7
  overseas 166–8
violence and mental illness 122, 123
Vomiting Lady in Italy sketch 203

Walliams, David 38–9, 43
  awards 2, 3
  and cross-dressing 30
  as Dennis Waterman 42
  and improvisation 45, 50
  influences 26, 29
  on *Little Britain Live* 36, 47, 48
  partnership with Matt Lucas 3–5
  and sexuality 141–2
Waterman, Dennis 42
Wedding Caterer sketch 106
Wedding sketch 104
wheelchairs 111, 112, 117,
    119, 120
Whelehan, Imelda 132
white social types 80–1
  see also working classes
WI (Women's Institute) 6
Wodak, Ruth 65
women 7, 27, 59, 89, 135–6, 140,
    158–60
  as abject body 124–5
  and race 83, 85–6, 88, 90–1
  see also Pollard, Vicky; transvestism
working classes 21, 84–5, 96,
    99–100, 102, 106, 108

X-ray sketch 56–7, 65–6